*f*P

ALSO BY SOLOMON VOLKOV

Testimony: The Memoirs of Dmitri Shostakovich

Balanchine's Tchaikovsky: Conversations with Balanchine on His Life, Ballet and Music

From Russia to the West: The Musical Memoirs and Reminiscences of Nathan Milstein

Joseph Brodsky in New York

Yuri Lyubimov in America

St. Petersburg: A Cultural History

CONVERSATIONS WITH

JOSEPH
BRODSKY

A POET'S JOURNEY THROUGH

THE TWENTIETH CENTURY

SOLOMON VOLKOV

TRANSLATED BY MARIAN SCHWARTZ
WITH PHOTOGRAPHS BY MARIANNA VOLKOV

THE FREE PRESS
New York   London   Toronto   Sydney   Singapore

THE FREE PRESS
A Division of Simon & Schuster Inc.
1230 Avenue of the Americas
New York, NY 10020

Designed by Carla Bolte

Manufactured in the United States of America

10 9 8 7 6 5 4 3 2 1

Library of Congress Cataloging-in-Publication Data

Volkov, Solomon.
    Conversations with Joseph Brodsky : a poet's journey through the
    twentieth century / Solomon Volkov ; translated by Marian Schwartz.
        p.   cm.
    Includes index.
    ISBN 0–684–83572–X
    1. Brodsky, Joseph, 1940–   —Interviews.   2. Poets, Russian—20th
century—Interviews.   3. Poets, Russian—20th century—Biography.
I. Schwartz, Marian.   II. Title.
PG3479.4.R64Z93   1998
811'.54—dc21
[B]   97–31012
                                                            CIP

Photographs courtesy of Marianna Volkov

Portions of the work have been previously published in Russian in substantially the same form in the
following publications: *Chast Rechi* (New York), no. 1 (1980), nos. 2–3 (1982); *Novy Amerikanets*
(New York), Sept. 5–11, Sept. 12–18, Sept. 19–25, Sept. 26–Oct. 2, 1983; *Kontinent* (Paris), no. 53
(1987); *Ogonyok* (Moscow), no. 7 (1991); *Stolitsa* (Moscow), nos. 46–47 (1991); *Iosif Brodskij v Nyu-
Yorke* (New York, 1990, in Russian); *Vspominaya Annu Akhmatovu* (Moscow, 1992, in Russian); *Svoyu
mezh vas yeshchyo ostaviv ten . . .* , Akhmatovskiye chteniya, vyp. III (Moscow, 1992).

CONTENTS

v

SOLOMON VOLKOV TALKING WITH JOSEPH BRODSKY IN
BRODSKY'S HOME, GREENWICH VILLAGE, NEW YORK, 1982

PREFACE

This book could serve as a guide, a kind of Baedeker, to the breathtaking, often beautiful, and at times forbidding territory of Brodsky's life and art. The idea for it came in the fall of 1978 when, out of curiosity, I attended lectures that Brodsky was giving at Columbia University in New York for a young American audience that consisted mostly of aspiring poets. Brodsky, thirty-eight at the time and in exile for more than six years, analyzed his favorite poets for his students. He was in his element, charming and inspiring his listeners with ease. I, too, was deeply struck.

I immediately approached Brodsky with the idea of starting a volume of conversations that would explore poetry and Russian culture through the lens of his experience. Such a book, I suggested, would bring new readers to Russian literature and give them a new understanding of the Russian literary world. To my surprise, Brodsky consented with alacrity. I didn't know that he was preparing to undergo his first open-heart surgery at the time. He had addressed mortality in his verse quite early. Yet it remains difficult to judge whether his concerns with his own mortality were fueled by his heart problems or by his immersion in existential philosophy. In any event, he faced the issue squarely, even if a bit nonchalantly at times.

We began meeting in Brodsky's apartment at 44 Morton Street to tape-record discussions of poetry as well as biographical matters that we thought were important for a proper understanding of his writing. As a memento of those days, I have a bookshelf packed with many volumes by and about Frost and Auden, whose work I had not known very well before these encounters.

The bypass operation went well, and our meetings continued. Why? Unlike my other interview subjects over the years—the composer Dmitri Shostakovich, the choreographer George Balanchine, and the violinist Nathan Milstein—Brodsky was eminently qualified to put his own words on paper. Yet, he obviously enjoyed this opportunity to converse seriously, sometimes for hours on end, with someone else who would take final responsibility for transforming the raw taped material into finished and edited form.

Such work is a perilous proposition, fraught with uncertainty and compromise. I would even venture to compare writing a book about someone whom the writer has been interviewing to marriage. Many shades of trust, admiration, and love bear upon the work, but so too do creeping suspicions, neuroses, and all kinds of psychological clashes. In the end, a completed book project, always years and sometimes decades in the making, is sustained by the belief of both parties that the arrangement is vital. By the time Brodsky's heart operation had proved a success, he and I already had a solid emotional investment in the process and also, I believe, a rather good rapport.

The productive atmosphere of our conversations could be explained initially in several ways. First of all, a musician by profession, I was outside the literary coterie that surrounded Brodsky, and he particularly enjoyed discussing the music he loved, especially that of Haydn and Stravinsky. Second, I had no need of his patronage. This was certainly a relief to Brodsky, whose phone rang incessantly (he would say, "as if it had been invented yesterday"), with calls from people asking for all kinds of favors, urgent requests for recommendations, blurbs, and so forth. Finally, I was not an academic or any kind of "Brodsky expert"—the kind of people he did not suffer gladly.

But the motivation for the project did not end there. Brodsky also saw that we achieved tangible results. Several chapters of the planned book appeared in print, over the course of twelve years, between 1980 and 1992. These included our conversations about Auden, Akhmatova, Brodsky's life in New York, as well as his travels to Venice. They were published first in various émigré Russian publications and then, after the momentous changes in Russia, were even picked up in Moscow.* Brodsky never interfered, insisting that this was my idea and my book, hence all editorial and publishing decisions were up to me.

Being a natural-born leader, Brodsky was never one to shy away from an opportunity to express his views in a public forum. He gave many inter-

---

*See especially *Chast Rechi* (New York), no. 1 (1980), nos. 2–3 (1982); *Novy Amerikanets* (New York), Sept. 5–11, Sept. 12–18, Sept. 19–25, Sept. 26–Oct. 2, 1983; *Kontinent* (Paris), no. 53 (1987); *Ogonyok* (Moscow), no. 7 (1991); *Stolitsa* (Moscow), nos. 46–47 (1991); Chapters on Brodsky's life in New York and on Akhmatova also appeared in, respectively, *Josif Brodskij v Nyu-Yorke* (New York, 1990, in Russian); *Vspominaya Annu Akhmatovu* (Moscow, 1992, in Russian). The latter was also reprinted in *Svoyu mezh vas yeshchyo ostaviv ten . . .* , Akhmatovskiye chteniya, vyp. III (Moscow, 1992).

views and told choice anecdotes on more than one occasion. He repeatedly emphasized, however, that this or that part of our conversation was being told for the first time. Many of these parts dealt with the most dramatic events in Brodsky's life, such as his arrests and detentions in the Soviet Union, as well as his trial and subsequent exile to the Far North. He also never, to my knowledge, discussed for public consumption his involvement in the defection of the Soviet ballet star Alexander Godunov in New York in 1979, which brought the two superpowers of the day to a dangerous political standoff. With respect to his relationship with Akhmatova, after our discussion of this friendship appeared in print, Brodsky simply stopped discussing it with journalists at any length, referring them instead to the published account.*

Brodsky also discussed with me themes that were central to his thinking and work, such as the poet's role in the modern world, his relationship to language, his position vis-à-vis the people and the authorities. Some of the commentaries and ideas that appeared throughout his life in his poems and prose were first articulated in our conversations and later incorporated elsewhere—never, of course, in exactly the same way, but with variations, alterations, and shifts in accent and mood. And here I must respond to the question of the *raison d'être* of our ongoing dialogue with the answer that is most fundamental.

The word *dialogue* is key. Brodsky's mind was essentially dialogic, to an extent I've never observed in anyone else. In this sense, he was a true follower of the ideas of the Russian thinker Mikhail Bakhtin, who proclaimed the dialogue the ultimate form of human self-expression, with everything existing in flux, subject to open-ended questioning by a free mind. Brodsky thrived on paradox, ambiguity, and contrariness. Here was a man in constant Socratic dialogue with himself, endlessly questioning, expanding, and shifting his mental position—and glad to have a sparring partner.

So, we Russians sparred. Brodsky could use our discussions as a kind of linguistic sounding board for his Russian prose writing—paradoxically, Brodsky first established his prose style in English. In Russia, he had never been asked to contribute an essay, a book review, or a commencement address. Commissions for prose materialized for Brodsky only in the West, and almost from the beginning he made a conscious decision to compose these pieces in English, "for the pure pleasure of it," as he explained, but also "to please the shadow" of his beloved W. H. Auden.

*See for example an interview with Brodsky in *Ogonyok* (Moscow), no. 31 (1988), reprinted later in two collections, *Tsena prozrenija* (Moscow, 1990) and *Posle Rossiyi* (Moscow, 1992).

Brodsky very rarely failed to achieve something in the intellectual realm if he really put his mind to it, so ultimately he did develop his highly idiosyncratic, effective, and memorable English prose style, of which he was rather proud. Ironically, Brodsky was less confident—or maybe more demanding and self-critical—of his prose skills in Russian. In his mother tongue, he tried to assimilate a much wider linguistic range than in his English essays. In the West his milieu was intellectual and this had its effect on his style of English expression. Not so in his native country, where Brodsky's unusual life trajectory had landed him in the factory and the morgue, on geological expeditions, and in prisons and squalid backwater villages, and had placed him in contact with criminals, paupers, street hustlers, mental patients, and peasants. In Russia, Brodsky faced—not in books but in real life—a staggering quantity of slang and dialect, which he tried to incorporate in various ways into his prose.

On one occasion, Brodsky orchestrated an exchange between us in the roles of "white" and "redhead" clowns. I had set him off by mentioning my plan (realized sometime later on) to write an essay about the heavily bowdlerized Soviet translation of the famous Stravinsky–Craft conversations. "Write an essay!" he began sarcastically, taking aim. "Ha! What a marvelous pronouncement! It's all very well for you, Solomon, really," he continued, doing a slow burn. "I would be ecstatic if I could utter a sentence like that: 'I think I'll write an essay!'" I muttered something in my defense. "I envy you tremendously, Solomon!" Brodsky continued to beat on me mercilessly. "Really, I envy you! Because writing essays, as you were so good to express it, is in fact a perfectly natural process. Certain ideas occur to you, and you just set them out in written form. It's an immediate reaction to reality. Ultimately, it is simply a more immediate relationship to reality. I would be a happy man if I could express my views and ideas like that. I'd write so many essays, ha!" This rather caustic monologue highlighted another explanation for Brodsky's desire to polish his prose in Russian through conversation: he was constantly tinkering with his oeuvre. His aversion to viewing his work as a finished product (another striking example of Brodsky's congenital dialoguism) is widely known. Even greater was Brodsky's reluctance to see his writing collected between two covers and published. He would procrastinate ad infinitum in an attempt to delay this event to the last possible moment. If I remember correctly, he managed to put off publication of his first collection of essays, *Less Than One,* first announced by the publisher in 1979, until 1986! In the whole history of

Russian literature, only Fyodor Tyutchev, the nineteenth-century poet, could compare to Brodsky in this respect.

Brodsky's candor and desire to be as self-analytical as possible, which will be obvious to readers of this volume, had their limits. He was reluctant to discuss his family life. Brodsky's marriage in 1990 to Maria Sozzani, a young beauty of Italian and Russian descent, with whom he had a daughter, Anna, in 1993, was, in my estimation, at least partly prompted by the poet's desire to escape the post–Nobel Prize pressure and chaos. As Brodsky himself sometimes put it, he saw his marriage and subsequent move from bohemian Greenwich Village to the much more tranquil and staid Brooklyn Heights as "an escape from all this madness. It's like there's a moat, and you raise the bridge."

But for a while, there was no moat, and our talk painted a self-portrait of a poet in all his contradictions, full of immense vitality and intellectual curiosity. These conversations, fifteen years in the making, were regarded by both of us as a kind of work in progress, with bits and pieces added along the way, expanding and enriching the original concept. For the sake of continuity and clarity, it was sometimes necessary to group together episodes recorded at different sessions. The last chapter was planned to be a summation of Brodsky's long-awaited, endlessly deferred return visit to his native shore. This wasn't meant to be . . .

Although obviously I cannot know for sure what Brodsky, notorious for endless tinkering with his own texts, might have said about this book in its final form, I truly believe that it represents both the letter and the spirit of the poet's thinking throughout the years. With their feel of immediacy and spontaneity, these conversations capture, I hope, a unique personality in a unique moment in history. Brodsky's vantage point as a Russian émigré living in New York gave him the impetus for pronouncements that combined a heartfelt Russian sensibility with the cosmopolitan outlook of a seasoned *philosophe*. Brodsky liked to compare his position with that of an observer sitting on top of a mountain, seeing both slopes. In my mind's eye I still see him passionately holding forth: "This is an absolutely special sensation."

VOLKOV AND BRODSKY ON MORTON STREET,
GREENWICH VILLAGE, NEW YORK, 1978

INTRODUCTION:
THE LONE WOLF OF POETRY

When a man dies,
His portraits change.

There is a chilling quality to these lines by Anna Akhmatova. Often, after I have learned of the death of a friend and been assigned the task of sorting through his or her photographs, I notice subtle, and sometimes striking, changes in the features of the deceased. In granting the person's fate a sense of false completion, death casts a new light on the fleeting poses imprinted in these portraits, robbing them of their casualness and imbuing them with a new perspective and meaning. Moreover, the stronger the posthumous legend, the more unsettling its effect on the artifact.

I experienced nothing like this after Joseph Brodsky died of a heart attack on January 28, 1996, in New York City, at the age of fifty-five. His portraits had already become indistinguishable from the legend that took shape during his lifetime. Its contours were already known to poetry connoisseurs all over the world: a rebellious youth spent in the grim spectral city of Leningrad, which had barely recovered then from the Nazis' horrible siege and Stalin's vindictive purges; his early attempts at nonconformist poetry with the encouragement and blessing of the "keening muse" of Russian poetry, the great Anna Akhmatova; and his skirmishes with overzealous Soviet authorities, culminating in the notorious 1964 trial against the twenty-three-year-old loner on charges of "social parasitism."

This Kafkaesque trial occupies a central position in the Brodsky myth. Little did Leningrad officials suspect, when they instigated this routine case, that the individual they considered a Jewish "pygmy in corduroy trousers, scribbling poems that alternated gibberish with whining, pessimism, and pornography," would turn their Soviet court proceedings into

3

an absurd drama at the intersection of genius and idiocy. In reply to the irritated question of the female Soviet judge, "Who made you a poet?" Brodsky thoughtfully replied, "And who made me a member of the human race?" and added hesitatingly, "I think it was God." Brodsky's friend, the poet Lev Loseff, observed that in an instant Brodsky's answer transposed the proceedings to a different plane. There was no doubt about which metaphysical power the poet's opponents were representing in this Manichean drama. This notorious dialogue became one of the most frequently quoted court exchanges in the history of twentieth-century culture.

Brodsky was sentenced to five years' hard labor in the Far North. There, in a cold, remote village near the White Sea where he shoveled manure, he wrote some of his finest poems. They reached Leningrad by circuitous routes and were distributed clandestinely, but widely, in typescript, enhancing Brodsky's underground literary standing immensely. In the West, meanwhile, the Brodsky affair became a *cause célèbre,* with prominent intellectuals such as Jean-Paul Sartre adding their weight to an already vigorous campaign for Brodsky's release being waged by such Soviet luminaries as Kornei Chukovsky and Dmitri Shostakovich. When the authorities relented and Brodsky was granted early release, many in Leningrad feted him as a cultural hero.

Cat-and-mouse games with the KGB ensued with their own harebrained logic. But in 1972, when the secret police decided Brodsky could not be bought, they expelled him and he settled in the United States. Soviet officials felt that by expelling Brodsky they were silencing him at last. At the time, the exile of a major Russian cultural figure was still an exceptional event and viewed as an extreme measure. On such occasions, virtually all ties with the homeland were severed, and the new émigré was expected, after an initial flurry of media appearances, to lose news value quickly for his Western handlers. With luck, he would plunge into oblivion and drink himself to death amid wails of despair and nostalgia.

Once again, the Soviets miscalculated badly. Brodsky made a great show of his reluctance to leave Russia, even writing a letter to the Party leader, Leonid Brezhnev, asking him to reconsider the explusion order. Yet Brodsky never appeared to slow down or lose heart after the explusion. He missed his elderly parents, who never saw their son again because the Soviet authorities would not grant them permission to visit him. And Brodsky must have longed for his son Andrei, who was four years old when he left. It was Andrei's mother, the Leningrad artist Marianna Basmanova, to whom Brodsky dedicated his 1983 collection, *New Stanzas to Augusta,* a compendium unprecedented in Russian poetry of eighty love poems written over the course of twenty years. He clearly ached for his friends and native city. Nonetheless, Brodsky immediately plunged into his work, lecturing, giving many poetry readings (over sixty in his first year and a half in the States), and eventually teaching Russian and comparative literature, specializing in his favorite poets: Tsvetaeva, Akhmatova, Mandelstam, Frost, and Auden, as well as Thomas Hardy and W. B. Yeats.

Brodsky's English was essentially self-taught. Increasingly, though, his literary output was in English, a consequence, in part, of his close involvement with some of the leading figures on the contemporary American and international literary scene, such as Susan Sontag, Derek Walcott, Octavio Paz, and Seamus Heaney. Russian remained his mode of communication with some of his new friends, including Isaiah Berlin and Czeslaw Milosz. However, Brodsky's essays, later collected in two volumes, were written largely in English, a matter of considerable pride for him. The English voice of Brodsky's essays is widely regarded as the uniquely powerful and spellbinding creation of a mature author.

At first, no doubt, Brodsky's renown in the West was based on the notoriety of his tribulations in Russia. But while some émigrés saw their politically propelled fame fizzle in the West, Brodsky's intellectual curiosity, openness, and energy endeared him to literary lions who were at first reluctant to engage in serious discussion with the anti-Soviet outcast. As Susan Sontag once told Brodsky, he helped make the "anti-Soviet" stance acceptable to her and like-minded Western liberals. No mean feat, this was a bitter disappointment to the wizards of the KGB who had planned Brodsky's speedy self-destruction in the West.

Brodsky's secret Moscow files—unlike Solzhenitsyn's—are not yet accessible, but internal KGB documents that reflect the agency's utter disarray and anger after Brodsky was awarded the Nobel Prize for Literature in 1987 have been published in the post-Soviet Russian press. Mikhail Gorbachev's reforms were in full swing then, but the KGB still characterized the event as a "political provocation on the part of reactionary circles in the West."

In contrast, Russian intellectuals, especially in Brodsky's native Leningrad, were ecstatic. This particular gesture of recognition by the international community vindicated their early belief in the literary genius of this "social parasite," and seemed to be the fitting end to a parable about a man who was unrecognized, vilified, and persecuted by the cruel and ignorant authorities at home but eventually found freedom, acclaim, and high status abroad. Poetry-loving Russians celebrated the close parallels to the story of the biblical Joseph.

Many times I have come across assertions that the trajectory of Brodsky's life was largely determined by the caprices of fate and that the mythological halo around him was to a great extent a providential gift, an accidental victory. One of Brodsky's friends from his youth wrote as much in a poem: "You, on your guard, carrot top . . . you've already snatched your brass ring." But Brodsky earned his legend. He faced many crossroads in his life, and each time he chose uncannily the more tortuous and ultimately more rewarding path.

For instance, right before his arrest in 1964, Brodsky turned up in Moscow, where his friends tried to talk him out of returning to Leningrad. The situation was obviously getting out of hand, and a dramatic turn of events was imminent. Brodsky insisted on returning, however, and his trial and exile ensued. Akhmatova joked grimly: "What a biography they're creating for our redhead! You'd think he'd put them up to it."

With similar clearheaded daring, Brodsky refused to sign on with the established and politically controlled literary world after his return from the Far North. His decision against collaborating with the KGB, which would have given him an opportunity to publish his first volume of poetry, was simple, inasmuch as it was morally unambiguous. By contrast, the tempting proposal by a popular magazine to publish a selection of Brodsky's poems if he would just agree with their choice of his work would have enticed most fellow poets. But not Brodsky. He refused to make even this seemingly minuscule compromise. This decision, along with several other equally innocuous actions, doomed him to expulsion. Brodsky's stance was rather unusual by the prevailing Soviet standards of the early 1970s. It can be traced to a half-forgotten Petersburg tradition. After the 1917 Bolshevik revolution, such disparate figures as Igor Stravinsky, Sergei Diaghilev, Vladimir Nabokov, and George Balanchine found themselves in the West. These four men succeeded in becoming pillars of the twentieth century's international modernist movement. Their artistic roots, however, lie in that crucible of dynamic cultural development and bold experimentation that was Petersburg at the turn of the century.

Then the capital of the tsarist empire, Petersburg had been founded by Peter the Great in 1703 explicitly for the purpose of challenging the ancient ways and habits of Old Mother Russia. Of course, this maddeningly complex culture also had a capacity for jingoistic feelings and ideas, but there was always a hard-core artistic elite for whom Western impulses and trends were of paramount importance. Employing Western devices to great effect, St. Petersburg culture produced such masterpieces as Pushkin's "French" elegies, Glinka's "Italianate" operas, and Tchaikovsky's "Germanic" symphonies. This was essentially Russian art that felt itself at home in Europe.

Stravinsky, Diaghilev, Nabokov, and Balanchine grew up in this environment. All of them leaned—as much by artistic and personal temperament as by aesthetic upbringing—toward the sophisticated "art-as-play" approach then very much in vogue in the West but not in Russia. Russia's primordial conflict between art and society, which subjugated the former to the immediate demands of the latter, explains, at least in part, why these four artists eventually found themselves outside Russia's borders. It is interesting that Nabokov and Balanchine both fled the Communist regime, while Stravinsky and Diaghilev were pushed abroad by their bitter battles with the tsarist cultural establishment. Regardless of current politics, Russia's body cultural could not stomach these irritants and so expelled them.

In the West, all four men became cultural arbiters in their respective fields not only because of their creative genius and intense drive but also, to some extent, because of this very "un-Russianness." Yet paradoxically, they all remained deeply Russian artists, not only in their "exoticism," which strongly colored even their most cosmopolitan works, but also in their deep-seated ambivalence concerning their obligation to the Russian people. Although they had fled the conventions and duties that Russian society imposed, they eventually found themselves within the broader Russian cultural tradition that they helped to forge.

Brodsky's life and work confirmed the vitality of this newly devised tradition. He could have chosen another strong Petersburg modernist lineage, represented in particular by Osip Mandelstam and Anna Akhmatova, for whom leaving Russia for the West would have been inconceivable. Akhmatova's sentiments in this regard were especially fierce. In her poems, she often lamented the bitter fate of the émigré, whom she likened to "a prisoner, or a patient." Both Mandelstam and Akhmatova paid dearly for their courageous decision to remain in Communist Russia, and Akhmatova, who survived the Stalinist terror, was always proud of the fact that she, as she put it, "was where my people had the misfortune to be."

Despite Akhmatova's powerful influence on Brodsky—more moral than artistic or professional—he chose the other Petersburg trajectory, which at the time was especially unappealing. Due to many factors, including effective Soviet propaganda, the existence of Petersburgians in the West was viewed as precarious at best, and not only by those inside Russia. Jean-Paul Sartre's hostile reaction to Nabokov, whom Sartre berated for not helping to build the socialist paradise on earth, was typical. The émigrés themselves were not entirely sure of their own vocation. Diaghilev's serious plans to return to Soviet Russia were quashed only by his sudden death in 1929. Stravinsky periodically toyed with the idea, too, and I happened to be present when Balanchine—admittedly weakened in body and spirit by his final illness—mused out loud about how much more esteemed he would have been had he stayed in the Soviet Union.

Only Nabokov seems to have been quite immune to the siren songs and entreaties of the totalitarian authorities, perhaps because the Soviets did not really put him to the test. In any case, Nabokov's example was not an attractive alternative to Brodsky, whose artistic vision placed poetry so high above prose and who saw Nabokov as a failed poet. Also, Nabokov's decisive and irrevocable switch in his work from Russian to English must have seemed to Brodsky, especially from inside Russia, more an act of artistic capitulation than of triumph. The prospect of losing his native language frightened the young Brodsky.

Nonetheless, Brodsky accepted "the condition we call exile," as he put it. With hindsight, we can see he began preparing for this condition quite early on, even before his exile to the Far North of Russia. He had just turned twenty-two when he described himself in a poem as a "fugitive." Addressing his native city, he surmised, startlingly, that fate had already decreed that he would die far away. (While always insisting that the words "poet" and "prophet" should not be confused, Brodsky, as it happens, made several incredibly accurate predictions of his own future in his poetry.)

One of Brodsky's favorite notions was that a poet's real biography was his poetry. He felt it was not only possible but inevitable that any crucial life decision would be reached first in a poem, dictated by the linguistic impulse. Only then would it come about in real life. It is a bold and even dangerous concept, but if taken seriously it can give the poet's verse that famous "drop of real blood" that distinguishes every profound artistic act.

Brodsky prophesied his own exile by introducing the notion of an "indifferent homeland" in his early work and trying on the garb of the quintessential poet in exile, Ovid. Russian culture always embraced Ovid as its own. During the time of Augustus he was exiled to the shores of the Pontus, now known as the Black Sea, and he died there surrounded by barbarian Getae many long, lonely years later. Pushkin, too, who was exiled by Emperor Alexander I in 1820 to those same lands, expressed kinship with Ovid. Brodsky was in his early twenties when he wrote a poem "in imitation" of Ovid ("Ex Ponto"). In it, he seems to rehearse the themes of separation from one's beloved and one's homeland and addresses the problem of freedom when far from one's home. At the same time, another key theme began to crystallize in his work: empire as a universal concept, the symbol of faceless state power attempting to control both time and space, and the poet's confrontation with this monster.

From a young age, Brodsky was betting on the individual's ability to imagine himself not as an independent entity but as a unique link in a great cultural chain. Paradoxically, this creative ability was connected, Brodsky believed, not to the habit of passive behavior or fatalism but, on the contrary, to bold action that eschewed predictability and inertia. Independence, freedom, and solitude became closely intertwined. In this way, Brodsky assumed the role of the lone wolf of Russian literature.

We first met in Leningrad in 1972, shortly before he was forced to emigrate to the West. To me, he even looked like a wolf, a hunted wolf aggressively baring his fangs to drive back the pressing chase. Later, however, in New York, when I had occasion to observe Brodsky moving through the relatively safe and friendly back streets of bohemian Greenwich Village, I was always struck by his lupine grace and the force of his movements, as well as by his air of animal independence and solitude. He cut through the crowd; passersby instinctively gave way to him in these crowded surroundings where practically everyone has some claim to being an artist or a leader. Brodsky was both.

This wolf image suggests a figurative explanation for the power of Brodsky's readings of his verse, when his rabbinical singsong pulled the reader into the vortex of his images, metaphors, rhymes, and alliterations, stealing the will to resist, bewitching and hypnotizing. Those who heard him, seemed to be witnessing a beast's dialogue with the full moon.

I do not mean to suggest that Brodsky lived like a proud hermit, shunning worldly pleasures and only rarely appearing in public with some earth-shattering pronouncement. He liked to sit in cheerful company over a bottle of vodka and plates of Russian delicacies. He was notoriously attracted to the fair sex. Frequently violating the strict rules of contemporary etiquette on college campuses, he enjoyed the company of his female students. Brodsky adopted two other unfashionable vices, consuming large quantities of espresso and strong cheap cigarettes (emulating his idol, W. H. Auden, he preferred the Italian brand MS), despite doctors' insistent warnings. Having undergone open-heart surgery twice and facing a third, he nonetheless started his day with a cigarette while still in bed ("Why bother to wake up if you can't light up?").

Brodsky was no stranger to social life either, taking an active part in what is called literary politics, and he adored gossip ("There are only two truly interesting subjects for serious discussion, gossip and metaphysics," he liked to say). But only a casual or inattentive observer—or a young woman he was trying to win over—could come away from an encounter with Brodsky with the impression that here was a charming, easygoing, even delightful individual. Even brief passing meetings with Brodsky had an upsetting effect. There were always overtones of menace, even if the tone of the conversation was quite civil. More than a few times I heard Russian acquaintances of Brodsky address him as *nachal'nik,* or "the boss," and Brodsky seemed to accept and even enjoy it. Once the writer Sergei Dovlatov, Brodsky's friend from their Leningrad days and later a fellow émigré in New York, inquired in all seriousness as to whether I'd ever had a nosebleed after a long tête-à-tête with Brodsky. After hearing my answer in the affirmative, he gave a sigh of relief. "Thank God. I thought I was the only one who was such a weakling." And Dovlatov was a giant of a man, six feet six inches tall, strong, fearless, and not easily excited; his prose style was sufficiently understated to earn him a secure place in the pages of *The New Yorker.*

Brodsky's presence could be overwhelming not only to his fellow Russians. I attended many of his readings for English-speaking audiences in New York, and any other poets appearing with him were inevitably upstaged by Brodsky's presentation. Their declamatory style, in accordance with local mores, would be rather taciturn and circumspect. American poets almost always affect an image of insecurity, of finding themselves on stage due to some untoward accident. They seem almost to be apologizing for appearing before the assembled audience. Their words are mumbled, their gestures timid, their posture awkward, as if to say, "Look, don't take us seriously, folks."

Not so Brodsky, who would grab his listeners by the throat and then move in for the kill, raising his voice to penetrate the dead zone of privacy that every New Yorker constructs around him- or herself. When Brodsky felt that all else, every other device in his repertoire, was failing to achieve the desired effect, he would switch to reading in Russian, shamanlike. Typically, the audience would then succumb uncomprehendingly.

No self-respecting individual likes to be hypnotized or assaulted in this manner. Perhaps among the barbarians in Russia it could be tolerated, but not in the cultural capital of the world. So is it surprising that many resented this man? Here was this animal of poetry who obviously needed cutting down to size. Thus, many of Brodsky's pronouncements and ideas were greeted with derision and howls. Brodsky would speak wistfully of the traditional Russian "longing for world culture" proclaimed long ago by Mandelstam, and he would be chided: "What world culture? There's no such thing!" Brodsky's belief in the transformative power of poetry would be ridiculed, and his adherence to traditional forms of poetry, with their special attention to strict meters and rhymes, rejected as old-fashioned. His insistence on poets' moral right to lead society, because of their linguistic superiority, was criticized as self-indulgent. Even Brodsky's demand that his students memorize poetry was rejected as absurd. I once spent two hours listening to an overwrought Harvard professor arguing that this particular idea of Brodsky's infringed upon American students' civil rights, inasmuch as it constituted cruel and unusual punishment and was absurd anyway. "Memorizing poetry may be useful in Russia, where you can't find all the books you need in the library, but not here in the free world."

For all the resentment and resistance, though, some of Brodsky's suggestions did take hold, if only tentatively. His advocacy of the nonmodernist tradition in poetry was grudgingly accepted, at least by some, and his close readings of Thomas Hardy, Robert Frost, and W. H. Auden, in particular, were admired, if not universally. (Some academics still cannot speak of these analyses by Brodsky without foaming at the mouth.) Brodsky's proposal to print cheap editions of poetry and make them available everywhere, like Gideon's Bible—in airports, motels, hospitals, prisons— was eventually implemented, if on a much more modest scale than Brodsky envisioned. Even Brodsky's insistence that students recite poetry from memory gained some currency in universities and colleges.

Brodsky's forceful presence on the American literary scene helped rekindle the discussion about the poet's role in a modern democratic society. Should he be sage, prophet, mystical oracle? Should he be a linguistic highwire artist and produce waterfalls of verbal eloquence, or should he be just

your typical man in the street and use a populist vocabulary, an unpreten-
tious bard of everyday life? Can poets nowadays be leaders of society, forc-
ing consequential changes in the political and personal spheres? Or is it all
just a dream, a remembrance of times past, when poets like Goethe, Byron,
Alexander Blok, and Vladimir Mayakovsky reigned like demigods in the
minds of their contemporaries and Russia's entire educated class saw Anna
Akhmatova as the keeper of the national memory? Perhaps, as one influential *New York Times* critic recently put it, the notion that poetry reveals essential truths is just an "old-fashioned belief" and the time has come to
reconsider "our inclination (or desire) to believe that art redeems."

These are all "eternal" questions, at least in a literate society, and as such
will be tangled and untangled by each successive generation in its own way.
However, they always revolve around extraordinary literary figures, reflect-
ing their impact both as living personages and as roaming ghosts after they
are gone. There is no doubt that, even dead, Brodsky survives, in the apt
metaphor of his friend Seamus Heaney, like some wild beast behind the
black bars of his printed work, and will continue to produce spasms of self-
doubt and self-examination in the American and European literary establishment for a long time. Despite all protestations to the contrary, even in
our cynical times, there seems to be a longing for a heroic cultural presence,
a niche for the poet as a moral sage. Brodsky, when he was around, fit well,
perhaps better than any other poet of his generation.

Brodsky's life and work probably had its greatest impact in his homeland. His contemporaries, myself included, still remember the shock of
first encountering, sometime in the early 1960s, the young poet's works in
samizdat. There was this tremendous liberating feeling of having discovered something utterly new and fresh. In the society we lived in, politics as
such were the forbidden province of a tiny ruling clique somewhere in the
distant Kremlin. For the rest of the country, political and semipolitical
thoughts and sentiments were expressed and circulated obliquely, and contemporary art and literature were loved and prized precisely for their ability to articulate, in Aesopian language, forbidden or discouraged ideas and
sentiments. Thus, the most popular young poets of the period were
Yevgeny Yevtushenko and Andrei Voznesensky, skillful practitioners of this
type of "civic" discourse. But Brodsky's poetry wasn't "civic"—in this
sense—at all. It wasn't anti-Soviet so much as it was un-Soviet, ignoring the
regime utterly and refusing to enter into any kind of dialogue with it.

Brodsky's poems opened up completely new vistas. Optimism was the mandatory mode of expression in daily life and art, but Brodsky's work dared to be intensely tragic. Collectivism was the watchword, but Brodsky's lyrical protagonist was a loner and a misfit. Brodsky reintroduced religious themes and vocabulary to Russian poetry at a time when religion had long been branded as capitalism's "opiate of the masses." It was outmoded, the closed realm of ignorant old people. The Soviet astronaut Yuri Gagarin had gone into space and he hadn't encountered any God there, had he? So the "ultimate argument" went.

Even more significantly, while still in his twenties, Brodsky soaked up many ideas from the great Russian religious philosophers Nikolai Berdyaev and Lev Shestov, whose work was strictly taboo in the Soviet Union. Brodsky's poetry was thereby enriched immensely, acquiring a distinctive and for that period highly unusual philosophical bent and depth. Brodsky's preoccupation with time, death, faith, and the power of language struck a chord with his generation of poetry readers in Russia.

None of this would have mattered had all these feelings and ideas not been expressed by an utterly self-assured poetic voice. Almost from the outset, Brodsky showed himself to be a remarkably accomplished writer, a true master, who wasted very little time scaling the heights of technical virtuosity. Brodsky's rhymes are especially rich and inventive, rarely if ever used for purely decorative purposes. They move the train of thought along, working in tandem with often complex meters and a great deal of enjambment, a typical and striking feature of Brodsky's verse. Brodsky's metaphors, one of his key devices and main strengths, are bold, often multilayered, and ingeniously constructed, allowing the poem to expand and soar.

This ability of Brodsky's verse to propel itself, often to considerable length (his "Great Elegy to John Donne," for example, runs to 308 lines), was one of the young poet's major accomplishments and lent his private readings in Leningrad a distinctive tone; it remained a Brodsky trademark. Nabokov once said that reading Pushkin enlarged one's lungs; the same could be said about some of Brodsky's long poems—a form he reintroduced to Russian poetry almost singlehandedly.

Brodsky also injected a strong dose of Anglo-Saxon influence into Russian literature. In and of itself this was not without precedent—Pushkin's fascination with Lord Byron's romanticism comes to mind—but Brodsky's models were decidedly novel for the Russian poetic tradition: the English metaphysical poets and the anglophone modernists. Very early on he translated Andrew Marvell, George Herbert, and John Donne into Russian, as well as plays by Brendan Behan (*The Quare Fellow*) and Tom Stoppard (*Rosencrantz and Guildenstern Are Dead*). At this point matters can get a bit complicated. Some of Brodsky's early baroquelike eloquence and tendency to overuse metaphors can be traced not only to seventeenth-century English poetry but also to the Russian classicists Kantemir and Derzhavin. On the other hand, Brodsky's predilection for prosaic expressions and even shocking vulgarisms—evidently stemming from his knowledge of modern Western poetry—can also be linked to some of his Russian predecessors, such as Mayakovsky, Sasha Chorny, and Boris Slutsky.

One thing is clear. By moving to the West and retaining his strong creative drive here, Brodsky managed to pave some new and exciting paths for Russian culture in the same way that his illustrious predecessors from the St. Petersburg modernist movement did. Stravinsky, Balanchine, and Nabokov all, in one way or another, helped unclog their homeland's hardened creative arteries, if only, as in the case of Nabokov, posthumously.

Brodsky was luckier. The political changes that came about in Russia in the late 1980s and the official recognition of his importance that followed allowed his poetry to return to his native shores during his lifetime. He saw virtually dozens of Russian editions of his poetry appear in the space of just a few years without even a hint of prodding on his side; the combined printings amounted to well over a million copies. Brodsky was inundated with letters from young poets from all over Russia. Many sent him their manuscripts for advice and approval, and Brodsky once complained to me that he was buried under an avalanche of Brodskylike poems seven feet deep. It was to be expected that most of these aspiring poets would imitate the master so slavishly: his pungent vocabulary, with its deliberate mix of high and low; the detached tone of his later poems, in which understatement and irony become dominant; his whole weary *weltanschauung*. To imitate such a master cannot be considered ignoble.

These young poets also eagerly awaited Brodsky's return to Russia, after an absence of more than twenty years, if not to settle (as another great exile, Aleksandr Solzhenitsyn, had), then at least for a visit, and if not to Moscow then surely to his native city, to which the grand historical name of St. Petersburg had been restored, at last, in 1991. They begged him to come, promising a triumphant welcome: "We will carry you through the streets!"

He never returned. He rationalized his decision many times and in many different—almost tired—ways. At its core, I believe, was the hard, desperate, obstinate feeling of being a lone wolf who should not look back.

"The best way out is always through," to quote Brodsky's favorite line from Robert Frost.

By maintaining his distance, Brodsky retained his mythic image, earned first in his confrontations with the authorities in Russia and then by leaving the country. Who knows? Maybe returning to his native shores and meeting all his countless admirers would have shattered this image. Maybe the legions of Brodsky fans would have been disappointed when they saw their aging idol face to face. Someone once quipped that the Russian public loves their poets young and dead. Brodsky outlived some certifiable literary legends in Russia (Pushkin was killed in a duel when he was thirty-seven, Lermontov when he was twenty-six; Esenin committed suicide at thirty, Mayakovsky at thirty-six), but he left Russia at thirty-two at a time when emigrating was tantamount to disappearing into the netherworld. The miraculous, Orphean return of Brodsky's poetry only reinforced this perception of him as a legend. His sudden death in distant New York propelled Brodsky into the very pantheon of Russia's literary gods.

Once I told Brodsky about a malicious comment from some Russian émigré journal, which accused him of "climbing to the heights of fame over the steps of the Russian language." Brodsky, who tended to take criticism hard, paled immediately; the blood drained from his face, he seemed about to break into a wolfish snarl, when suddenly he laughed out loud and said: "Lord! What could be better, right?"

Having known during my lifetime a few creatures who belonged to this rarest category of humanity, vaguely described as geniuses, I can say that Brodsky was the most forceful of them all. Strangely enough, this force manifested itself not only during Brodsky's life, which would be understandable, but also after his death. One of the most striking episodes of this kind occurred during the memorial service for Brodsky held at the Cathedral of St. John the Divine in New York on March 8, 1996. By pure coincidence, the service was held on the fortieth day after Joseph's death, when, according to Russian Orthodox tradition, the soul of the deceased, having quit his earthly body, finally transposes to the other world.

Brodsky's friends read his work at this ceremony, both in Russian and in English translation. Then, at the close of the service, a tape of Brodsky himself reading one of his poems was played. Among the previous readers had been some great poets accustomed to performing at public occasions, and their delivery had been strong and masterful. But Brodsky's voice soared, reminding me of what Nadezhda Mandelstam once said about him: "This isn't a man, it's a wind orchestra!" Here was music-making of a completely different order. It was as if Brodsky's soul had refused to obey tradition and start on its way up. It wanted to be here, among his fellow poets, with the audience. It wanted to be heard, to participate in this most unusual bardic competition—and it wanted to win. Which it did. In the huge confines of the cathedral, the powerful, vital, unstoppable voice of Joseph Brodsky soared, another triumph for the lone wolf of poetry.

BRODSKY, GREENWICH VILLAGE, NEW YORK, 1978

1

A LENINGRAD YOUTH

Volkov. You were born in May 1940, which is to say, a little more than a year before Hitler's army invaded Russia. Do you remember the blockade of Leningrad, which began in September 1941?

Brodsky. One scene I remember quite well. My mother is pulling me on a sled through streets adrift in snow. It's evening, and searchlight beams are sweeping the sky. My mother is pulling me past an empty bakery. This is near the Cathedral of the Transfiguration, not far from our apartment house. This is my childhood . . . I remember my mother talking about which of the people she knew had died and how, and which had been found in their apartments—dead. When my father came back from the front, he and my mother often talked about this. They discussed who had been where during the blockade.

Volkov. But did they talk about the cannibalism in besieged Leningrad?

Brodsky. Yes, they did. Naturally.

Volkov. You were evacuated from Leningrad for less than a year, to Cherepovets. Do you remember coming back to Leningrad?

Brodsky. Very well. One of the most terrible memories of my childhood is connected with my return from Cherepovets. At the train station, a crowd of people mobbed the train. When it started moving, some old invalid hobbled after it, still trying to climb onto a car, and someone poured boiling water on him. It was like some scene out of Noah and the ark.

Volkov. What were your emotions on Victory Day, 1945?

Brodsky. Mama and I went to see the military salute. We were in that huge crowd on the banks of the Neva by Liteiny Bridge. But I have absolutely no memory of my emotions on the occasion. I was only five years old.

Volkov. Precisely where in Leningrad were you born?

Brodsky. I think it was in a small hospital on the Petrograd side. But I grew up mostly on Ryleyev Street. During the war my father was in the army. Actually, my mother was in the army, too. She was an interpreter for the German prisoners of war in the prison camp. Toward the end of the war, though, we went to Cherepovets.

Volkov. And you returned to the same place?

Brodsky. Yes, the very same room. At first we found it sealed, whereupon all hell broke loose, and we got into a battle with the authorities and the management. Later they did give us the room back. Actually, we had two rooms. My mother had one on Ryleyev Street, and my father had another, on Gaz Boulevard, at the corner of the Obvodny Canal. Really, I spent my entire childhood between those two points.

Volkov. In your poems, practically from the very start, a distinctly untraditional view of Petersburg comes through. Even in your very early poems, Petersburg is a city of outlying workers' districts rather than a museum. Just look at your poem, "From the outskirts to the center," which was written when you were twenty-something. In it you describe Leningrad as "a peninsula of industries, a paradise of workshops, an arcade of factories."

Brodsky. Yes, that's Little Okhta!

Volkov. How did you choose to refer to the city, as Leningrad or Petersburg?

Brodsky. As Peter, really. And for me, Peter is the palaces and the canals. But, of course, my childhood predisposed me to an acute perception of the industrial landscape. I remember the sensation of this enormous expanse, open, filled with these not very imposing but jutting structures. Like smokestacks. All those new construction sites, the spectacle of the Okhta Chemical Factory. That whole poetics of a new era.

Volkov. You might even say that this went *against* the poetics of the new—which is to say, Soviet—era. But reading your poem immediately brings to mind the actual city, the actual landscape—its colors and smells.

Brodsky. You know, as far as I remember, I packed so much of everything into that poem that it's hard for me even to talk about. Under no circumstance could you express it in a single word or phrase. In fact, this is a poem about the 1950s in Leningrad, about the era of our youth. There is even, literally, a comment in it about the appearance of narrow trousers.

Volkov. " . . . your still wide trousers"?

Brodsky. Yes, absolutely correct. It was an attempt to preserve the aesthetics of the 1950s. A great deal gets thrown in, including the contemporary cinema—or at least what we thought was the contemporary cinema at the time.

Volkov. This whole poem could be interpreted as a polemic with Pushkin's "Once again I paid a call."

Brodsky. No, it's more of a paraphrase, but everything seems so dubious from the very first line, doesn't it? I was always very much hung up on the industrial landscape. In Leningrad, it's like the antithesis of the center. And really, no one at the time was writing about that world, about that part of the city, about the outskirts. The main thing in this poem is really the music, that is, the tendency toward that kind of metaphysical resolution. Is there anything important or key in what you see? Even now I can remember how the poem ends. There's an idea there . . .

Volkov. Do you mean the line, "Thank God I was left on this earth without a homeland"? Those words proved prophetic. How did they pop out of you then, in 1962?

Brodsky. Well, there was this idea of solitude . . . of detachment. After all, in that Leningrad topography, there is really a very powerful split. There's a tremendous difference between the center and the outskirts. And suddenly I realized that the outskirts were the beginning of the world, not the end. They were the end of the familiar world but the beginning of the unfamiliar world, which is much bigger, much vaster. In principle the idea was that, in leaving for the outskirts, you're distancing yourself from everything you know and setting out for the real world.

Volkov. I sense in this a certain rejection of traditional decorative Petersburg.

Brodsky. Well, in the first place, there's a slightly lunatic tinge to all this decorativeness in Petersburg. Which is what makes it so interesting. Secondly, the outskirts suit me even more because they provide the sensation of space. It seems to me that in Petersburg the most powerful impressions of my childhood and youth are connected with this unusual sky and the idea of infinity. When that vista opens up before you, it drives you mad. You think that something utterly remarkable must be happening on the far shore . . . And even though you know everyone who lives there and you know everything in advance, still, when you look, you can't help this feeling. The impression's especially strong when you look out, say, from the Trubetskoy tower of the Peter and Paul Fortress toward New Holland, downstream and toward the opposite bank. You see all those spouts there, all this devilment.

Volkov. The land of Alexander Blok.

Brodsky. Yes, it's what Blok was so stoned on. After all, he got stoned on the Petersburg sunsets, didn't he? And he prophesied this, that, and the other. In fact, the point is not the color of the sunset but the perspective, the sensation of infinity, right? Infinity and, more generally, a certain unknown quality. I think too that Blok, for all his apocalyptic visions, was trying to tame all this. I don't want to say anything bad about Blok, but it really is a banal resolution for the Petersburg phenomenon. A banal interpretation of the space.

Volkov. Might this love of yours for the outskirts be connected with your position as an outsider in Soviet society? After all, you didn't follow the intellectual's well-trodden path: school, university, a respectable job, and so on. How did this come about? Why did you drop out of school?

Brodsky. It just happened.

Volkov. Where was your school?

Brodsky. Oh, there were so many of them!

Volkov. You changed schools?

Brodsky. Yes, like gloves. Partly because I would be living with my father and then with my mother. More with my mother, of course. Right now I get all those numbers mixed up, but first I went to School No. 203, if I'm not mistaken, the old Peterschule. Before the revolution it was a German academy, and its pupils included quite a few rather remarkable people, but in our day it was an ordinary Soviet school. After the fourth year, for some reason I had to leave there—something connected to the fact that I turned out to live in a different district—so I transferred to School No. 196 on Mokhovaya Street. Something happened there, too. I don't remember what anymore. And after three years I had to transfer to School No. 181. I went there for a year, my seventh. Unfortunately, I was held back a year, and because I was held back, I was just too fed up to go back to the same school. So I asked my parents to transfer me to the school for my father's place of residence, on the Obvodny Canal. There I fell on marvelous times because this school had a completely different contingent— the working class, really, workers' children. It was a completely different feeling. That quasi-intellectual rabble used to turn me off. It wasn't that I had any kind of class feelings at the time, but in this new school everything was *simple,* right? After my seventh year I tried to get into the Second Baltic Academy, where they trained submariners. That was because my papa was in the navy, and like any kid, I was hung up on all that stuff, you know?

I really have quite wonderful feelings for the navy. I don't even know where I get them, but my childhood, my father, and my native city all come into play. There's nothing to be done about it! The moment I remember the Military Naval Museum, the flag of St. Andrew, the blue cross on the white field . . . There's no better flag in the whole world! I can say that now for certain. But nothing ever came of this enthusiasm of mine, unfortunately.

Volkov. What got in the way?

Brodsky. My nationality, point five [in the passport documents]. I passed the exams and the medical commission, but when it became clear that I was a Jew—I don't even know why it took them so long to figure it out. They sent me through again, and I think they found some problem with my eyes, an astigmatism of the left eye, not that that ever got in anyone else's way. Given whom they took . . . That whole business went up in smoke. As a result, I went back to school on Mokhovaya Street and studied there another year, but by that time I was already sick and tired of the whole business.

Volkov. Did one of your teachers have it in for you especially?

Brodsky. Yes, there was one especially remarkable teacher there. I think he taught the Stalin Constitution. He had come to the school straight from the army, where he'd been a commissar. His face was a total caricature. You know, the way they depict Soviets in cartoons in the West: the hat, the jacket, all square and double-breasted. He hated me with a vengeance, actually. And because he was the secretary of the school's Party organization, he did everything he could to make my life miserable. And that was the end of it. I went to work as a milling machine operator at the Arsenal Plant, P.O. Box 671. I was fifteen years old.

Volkov. That's a pretty rebellious decision for a young Leningrad Jew. How did your parents react?

Brodsky. Well, first of all, they could see nothing was ever going to come of me anyhow. Secondly, I really did want to work. And there just wasn't any dough in the family. Sometimes my father had work and sometimes he didn't. Those were the times, troubled times. Gutalin [shoe polish] had only just kicked the bucket. It was under Gutalin that my papa had been driven out of the army because of Zhdanov's decree forbidding Jews higher than a specific rank (by then my father was a *kavtorang*, that is, a major) from engaging in political work.

Volkov. Who was Gutalin?

Brodsky. Gutalin—that's Joseph Vissarionovich Stalin. Dzhugashvili really. After all, in Leningrad all the shoemakers were Georgians.

Volkov. Didn't the school try to talk you into staying?

Brodsky. Sure, the whole class came to see me. Meanwhile, I was already wooing some girl Pioneer leader, or at least I thought I was, right? I remember coming home from my courting completely torn up. I walk into the room—and we only had two rooms there, one a little bigger, the other a little smaller—and I see almost the entire class sitting there. I must say, this incensed me. That is, my reaction was absolutely not what you'd expect in a Soviet movie. I wasn't touched at all. Quite the contrary, I got angry. And of course I never went back to school.

Volkov. And you never regretted it later?

Brodsky. I don't think I missed out on anything as a result. Although, of course, I did regret not graduating and going to the university and so on. Later I tried to take the high school equivalency exam. I thought I'd flunk physics or chemistry, but I passed those. I know it's funny, but I flunked astronomy. I didn't read anything on astronomy that summer. Really, I never touched it! They asked me something and I started pacing back and forth around the blackboard. I could have tried to retake it, but I was already turned off by the whole thing. I was sick of it all, all those kiddie games, and I had already a taste for work. First the factory, then the morgue in the district hospital. Then the geological expeditions began.

Volkov. What precisely did you do in the morgue?

Brodsky. You know, when I was sixteen, I got the notion of becoming a doctor. A neurosurgeon, naturally. Well, it's the normal dream of every Jewish boy. And after that I had another romantic idea—to begin with what was most unpleasant, most intolerable, that is, with the morgue. My aunt was working in the regional hospital, so I got a job there, at that morgue, as a dissector's assistant. That is, I dissected corpses, removed their guts, and then sewed them back up. I removed their skulls, the lid. And then the doctor made his analysis and reported his conclusions. But my work at the morgue lasted a relatively short time. My father had suffered a heart attack that summer, and when he got out of the hospital and learned I was working in the morgue, he was not pleased, naturally. That's when I left. I should say that I left without any regrets whatsoever. Not because I didn't like the idea of a career as a doctor anymore, but partly the idea had sort of flown out the window. I was already wearing a white jacket, right? Evidently this was what had attracted me mostly about the profession.

Volkov. Working at the morgue didn't revolt you?

Brodsky. You know, right now I couldn't hack it at all, but when you're young you don't think about anything that metaphysical. There were just a number of unpleasant sensations. Say you're lifting an old lady's corpse and turning her over. She has yellow skin, very flabby, it bursts open, and your finger slips into a layer of fat. To say nothing of the smell. Because most people die before shitting, and all that gets left inside. So the smell—it's not only the smell of rotting, but there's all that other stuff, too. That was one of my greatest ordeals.

I left the morgue primarily because of one nasty scene. This was the regional hospital, and in the summer they brought quite a few children there. The problem is that in the summer (and this was July) child mortality jumps. Brucellosis runs rampant through the region. There are numerous cases of toxic dyspepsia, and small children suffer especially. They eat or drink something they shouldn't—say the milk is off—and that's it. Infants are highly susceptible to this. So a gypsy came to see us in the morgue. I gave him his two children—twins, if I'm not mistaken. When he saw them all cut up, he reacted in a rather turbulent fashion. He decided to pin me right where I was. So this gypsy, knife in hand, started chasing me all around the morgue, and I ran in between the tables where the sheet-covered corpses were lying. Jean Cocteau was a piker compared to the surrealism that went on there! Eventually he caught me, grabbed me by the lapels, and I realized something irreparable was about to happen. That was when I managed to grab the surgical hammer—you know the kind, stainless steel—and struck the gypsy's wristbone. His hand unclenched, and he sat down and wept. And all of a sudden I didn't feel so good.

The morgue shared a wall with the Crosses [the notorious Petersburg prison]. Prisoners would toss notes out to us and send each other "horses." A horse is a means of communicating in prison. A way to transmit various kinds of information, as well as bread and things. Say you're a "pigeon." You land in prison, and someone else is getting released, but he doesn't have anything to wear. They take your jacket from you and then wind rags or socks or sheets into a long rope. The jacket gets bundled up and attached to this contraption. Then someone sticks his hand through the window bars and swings this rope and jacket until it lands in the window of the next cell, where they catch it by poking out a hand or a stick. This is called sending something by horse. I could observe all this from the morgue. The funniest part is that later, when I landed in the Crosses my-self, I observed all this from the other side.

Volkov. After the morgue, I believe you worked as a stoker in a boiler-house.

Brodsky. Yes, but that was relatively brief—a few months maybe. Then began my work on geological expeditions. I had had the notion of travel-ing all over the world. But I had absolutely no idea how to make it happen. Then someone—I don't remember who anymore—said there were these geological expeditions. The idea really turned me on, and I found out that every summer geological teams were sent out into the field and that they just needed hands there. Which I had. And legs. And backs, as later became clear. All of this I had as well. I found the Fifth Geological Administration and offered them my modest services, and they took me on.

Volkov. Your nationality didn't matter?

Brodsky. Oh, no! Geology was such a mother hen. It took in anyone who crawled under its wing. Geology became nursemaid to so many people!

Volkov. Where did you go?

Brodsky. We went to the White Sea.

Volkov. So that's when you saw the North for the first time! What im-pression did it make on you?

Brodsky. Those were remarkable places. I mean, there was nothing good about them. This was to the north of Obozyorsk—half-taiga and half-tundra. The mosquitoes were incredible! Everything that happened to me on later geological expeditions—all through Siberia, Yakutia, and the Far East—that was all kindergarten compared with those mosquitoes. It never got worse than that. So it was quite a remarkable tempering. The crew was pretty much picked at random. *Bichi* mostly. Do you know what *bichi* are?

Volkov. Tramps. What they call hobos in America.

Brodsky. Yes, but hobos are a much meeker tribe than *bichi*. *Bichi* had done time. They carried knives.

Volkov. What did you do there?

Brodsky. At the time they were compiling a millionth-scale geological map of the Soviet Union, so we were making a map of the rock deposits in that area, in the North. It was a map of the quaternary beds, that is, the strata of soil that lie relatively close to the surface, clay and so forth. The bore pits get hammered through a meter or a meter and a half. In one day we would cover thirty kilometers on foot and drive in four bore pits. Or, since this was in the tundra, the swamps—they would do a tap. They would just take a pole, drive it in, and pull something out, whatever was there. As a rule, nothing.

Volkov. What were they hoping to find?

Brodsky. Uranium, naturally. So that later . . . Well, we know why they needed uranium. Once, in the Far East, I actually did find a uranium deposit—a small one, but I found it.

Volkov. Was that hard work?

Brodsky. You drag yourself across the taiga, through those perfectly flat, endless swamps. Hunched over. You never straighten up afterward.

Volkov. What were you hauling?

Brodsky. Mainly all kinds of geological instruments. Since this was uranium exploration, dosimeters. At first this was a Geiger counter, to measure radiation, and then later better instruments, fairly sensitive, with a remarkable scale, that gave approximate readings on the radioactivity of a given rock. You were asking me about my impressions of the northern landscape. You see it all, but in completely the wrong key. You perceive the landscape exclusively on the functional level, since psychologically you're not up to anything else.

Volkov. What did you eat and drink there?

Brodsky. Domestically produced canned meat, which we heated up over a campfire. We drank water. And vodka, naturally. We also drank *chifir* [espresso-strength black tea with a narcotic effect favored by prisoners in Siberia] since the main contingent on these geological teams had had considerable experience in that regard. We drank grain alcohol, brake fluid. Anything at all. More precisely, anything we could get our hands on.

Volkov. Were there any women on these expeditions?

Brodsky. Very few. But some. Although in the field sexual problems get resolved and viewed somewhat differently. The situation is both simple and complicated at the same time. The work wipes you out, of course, but that doesn't turn you into some asexual being—quite the opposite. On the other hand, the females on geological expeditions are viewed in the same vein as the males to a significant extent because they're doing the same work. And it's hard to tell: Maybe they aren't really up for that. Or on the contrary, maybe the way's wide open. At any rate there was a strict sex code—if not of honor then of conduct. Because if you started fooling around with someone, that meant everyone else came off a loser, right? So there were all kinds of psychological nuances. Often we would stop over at lumber camps, and there would always be some women there who'd been released from police custody, and they would go at it right away. As a rule, you don't linger anywhere; you stop for a night, then you're off. So sexual liaisons are like a picaresque novel, adapted to that landscape and that contingent. Generally speaking, though, during all my years on expeditions, I didn't notice any particular erotic tension or unruliness. A few times I came across couples that worked together, a husband and wife or lovers. People tended to tease them, so they behaved more or less discreetly, trying not to provoke too much gossiping—which was inevitable, of course.

Volkov. How many years did you spend going on expeditions?

Brodsky. Five or six, beginning in about 1956 or 1957, that is, when I was sixteen or seventeen, and ending in about 1962.

Volkov. For a beginning poet, the life experience you had was awfully diverse even for Russia.

Brodsky. As far as being useful in literature? Like in Gorky's *My Universities?* All that *was* my university education, and in many respects, it was a rather remarkable time. At that age you take in and absorb everything with such avidity and intensity, and you look on absolutely everything that happens to you with such incredible interest, as if it were happening for the first time. Yet even now I believe that not all experience is useful and entertaining. There is nothing really bad in life, in my opinion. The only thing that's bad in it is predictability. And whenever I've sensed this predictability in some life situation, I've always bailed out. So that the saying "repetition is the mother of learning" doesn't apply to me. Unless it's the repetition Georg Christoph Lichtenberg spoke of. His saying ran approximately like this: "It's one thing to believe in God and something else to believe in Him again." That is, when you come to God after the experience of disbelief, then it's a completely different story, a different belief. Kierkegaard talked about this, too.

Volkov. You once told me that predictability was one of the main conventions of the poetic art. You said that, in order to have the possibility of writing, the poet has to exist in a state of inertia.

Brodsky. Well, certainly. An existential echo has to arise. That principle of metaphysical music we've already mentioned. Certainly, there is a definite plus to predictability. Personally, though, I've always aimed to make myself scarce to avoid becoming a victim of inertia.

Volkov. Not that there have been that many predictable situations in So-viet life. Especially in Stalin's day, when one mortal threat or another al-ways hung over the average intellectual. Do you remember, say, the Central Committee's "Zhdanov resolution" about Zoshchenko and Akhmatova being discussed in your family?

Brodsky. No, that went absolutely right by me. I was six years old then! I've retained a different vivid memory from those years—my first white bread, the first French roll I bit into. The war had recently ended. We were at my mama's sister's house, my aunt's, Raisa Moiseyevna's, and somewhere they got a hold of that roll. I stood on a chair and ate it while they all watched me. That I've remembered.

Volkov. What about the later campaign, in 1948, against Prokofiev, Shostakovich, and the other composers?

Brodsky. I read about that in the papers. I remember them discussing Vano Muradeli and his opera, *A Great Friendship,* but I didn't really under-stand what it was all about. We didn't discuss that in our family. I do re-member conversations about the "Leningrad affair," though. My father said that Popkov was a good man.

Volkov. How did you perceive the anti-Semitic campaign of the early 1950s, that is, the affair of the "doctor assassins"?

Brodsky. Now that story I remember quite distinctly. I remember com-ing home from school and finding my mother and father, who were sup-posed to be at work at that time, sitting in our room, oddly enough. They looked at me so strangely, and one of them—I don't remember if it was my father or my mother—said they would probably have to go on a long trip soon, and because of that they would have to sell the piano and the other furniture. Then I asked them what kind of trip it was. And my father tried to explain it all to me very simply. He told me about the open letter to *Pravda* that supposedly had been signed by all the leading Jews. It was rumored that in it they confessed and expressed all kinds of loyal sentiments.

Volkov. I didn't know about this alleged letter then, in 1953, but I re-member how uncomfortable I felt in that widespread anti-Jewish hysteria. To put it simply, I was frightened. Were you frightened as well?

Brodsky. You know, I wasn't. No. But I wasn't particularly enthusiastic ei-ther, I must say. It was clear that my parents were not very happy with the situation, and I felt sorry for them. We'd have to take out the furniture, deal with it all. I was just thinking about the disruption.

Volkov. How did you react to Stalin's death in March of 1953?

Brodsky. At the time I was studying at the Peterschule. They called us all into the auditorium. The secretary of the Party organization at the Peterschule was my class directress, Lydia Vasilyevna Lisitsyna. Zhdanov himself had pinned the Order of Lenin on her, which was a very big deal, and we all knew about it. She climbed up onto the stage and started talking, but at a certain point she broke off and shrieked in a heartrending voice: "On your knees! On your knees!" Then all hell broke loose! All around me everyone was howling, and I was supposed to be howling, too, apparently, but—at the time to my shame, but now, I think, to my credit—I wasn't. It all seemed so barbaric to me. Everyone around me was standing there sniffing. Some were even sobbing, and a few were really seriously weeping. They let us go home early that day, and again, strangely, my parents were waiting for me at home. My mother was in the kitchen. Our apartment was communal. In the kitchen, the pots, the neighbor ladies—and everyone weeping. Even my mother was weeping. I went back to our room somewhat amazed. Then suddenly my father winked at me, and I realized that there really was no reason for me to get particularly upset over Stalin's death.

Volkov. What did you hear about Khruschchev's anti-Stalin speech at the Twentieth Party Congress?

Brodsky. You know, I heard about the report, but it was "secret," after all, for Party members only, and the secret was kept fairly strictly. For instance, my uncle, who was a Party member, never did tell us anything. So that I didn't read the text of the report until I got here, to the West.

Volkov. What were your feelings in connection with Stalin's unexpected posthumous disgrace?

Brodsky. That disgrace suited me just fine. At the time Stalin died I was—how old?—twelve, right? I certainly didn't feel anything special for Stalin, that's for sure. Or rather, I was sick and tired of him. Word of honor! Well, his portraits everywhere! And that generalissimo uniform—the red trouser stripes and so forth. Even though I adore a military uniform, in Stalin's case it always seemed to me that something behind it was rotten. That service cap with the insignia and the brass, and the other things—all that somehow didn't jibe with Stalin, it didn't seem very convincing. And then that mustache!

Meanwhile, parenthetically, do you know who Stalin made a very strong impression on? Homosexuals! This is terribly interesting. There was something southern, something Mediterranean in that mustache. A real-live mustachioed daddy! I think that a significant percentage of the support for Stalin among the intelligentsia in the West had to do with their latent homosexuality. I would guess that many people in the West turned to the Communist faith precisely for this reason. That is, they simply worshipped Stalin!

To my taste, the best thing written about Stalin is Mandelstam's "Ode" of 1937. In my view, this may be the grandest poem Mandelstam ever wrote. Even more. This poem may be one of the most significant events in all of twentieth-century Russian literature. That's my belief. Because this poem of Mandelstam's is simultaneously both an ode and a satire, and out of the combination of these two opposite aspirations arises an utterly new quality. This is a fantastic work of art.

You know, it's like in Russia at a bazaar, when a gypsy would come up to you, grab you by the button, look into your eyes, and say: "Want me to tell your fortune?" What was she doing, diving in your face? She was violating a territorial imperative! Because otherwise, who on earth would agree? Who would cough up? So you see, in his "Ode," Mandelstam carried off more or less the same trick. That is, he violated that distance, he violated that same territorial imperative—and the result is simply fantastic. To say nothing of the poem's phenomenal aesthetics: cubist, almost posterlike. It reminds you of a John Hartfield photomontage, or better yet, Rodchenko. You do know that Mandelstam has a poem entitled "Slate Ode"? So then, this is his "Coal Ode": "If ever coal I took for praising higher still, A drawing for delight immutable . . ." This is where you get the fantastic, constantly changing angles in the poem.

Volkov. It's noteworthy that first Mandelstam wrote a satirical poem about Stalin, which got him arrested, evidently, in 1934. But his "Ode" was written later. Usually it happens the other way around. First they compose odes and later disenchanted pamphlets. And Stalin's reaction, at first glance, was illogical. Mandelstam was exiled to Voronezh for the satire, and then they let him go, but after the "Ode" they destroyed him.

Brodsky. You know, if I were Joseph Vissarionovich, I wouldn't have been at all cross over the satirical poem, but after the "Ode," if I were Stalin, I would have slit Mandelstam's throat immediately. I would have realized that he'd violated me, he'd moved in, and there's nothing more frightening or shocking than that.

Volkov. Is there anything else in Russian literature about Stalin that seems significant to you?

Brodsky. Nothing else on the level of Mandelstam's "Ode." After all, he was taking a remarkable theme that runs all through Russian literature, "the poet and the tsar." In the final analysis, this theme is resolved to a certain degree in the poem inasmuch as it points to how close the tsar and the poet are. To do this Mandelstam makes use of the fact that he and Stalin share the same first name [Osip=Iosif=Joseph]. So his rhymes become existential.

Volkov. Mandelstam declaimed his satire on Stalin right and left, but those were dangerous times. You could crash and burn for an innocent joke. Still, the poet had to read his new poem out loud, at least to some of his acquaintances, to share it. That was very important to him. Do you remember reading a poem of your own to someone else for the first time?

Brodsky. You know, I don't. I really don't. One of the first was a Leningrad writer, Yakov Gordin, a remarkable man, one of my first literary friendships. I remember reading my poems to the literary group attached to *Smena,* the young people's newspaper. The leaders of this group, as I recall, were two very unfortunate men. That's instead of saying "two great scoundrels."

Volkov. When did you begin writing poetry?

Brodsky. At eighteen or so, more or less, although this was still pretty bad stuff. I think I heard about the *Smena* literary group from some people on a geological expedition. There were always a lot of people writing poetry on those expeditions.

Volkov. What inspired you to write poetry?

Brodsky. There were two impulses, actually. The first was when someone showed me *Literaturnaya Gazeta,* which had published a poem by Boris Slutsky. I was probably sixteen at the time. In those days I was busy educating myself, frequenting libraries. That's where I found Robert Burns in Marshak's translations, for instance. All this was terribly much to my liking, but I myself didn't write anything and wasn't even thinking along those lines. Then they showed me a poem by Slutsky that made a very big impression on me. The second impulse, which is what actually inspired me to try my hand, came in 1958, I think. There was a poet, Vladimir Britanishsky, who used to knock around on geological expeditions about that time. A student of Slutsky's, by the way. Someone showed me his book, which was called *Quest.* I remember the cover as if it were yesterday. Well, I thought that surely someone could write better on that topic. So I started composing something myself, and that's how it all began.

Volkov. What were your emotions when your first book of poetry came out? After all, it came out in Russian in the USA. At the time, in 1965, that kind of foreign publication was still an extraordinary phenomenon. The memory of the incredible international scandal over the publication of Pasternak's *Doctor Zhivago* in Italy in 1957 was still fresh in everyone's mind. As was the 1965 trial of Sinyavsky and Daniel, who were accused specifically of publishing in the West.

Brodsky. Yes, that collection came out in the United States under the aegis of Inter-Language Literary Associates. At the time, I was in exile. I remember when I was released they showed it to me. A little gray volume filled with poems. I looked at it—well, it was a sensation of utter nonsense. You know, it felt as if these were poems that had been confiscated during a search and published.

Volkov. You mean, you had nothing to do with putting it together?

Brodsky. Absolutely nothing.

Volkov. What about your second book of poetry. *A Halt in the Wilderness?* It came out in America, too, with the Chekhov Russian-language publishing house. Did you put that one together yourself?

Brodsky. You know, not much of it. I remember they compiled it for me, and I tossed some things out.

Volkov. A Halt in the Wilderness was divided into sections: "Hills," "Anno Domini," "Fountain," "Verse Epics," "Gorbunov and Gorchakov," and "Translations." Did you lend these titles any particular significance?

Brodsky. Maybe, but right now I don't remember what that was anymore. Well, maybe "Anno Domini," which are lyrical poems devoted exclusively to the love drama. On the other hand, "Verse Epics" was inaccurately titled. In fact, these are not verse epics but long poems. There are things in there that belong in "Anno Domini," both thematically and chronologically. "Hills" are simply earlier poems, I think. I just liked that poem, "Hills."

Volkov. You're so nonchalant, so unpaternal about your books.

Brodsky. You know, in that sense I very much like one thing I read once about the painter Utrillo. Basically, he was an alcoholic, a very bad alcoholic. Which Utrillo's mother, Suzanne Valadon, did everything she could to encourage. Madame basically felt that she was the principal artist in the family. When Utrillo arrived at an exhibition of his pictures and they asked him to point out which were his paintings and which were the fakes, he simply couldn't do it. Not because he didn't remember, but simply because he didn't care. He never did remember when he had or hadn't painted a given picture. I don't remember these things either.

Volkov. To get back to *A Halt in the Wilderness,* what did you feel when you saw it?

Brodsky. I realized that I would never have another like it in my life. Because your humble servant was another person by that time. The author of *A Halt in the Wilderness* was a man with certain normal sentiments. He got upset over a loss, he rejoiced over—well, I don't know over what anymore. Over some inner discovery, right? By the time the book came out I knew for certain that I would never write anything like it again. I wouldn't have those same sentiments, that openness, those specific solutions.

Volkov. In her day, Akhmatova was very much caught up in the forays to the Stray Dog. Did she ever tell you stories about it?

Brodsky. Fairly often, fairly often.

Volkov. What impression did you get of the Stray Dog?

Brodsky. That it was a smelly hole where the Petersburg bohemia of the turn of the century gathered. Nonetheless, I still have a somewhat romantic impression: a half-basement, arches painted by Sudeikin . . .

Volkov. Do you like Akhmatova's poem about the Stray Dog—"All of us are drunkards here, loose women . . ."?

Brodsky. It's a good poem, but I don't like it. Although the diction in this poem is marvelous.

Volkov. Have you ever felt a nostalgia for that prerevolutionary bohemian life? Or did you have other more modern notions of how a poet or writer should live?

Brodsky. Personally, I never experienced that kind of nostalgia. For me all that smacked rather too much of someone like Alexander Grin, his version of the *dolce vita,* shall we say. That kind of life has never held any special mystery or charm for me. The Stray Dog always seemed to me like a much less interesting place than one of Fyodor Dostoevsky's inns.

Volkov. But how did the *dolce vita* of Leningrad look in your day?

Brodsky. Probably it was represented by artists and their studios. "Let's go see the artist in his studio!" That's how I remember that. I had two artist friends who had a studio in a perfectly marvelous place, near the Academy of Fine Arts. The artists were mediocre, although talented in their own way, designers. Fairly amusing companions, terribly witty. Every once in a while they'd have a gathering of bohemians, or what passed for bohemians. They laid around on rugs and pelts. They drank. Young girls would show up. Because what's so attractive about artists anyway? They have models, right? According to that particular hierarchy, a model was somehow above a mere mortal.

Mainly we had erotically charged conversations. A kind of light entertainment or, rather, clowning around. And tragedy, too, of course. All those tortured emotions over who was leaving with whom, because the disposition of couples was, as usual, totally wrong. Your usual spectacle. There were people who came simply to watch; they were the audience. And then there were the actors. I, for example, was an actor. I think the same thing went on at the Stray Dog to a certain degree.

Volkov. Did you drink hard?

Brodsky. What do you think?

Volkov. What exactly did you drink?

Brodsky. Well, whatever was there, because we didn't always have money. Vodka, as a rule. Although subsequently, when we inched up toward thirty, the vodka started being replaced by dry wine. Which absolutely enraged me, because I never could stand dry wine. It gave me heartburn, as a rule. This really was not the "dolce vita" because the *dolce vita*—especially the way engineers imagine it—is champagne and chocolate.

Volkov. Did you drink cognac?

Brodsky. Yes, Armenian, and Courvoisier when it turned up. Cognac never did much for me. What interested me most about cognac was the foreign bottles, not what they contained. For quite a long time I held to that Russian notion that "cognac smells like bedbugs." To this day cognac leaves me cold. Vodka is another matter. And whiskey, when we had it.

Volkov. Where did you ever get whiskey in Leningrad in the 1960s?

Brodsky. The whiskey was a Budapest bottling. Which didn't even bother me, since the label was in English. The most wonderful bottles were for gin, though. I remember, some American came to see Volodya Ufliand, and he brought a bottle of Beefeaters. This was a very long time ago, in 1959. So we're sitting there looking at this picture: a Guardsman in the Tower in all this red paraphernalia, and Ufliand made one of the most perceptive comments I remember. He said, "You know, Joseph, here we are getting stoned on this picture, and those people there, in the West, they're probably getting stoned on the absence of some picture on our vodka."

Volkov. I believe there is some picture on our Russian vodka, some Stalinist skyscraper!

Brodsky. You're talking about our Hotel Moscow on the Stolichnaya label, but here on the vodka it was just called "Moskovskaya," and there was this white and green picture—you could never imagine anything more abstract. When you look at this green and white, at those black letters—especially in the condition you're in drinking—you get absolutely freaked out. Half is green and the rest is white, right? This horizon, a hieroglyph for infinity.

Summer 1981–Winter 1992

BRODSKY TALKING WITH VOLKOV (NOT SHOWN) AT
COLUMBIA UNIVERSITY, NEW YORK, 1978

2

MARINA TSVETAEVA

Volkov. People have referred to you as a poet belonging to Akhmatova's circle. She loved you and supported you at difficult moments, but from talking with you I know that the work of Marina Tsvetaeva had a much greater influence on your development as a poet than did Akhmatova's. Tsvetaeva was the poet of your youth. When you speak about Tsvetaeva's poetry, you often call it Calvinistic. Why?

Brodsky. Above all, bearing in mind just how unprecedented her syntax was. This allowed—or rather, forced—her to spell everything out in her verse. In principle, Calvinism is a very simple matter: it is man keeping strict accounts with himself, with his conscience and consciousness. In that sense, by the way, Dostoevsky is a Calvinist as well. A Calvinist, to put it briefly, is someone who is constantly declaring Judgment Day against himself—as if in the absence (or impatient for) the Almighty. In this sense, there is no other poet like her in Russia.

Volkov. What about Pushkin's "Remembrance"? "And with disgust I read my life,/ I tremble and I swear . . ."? Tolstoy always pointed to these lines of Pushkin as an example of harsh self-condemnation.

Brodsky. The accepted notion is that you can find anything in Pushkin, and for the almost seventy years that followed his duel, this was very nearly the case. After which came the twentieth century . . . But there's quite a lot you can't find in Pushkin, and not only because of the changing times and history. Quite a lot is not in Pushkin by reason of his temperament and sex: women have been much harsher in their moral demands. From their standpoint—from Tsvetaeva's, at least—there simply is no Tolstoy. At least not as a source of judgment about Pushkin. In this respect, I'm even more of a woman than Tsvetaeva. What did our prolific count know of self-condemnation?

Volkov. What about, "There is a thrill in battle,/ An abyss of gloom on the brink . . ."? Don't these lines of Pushkin convey a sense of the elements and rebellion that is close to Tsvetaeva?

Brodsky. Tsvetaeva is not rebellion. Tsvetaeva is the cardinal statement of "the voice of heavenly truth/ against the earthly truth." In both instances, you'll note, we have truth. You won't find this in Pushkin, the latter truth in particular. The former is obvious and has been wholly usurped by Orthodoxy. The latter—at best—is a reality, but in no way a truth.

Volkov. It has always seemed to me that Pushkin does talk about this.

Brodsky. No. This is a huge topic, and it might be better not to get started on it. This is a matter of the judgment, which is actually final if only because *all* the arguments in favor of earthly truth have been enumerated. Tsvetaeva reaches the very end of this enumeration; she even tries to add onto it. Exactly like the heroes in Fyodor Mikhailovich Dostoevsky. Pushkin, after all—and don't forget this—is a nobleman. And, if you like, an Englishman in his attitude toward reality, a member of the English Club; he's restrained. He doesn't have anything you could call a violent expression of emotion. Tsvetaeva doesn't either, but her very statement of the question, à la Job—either-or—gives rise to an intensity that is not characteristic of Pushkin. The two dots over her *ë* have nothing to do with proper notation, nothing to do with her era, nothing to do with her historical context, nothing to do even with her personal experience or temperament. Those two dots are there because a space exists over the *e* to put them.

Volkov. The violent expression of emotion is indeed absent in the artists ordinarily deemed universal—Pushkin and Mozart, for example.

Brodsky. There is no violent expression of emotion in Mozart because he is above that. Whereas in Beethoven and Chopin everything rests on this.

Volkov. In Mozart we find glimmers of the supraindividual, which Beethoven, to say nothing of Chopin, does not have. And, since you prefer, as I know, Mozart, Tsvetaeva's elevated emotional tone actually ought to scare you off.

Brodsky. Quite the contrary. No one understands this.

Volkov. When you and I spoke in connection with Auden about the neutrality of the poetic voice, at the time you defended this neutrality.

Brodsky. This is not a contradiction. The source of rhythm is time. Remember I said that any poem is reorganized time? The more technically diverse a poet is, the more intimate his connection with time, with the source of rhythm. And Tsvetaeva is one of the most rhythmically diverse poets. Rhythmically rich and generous. Actually, "generous" is a qualitative category: let's stick to quantitative categories, all right? Time speaks to the individual in various voices. Time has its own bass, its own tenor—and it has its own falsetto. If you like, Tsvetaeva is the falsetto of time. The voice that goes beyond the range of proper notation.

Volkov. You mean, you think that Tsvetaeva's emotional intensity serves the same purpose as Auden's neutrality? That she achieves the same effect?

Brodsky. The same and even more. In my opinion, Tsvetaeva as a poet is in many respects greater than Auden. That tragic sound . . . Ultimately, time itself understands *what* it is. It has to. And it has to make itself known. Hence—from this function of time—arose Tsvetaeva.

Volkov. Yesterday, by the way, was her birthday, and I thought, how few years have passed really since her death. The poets you and I have been discussing are almost our contemporaries. And at the same time they are already historical figures, fossils almost.

Brodsky. Yes and no. This is very interesting, Solomon. The fact of the matter is that the view of the world you discover in these poets' work has become a part of our perception. If you like, our perception is a logical (or perhaps alogical) extension of what is set out in their verse. It is the development of principles, notions, and ideas whose expression was the work of these authors. Once we recognized them, nothing more important ever happened in our lives, right? I, for example, have never encountered anything more important. My own thinking included. These people simply created us. That's it. That is what makes them our contemporaries. Nothing else did so much to form us—me at any rate—as Frost, Tsvetaeva, Cavafy, Rilke, Akhmatova, and Pasternak. Therefore they are our contemporaries until we kick the bucket. For as long as we live. I think that a poet's influence—this emanation or radiation—lasts for a generation or two.

Volkov. When exactly did you first come across Tsvetaeva's poetry?

Brodsky. I was nineteen or twenty. Times being what they were, I read Tsvetaeva not in books, of course, but exclusively in *samizdat* typescript. I don't remember who gave it to me, but when I read "Poem of the Mountain," everything clicked. Nothing I've read since in Russian has produced such an impression.

Volkov. I don't like Tsvetaeva's pointing finger, her eagerness to chew everything up and regurgitate a rhymed prescriptive truth that may not have been worth all the fuss.

Brodsky. Nonsense! There's nothing like that in Tsvetaeva! There is a thought—as a rule, an extremely uncomfortable thought—taken to its conclusion. Hence, perhaps, your impression that this thought is wagging its finger at you, so to speak. One can speak of a certain preachiness with respect to Pasternak—"Living a life is not crossing a field"—and so forth, but definitely not Tsvetaeva. If the content of Tsvetaeva's poetry could be reduced to some formula then it's this: "To your insane world/But one reply—I refuse." And Tsvetaeva actually derives a certain satisfaction from this refusal. She says no with a palpable satisfaction: *nye-e-t!*

Volkov. Tsvetaeva has an aphoristic quality. She can be pilfered quote by quote, almost like Griboedov's *Woe from Wit*.

Brodsky. Oh, definitely!

Volkov. But for some reason this aphoristic aspect of Tsvetaeva's has always repelled me.

Brodsky. I've never had that reaction. In Tsvetaeva the main thing is the sound. Do you remember that famous anthology from the Khrushchev era, *Tarusa Pages?* I think it came out in 1961. In it there was a selection of poems by Tsvetaeva (for which, by the way, a deep bow to all the anthology's compilers). When I read one of these poems—from the "Trees" cycle—I was utterly shaken. In it, Tsvetaeva says: "Friends! Fraternal throng! You, whose stroke has swept/ The track of earthly insult./ Forest! My Elysium!" What is this? Is she really talking about trees?

Volkov. "My soul, Elysium of shadows . . ."

Brodsky. Of course, calling a forest "Elysium" is a marvelous formula. But it is not just a formula.

Volkov. In the United States, and subsequently throughout the world, a great deal of attention has been paid to the role of women in culture. They study the characteristics of women's contribution to painting, theater, literature. Do you think that women's poetry is something specific?

Brodsky. You can't apply adjectives to poetry—or to realism, for that matter. Many years ago (in 1956, I believe), I read somewhere how at a meeting of Polish writers where they were discussing socialist realism someone got up and stated: "I'm in favor of realism without adjectives." Those Poles.

Volkov. Still, does a woman's voice in poetry really not differ in any way from a man's?

Brodsky. Only in the verb endings. When I hear, "There are three eras of memory. And the first is as if it were just yesterday," I don't know who's saying it, a man or a woman.

Volkov. I could never separate those lines from Akhmatova's voice. Those lines are spoken by a woman with a regal bearing.

Brodsky. The regal bearing of these lines is not the bearing of Akhmatova herself but of *what* she is saying. It's the same with Tsvetaeva. "Friends! Fraternal throng!" Who is saying that? A man or a woman?

Volkov. Well, what about, "Oh, the howl of women from all time: 'My sweet, what have I done to you?'" That is such a female cry.

Brodsky. Yes and no. Of course, its content says it's a woman, but its essence . . . Its essence simply says that it's the voice of tragedy. (By the way, the muse of tragedy is female, as are all the other muses.) The voice of stupendous misfortune. Is Job a man or a woman? Tsvetaeva is Job in a skirt.

Volkov. Why is Tsvetaeva's poetry, which is so passionate and stormy, so rarely erotic?

Brodsky. My friend, reread Tsvetaeva's poems to Sofia Parnok! When it comes to erotica, she outdoes everyone there—Kuzmin and everyone else included. "I learn love through the pain all down my body." What more do you need! The fact is that sound, not erotica, is the real point here. In Tsvetaeva, sound is always the main point, regardless of what she is talking about. And she's right.

Volkov. For a hundred years or so, from Karolina Pavlova to Mirra Lokhvitskaya, women made up only a marginal part of Russian poetry. Then suddenly, all at once, we find two such talents as Tsvetaeva and Akhmatova standing alongside the giants of world poetry.

Brodsky. This may not have anything to do with time. Then, again, maybe it has. The point is that women are more sensitive to ethical transgressions, to psychological and intellectual immorality. And universal amorality is precisely what the twentieth century has offered us in abundance. There's something else I want to say, too. Man's biological role is as time-server, right? A simple, mundane example. A husband comes home from work and brings his boss with him. They have supper, and then the boss leaves. The wife says to her husband, "How could you bring that scoundrel into my home?" Although the home in fact is maintained with the money this very same scoundrel gives her husband. "Into my home!" The woman is taking an ethical stance, because she can allow herself that. Men have another purpose so they shut their eyes to a great deal. In fact, though, the result of existence ought to be an ethical stance, an ethical assessment, and women are in much better shape as far as that goes.

Volkov. Then how do you explain Tsvetaeva's conduct around that rather slippery Soviet espionage case involving her husband, Sergei Efron: the murder of the defector Ignace Reiss, and Efron's subsequent escape to Moscow? Efron was a Soviet spy during the grim Stalinist years. From the ethical standpoint, it's very easy to condemn a figure like that, but Tsvetaeva, evidently, accepted and supported Efron wholeheartedly.

Brodsky. There's a saying: "Love is a curse. You can fall in love even with a goat." Tsvetaeva fell in love with Efron when she was young—and thus forever. She had great personal integrity. She followed Efron like a dog, as she herself said. Those were the ethics of her act: being true to herself. Being true to the promise she gave when she was a young girl. That's all.

Volkov. If the dramatic events connected with Reiss's murder were a surprise for her, Tsvetaeva would never have followed Efron to Moscow. More than likely, Efron did not initiate her into the details of his espionage work, but Tsvetaeva knew, or at least guessed, most of it. That much is obvious from her letters.

Brodsky. The poet's role in the society is to animate it: the people no less than the furniture. Tsvetaeva did possess this ability—this inclination—to an extremely high degree. I have in mind her inclination to mythologize the individual. The more insignificant and pathetic the person, the nobler material he was for this mythologizing. I don't know how much she knew about Efron's collaboration with the Soviet secret police, but I think that even had she known everything, she would not have hesitated. The ability to see meaning where for all intents and purposes there is none is a professional feature of the poet's calling. Maybe Tsvetaeva could animate Efron only because there she faced a total disaster of the individual. Aside from everything else, this was a tremendous object lesson in evil for Tsvetaeva, and a poet does not squander those kinds of lessons.

Marina behaved in this situation in a much more dignified—and much more natural—manner than we have been taught. We do what? What is our principal reaction if something rubs us the wrong way? If we don't like a chair, we carry it right out of the room! If we don't like someone, we chase him the hell away! Marry, divorce, remarry—for a second, third, fifth time! It's pure Hollywood. Marina realized that a catastrophe is just that, and there's a lot you can learn from a catastrophe. Apart from anything else—and what was for her much more important at that time—she had had three children by him, and the children had turned out differently, not especially like their papa. Or so it seemed to her in any case. In addition, there was the daughter she had not been able to protect, for which she evidently punished herself severely—so much so that in any case she did not try very hard to appoint herself a judge of Efron.

Once Susan Sontag said that a person's first reaction in the face of a catastrophe is basically to ask, "Where did the mistake occur here? What should have been done to take this situation in hand? So that it doesn't happen again?" But there is another, alternate behavior, she says: to let the tragedy steamroll you, to let it crush you. As the Poles say, "to lie down under it." If you ever do manage to get back on your feet after that, then you rise up a different person. The phoenix principle, if you like. I often recall those words of Sontag's.

Volkov. It seems to me that after the catastrophe with Efron, Tsvetaeva was beyond recovery.

Brodsky. I'm not so sure about that.

Volkov. Her suicide was a response to misfortune that had built up over many years. Isn't that true?

Brodsky. Certainly. You know, though, only the suicide himself can analyze his suicide, can speak authoritatively about the events that led up to it.

Volkov. At one time I was interested in the political assassinations in Europe in the 1930s, because the great Russian singer, Nadezhda Plevitskaya, turned out to be mixed up in them. Nowadays, people try to present all those spies as idealists who agreed to do "wet jobs" out of intellectual conviction. In fact, both Stalin and Hitler used them to do away with independent figures they thought were in their way. They became spies for the money, for the perks, and some, in pursuit of power.

Brodsky. I think that the incident with Efron is a classic catastrophe of the individual. In his youth he has ambitions and hopes. But he ends up acting in some amateur theater in Prague. What can he do after that? Either lay hands on himself or else go into someone's service. Why the Soviet secret service specifically? Because his family tradition was antimonarchistic. Because he left Russia with the White Army when he was practically a kid, and once he grew up and saw all those defenders of the fatherland in emigration, the only way to go was in the opposite direction. Plus, there were also all those fellow travelers, the Eurasianism, Berdyaev, Ustryalov—the very best minds, and the idea of building a Russian Communist superpower. The idea of being a great power! To say nothing of the fact that it's easier being a spy than getting maimed on a Renault assembly line. Anyway, being the husband of a great poet is no bed of roses. Whether Efron was a soundrel or a nonentity, I don't know. The latter, more likely, although in the practical sense, of course, he was a scoundrel. If Marina loved him, though, it's not for me to judge. If he gave her something, then it was no more than he took, after all. He'll be saved just for what he *gave*. It's like that poor proffered onion that opens the gates in the other world. Where have you ever seen happy marriages in this profession? A poet's supposed to be happy in marriage? No, it's a disaster that when it comes, it comes like a gang of thieves, and it's either the husband or the wife in the lead.

Volkov. How do you account for Tsvetaeva's invariably ecstatic opinion of Vladimir Mayakovsky? She dedicated a poem to him while he was still alive and responded to his suicide with a special cycle. Whereas Akhmatova's opinion of Mayakovsky kept changing. For example, she was angered when she found out that Mayakovsky had sung her "Gray-Eyed King" to the tune of "A Dashing Merchant Was Riding to the Fair."

Brodsky. That was nothing to get angry about, I don't think, because Mayakovsky himself could be sung to just about anything. All his poems can be printed either step-fashion or as a column or simply in quatrains— and everything will still be in its proper place. And this would be a much riskier experience for Mayakovsky. That kind of thing often happens, by the way, that a poet likes exactly what he himself would never attempt in real life. Take Mandelstam's attitude toward Khlebnikov. To say nothing of the fact that Mayakovsky behaved so very archetypically. The whole shebang: from avant-gardist to courtier to victim. And you're always consumed by the suspicion that maybe that's how it ought to be. Maybe you're too shut up inside yourself, whereas here was a genuine nature, an extrovert, doing everything on the grand scale. If his poems are bad, there's good reason for it. Bad poems are a poet's bad days. And Mayakovsky did have quite a few bad days in his life, but when things got their absolute worst, he came up with some great poems. Of course, he let his tongue run away with him completely. Mayakovsky was the first major victim, for he had a major gift. What he did with it was another matter. Marina, of course, could play this role of poet-tribune as well. Within her sat that beast.

As for Mayakovsky and Tsvetaeva, here's one more thought. I think she was drawn to him for polemical and poetical reasons both. Moscow and the Muscovite spirit. The pathos of applied poetry. I assure you that on the purely technical level, Mayakovsky is a very attractive figure. Those rhymes, those pauses, and most of all, I think, the unwieldiness and free-wheeling quality of Mayakovsky's verse. Tsvetaeva has the same tendency, but Marina never slackens the rein, as Mayakovsky does. For him, this was his only idiom, whereas Tsvetaeva could work in several, and really, no matter how freewheeling Tsvetaeva's verse, it is always drawn toward harmony. Her rhymes are more exact than Mayakovsky's, even when their poetics come very close.

Volkov. In one instance your tastes and Mayakovsky's converge—neither one of you likes Tyutchev.

Brodsky. It's not that I don't like Tyutchev, but, of course, I find Batyushkov much more to my taste. Without question, Tyutchev is a very important figure, but for all those discussions of his metaphysicality and so forth, somehow the fact that our country's letters have never given birth to a more loyal subject gets forgotten. Compared with Tyutchev, our lackeys from the days of Joseph Vissarionovich Stalin are milksops, not only in talent but above all in the authenticity of their sentiments. Tyutchev did not simply kiss the imperial boots, he licked them. I don't know why Mayakovsky was so put out with him—possibly because of the similarity of their situations. As for me, I can't read the second volume of Tyutchev's works without astonishment. On the one hand, the chariot of the world edifice seems to be rolling through the sanctuary of the heavens. On the other, there are these servile "overcoat odes," to use Vyazemsky's expression. Russia's jingoists are this close to carrying Tyutchev around on their shield. It's so ugly. Batyushkov was no less a patriot than Tyutchev. He served in the army, too, for that matter, but he never once permitted this disgraceful sort of thing. When you come right down to it, Batyushkov has been tremendously underrated, both in his day and now.

Volkov. I first became interested in Batyushkov after reading Tsvetaeva. She opens her poem "In Memory of Byron" with a line from Batyushkov: "I quit the foggy shores of Albion." Nonetheless, Batyushkov can't compare with Tyutchev.

Brodsky. You know, Solomon, I probably have my own prejudices and, if you like, my own professional quirks, and of course, it can all be written off to that, but I advise you to reread Batyushkov in New York.

Volkov. There's nothing better than rereading Batyushkov while gazing at the Hudson. And even lesser poets. Here, in New York, I reread Golenishchev-Kutuzov two or three times a year.

Brodsky. Not a bad idea. All in all, Russian poets—I don't want to say second-rank but second-tier—have included some remarkable individuals. Dmitriev, for example, with his fables. What verse! The Russian fable is an absolutely stunning thing. Krylov is a brilliant poet who had a mastery of sound comparable to Derzhavin's. And Katenin! No one has anything more perceptive about the love triangle. Look at how the Hudson sunsets fit Katenin. Or Vyazemsky. I think he is the preeminent phenomenon in the Pushkin Pleiad. Unfortunately, society, especially an authoritarian society, always makes one poet the leader. It's because of that idiotic parallelism, the poet-tsar. But poetry requires much more than just one master of minds. By choosing just one, society condemns itself to one form or another of autocracy. By reading selectively, it rejects the democratic principle, so it has no right afterward to dump everything on the sovereign or the first secretary. It's society's own fault. Society pays for its indifference to culture primarily with its civic freedoms. Narrowing the cultural scope is mother to narrowing the political scope. Nothing paves the way for tyranny like cultural self-castration. So it actually makes sense when they start lopping off heads later on.

Volkov. You've just listed Russian poets of the so-called second tier: Dmitriev, Katenin, and Vyazemsky. They are all major, attractive individuals, and not simply marvelous writers. The life of each one of them is an entertaining novel.

Brodsky. What interests me most in these cases is the human aspect. Here a man is writing, and he either has success or he doesn't, but he's not thinking about that mainly but sort of gazing into the future. It's not that he's counting on posterity, but the language he uses is. There's something in the poet, in his ear, that ensures his labors if not of immortality then at least of an existence much lengthier than anything the poet can envision.

Volkov. As long as the Russian language exists, Ivan Krylov's fables will be read. Even though Russian schools do everything in their power to poison the pleasure we derive from him.

Brodsky. No, if there was one thing school did not poison for me, it was Krylov. Here they didn't accomplish their task.

Volkov. We were talking about Tsvetaeva's statement—"To your insane world/But one reply—I refuse." These lines appeared in a poem written for an "occasion," as we say: in connection with the invasion of Czechoslovakia by Hitler's army in March 1939. All her life she wrote political poems; we have only to recall her cycle, *The Swan's Encampment,* which sings the praises of the White movement. In this respect Tsvetaeva was not at all a typical figure for modern Russian poetry. Look at the nineteenth century: Pushkin's "To the Slanderers of Russia," Vyazemsky's poems, Khomyakov's "To Russia," the poems of your unfavorite Tyutchev, are all first-class political verse, textbook examples. But where are poems of this caliber devoted to the major events of the second half of the twentieth century? Upon the death of Emperor Paul I, Derzhavin produced "Silenced is the husky bellow of the North." Where is the verse on the fall of Khrushchev? Why didn't Russian poets respond to the invasion of Czechoslovakia in 1968 with the same force as Tsvetaeva did to his occupation of 1939? After all, she too was in fact writing "for the drawer," with no expectation of immediate publication.

Brodsky. That's not altogether fair. I think there's a lot we still don't know. But it's true, I've never read anything directly describing the seizure of Budapest or Prague by the Soviet army, although I do know a group of Russian poets whose references to the Hungarian uprising of 1956, say, or the Polish upheavals of the 1950s, were very powerful.

Volkov. You can't piece together modern history on the basis of these poems.

Brodsky. No, neither the moral nor the political history, and this is what is interesting: the World War II experience is scarcely reflected in Russian poetry. There is, of course, the generation of "war" poets, beginning with that total nonentity Sergei Orlov, may he rest in peace. Or those Mezhirovs—snivelers who really beat all. Well, there's Gudzenko and Samoilov. Boris Slutsky has some good poems—some very good poems—about the war, and Arseny Tarkovsky has five or six. All those Konstantin Simonovs and Surkovs (the kingdom of God to them both, though I'm afraid they'll never see heaven)—that's not about our national tragedy or about the destruction of the world; that's much more about self-pity. A plea for mercy. I'm not talking about that whole postwar mud stream, about the fist-waving that comes after the fight. At best, it is drama taken in exchange, for want of one's own; at worst, it is exploitation of the dead and grist for the Defense Ministry's mill. Put simply, propaganda for the recruits. There's not one iota of understanding of what happened to the nation, which is actually pretty wild. After all, twenty million were cut down . . .

Just recently, though, I compiled—to a certain extent I was lucky—the selected works of Semyon Lipkin, which include a huge number of poems on this very topic: the war and things connected with the war in one way or another. You get the impression that he alone was speaking out for everyone, for all of our *belles lettres.* He saved our national reputation, so to speak. Meanwhile, he is one of the very few who looked after Tsvetaeva upon her return to Russia from emigration. I think he's a remarkable poet—not on the hot topic of the day but on the horror of the day. In this sense, Lipkin is in fact a Tsvetaeva disciple. As long as we're talking about Tsvetaeva's poems to Czechoslovakia, or about *The Swan's Encampment,* then the former are a variation on her themes in "Ratcatcher," and in the latter, too, the main thing is their vocal element. I even think that the White movement attracted Tsvetaeva more as a formula than as a political reality.

Volkov. When it comes to topical poems, Russian authors in the twentieth century, which has been so rich in suitable "occasions," have not had the temperament or sweep for "occasional" poetry. In this sense, your poem "On the Death of Zhukov" stands out. It restores the old Russian tradition that goes back to Derzhavin's "Bullfinch," which is an epitaph for another great Russian commander, Suvorov. This is what is called a "state," or, if you prefer, "imperial" poem.

Brodsky. In this instance I actually like the definition "state." I really believe that this poem ought to have been published at the time in *Pravda.* I've taken a lot of shit in connection with this poem, I must say.

Volkov. Why is that?

Brodsky. Well, the earlier émigrés, the D.P.s, have extremely unpleasant memories of Zhukov. They ran away from him, so they have no sympathy whatsoever for Zhukov. Then there are the Balts, who took so much from Zhukov.

Volkov. But your poem doesn't express any particular sympathies for the marshal. On the emotional level, it's quite restrained.

Brodsky. That's very true, but after all, a person who isn't intelligent enough—he doesn't particularly care about those things. He's responding to the red flag. Zhukov? That's all it takes. I've also heard all kinds of things from Russia. Up to and including the perfectly comic. They say I'm plonking myself down at the bosses' feet. After all, though, many of us owe Zhukov our life. We would do well to remember that it was Zhukov and nobody else who saved Khrushchev from Beria. It was his Kantemirov

Tank Division that entered Moscow in July 1953 and surrounded the Bolshoi Theater.

Volkov. Did Zhukov's tanks stop by the Bolshoi or the Ministry of Internal Affairs?

Brodsky. Well, I think it's the same thing . . . Zhukov was the last of the Russian Mohicans.

Volkov. Once—it was probably in the late 1960s—in a symphony hall just outside Riga, at Dzintari, I noticed a man sitting in front of me. He had four gold stars on his jacket, which is to say he was a four-time Hero of the Soviet Union! The lights dimmed soon after, so I didn't get a good look at his face. I kept looking at the stranger's gray crewcut and solid red neck and trying to guess right up until intermission. Who could this be with such an unprecedented number of "Heroes" on his chest? When Marshal Zhukov stood up for the intermission—and this was, naturally, he—the whole audience watched him avidly. I remember being amazed that Zhukov, who had won all the glory and respect during his lifetime that anyone could ever have, needed to go out to a concert wearing all his regalia on his civilian jacket.

Brodsky. I think it's perfectly natural. It's a different mentality, a military mentality. It's not about the thirst for glory. After all, by that time he had been driven out of everywhere, hadn't he?

Volkov. Yes, he'd been in full retirement for about ten years.

Brodsky. All the more so then. And as we know, Heroes of the Soviet Union don't have to stand in line for their beer.

Volkov. What was the impulse behind your "Poem on the Winter Campaign of 1980"? That poem, about the invasion of Afghanistan by Soviet troops, was as great a surprise for your readers, I think, as "On the Death of Zhukov."

Brodsky. This was a reaction to what I saw on television. Budapest and Prague we had heard about on the BBC and read about in the newspapers, but we hadn't seen it. The invasion of Afghanistan, though . . . I don't know anything else in world events that has ever made such an impression on me. And after all, they weren't showing any of the atrocities on television. I just saw tanks driving across a rocky plateau, and I remember I was struck by the thought that this plateau had never before known tanks or tractors or iron wheels of any kind. This was a collision on the level of the elements, iron striking stone. If they had shown killed or wounded Afghans, well, the human eye—especially here—has become inured to this; there is no news without corpses. In Afghanistan, apart from everything else, there was a violation of the natural order. That's what sends you through the roof, apart from the blood. I remember it took me three days to climb back down. Later, when we discussed the invasion, I suddenly thought about how those Russian soldiers in Afghanistan right then were nineteen and twenty years old. That is, if I or my pals, together with our lady friends, hadn't behaved in a more or less responsible manner in the 1960s, then our children could very easily have been there, among the occupiers. This thought made me absolutely sick to my stomach. That's when I started writing this poem. When the same thing happened in Europe, when we meddled in Hungary and Czechoslovakia and Poland, that was almost to be expected. In the final analysis, it was just another repetition of European history, with a twist. But when it came to the Afghan tribes, this was an anthropological crime as much as a political one. A tremendous evolutionary transgression. It was like the Iron Age invading the Stone Age. As for your comment on the unexpectedness of my "Poem on the Winter Campaign" . . . Stylistically, I don't see any difference between it and my poems on nature or the weather. And of course, when I began working on "Poem on the Winter Campaign," I was attempting to resolve other problems—not so much purely formal as intonational.

Volkov. Tsvetaeva, Mandelstam, Pasternak, and Akhmatova are known to the reading public in the West, especially the latter two. They know Pushkin primarily from Tchaikovsky's operas. Baratynsky and Tyutchev—even to the educated Western reader, these names say nothing. That is, Russian poetry in the West is above all the poetry of the twentieth century, whereas they know Russian prose primarily from the authors of the nineteenth century. How did this come about?

Brodsky. I have a very simple answer for this. Take Dostoevsky, for example. The problem of Dostoevsky, sociologically speaking, is the problem of a society that ceased to exist in Russia after the 1917 revolution. Whereas here, in the West, society is still the same, which is to say, capitalist. That's why Dostoevsky is so vital here. On the other hand, take the modern Russian. Certainly, Dostoevsky may be of interest to him; he might even play a tremendous role in an individual's development, in the awakening of his self-awareness, but when the Russian reader goes outside, he comes face to face with a reality that Dostoevsky did not describe.

Volkov. Akhmatova spoke of this, too.

Brodsky. Absolutely. Do you remember? Like a man who has just executed yet another group of political convicts and comes home from work to get ready to go to the theater with his wife. He'll still raise a stink because she had her hair done! And no pangs of conscience, none of that Dostoevsky stuff! Whereas for the Western man, Dostoevsky's situations and dilemmas are his own situations and dilemmas. He recognizes them. Hence Dostoevsky's popularity in the West. And hence the untranslatability of much of twentieth-century Russian prose. In order to read it, you have to be able to picture the reality behind it more or less, but the Soviet reality described in the best Russian prose works of this period is totally alien to the Western mind. Understanding the prose that reflects this distorted reality inevitably requires a certain knowledge of the history of the Soviet Union, and not every reader is prepared for that effort of the imagination. Whereas reading Dostoevsky or Leo Tolstoy does not require any particular effort of imagination from the Western reader; the only effort is slogging through those impossible Russian names and patronymics.

Volkov. Why has nineteenth-century Russian poetry turned out to be so insurmountable?

Brodsky. As for the reaction of the English-speaking public, I have a theory. The problem is that nineteenth-century Russian poetry is metric, naturally, so translating it into English requires preserving the meter. As soon as the modern English-speaking reader encounters regular meters, though, he immediately thinks of his own native poetics, which set his teeth on edge a long time ago. By the way, I don't find those highly sophisticated discussions by local snobs of twentieth-century Russian poetry very convincing either, because their knowledge of Pasternak and Akhmatova rests on translations that allow tremendous deviations from the original. The emphasis in these translations is usually on transmitting the "content" at the expense of the structural features, which they justify by saying that the principal idiom in twentieth-century English poetry is free verse. What I would like to say is this: the use of free verse in translations does, of course, allow us to get more or less complete information about the original—but only at the level of "content," no higher. Therefore, when people discuss Mandelstam here, in the West, they think he falls somewhere between Yeats and Eliot, because the music of the original flies out the window. Local connoisseurs, however, feel this is permissible and even justifiable in the twentieth century.

Volkov. If you wanted to clarify the essence of Tsvetaeva to your American students who do not know Russian, which English-language poets would you compare her with?

Brodsky. When I talk to them about Tsvetaeva, I speak of the Englishman Gerard Manley Hopkins and the American Hart Crane. Although, as a rule, I do so in vain, because young people don't know either one. If they do force themselves to look up Hopkins and Crane, however, then at least they will see this complex—"Tsvetaevan"—diction, that is, what in English one just doesn't encounter very often: difficult syntax, enjambments, leaps over what can be assumed. This is what Tsvetaeva is famous for—technically, at least. If we extend the parallel with Crane (on second thought there really is no genuine similarity here), their end was the same, suicide, although I think Crane had fewer grounds for suicide. Once again, that is not for us to judge.

Volkov. By the way, about parallels. Frost and Akhmatova probably considered emigration but remained in their native land. Whereas Tsvetaeva and Auden both emigrated—only to return just before they died. Of course, these are all purely superficial coincidences, but they make me think nonetheless about how, in the final analysis, a poet is given a limited number of life "roles" to choose from. I wanted to ask whether Tsvetaeva has become closer to you now that you have emigrated. Do you understand her from the inside out now?

Brodsky. Understanding has nothing to do with territorial displacements. It has to do with age. I think that if I understand something in Tsvetaeva's verse differently now, then that's mainly because I now recognize her sentiments. In fact, Tsvetaeva was extremely unforthcoming about whatever was happening to her. She did not put her biography to much use in verse. Take "Poem of the Mountain" or "Poem of the End." She is talking about ruptures in general, not about ruptures with a real person.

Volkov. You yourself said that she was the sincerest of Russian poets.

Brodsky. Absolutely.

Volkov. Didn't you have in mind the biographical candor in her verse? What about Tsvetaeva's prose? Is it autobiographical throughout!

Brodsky. Tsvetaeva is indeed the sincerest Russian poet, but this sincerity is, above all, a sincerity of sound—as when people cry out in pain. The pain is biographical; the cry is apart from any individual. This "refusal" of hers that we were just talking about blankets everything, including what's inside her. Including her personal grief, her homeland, foreign lands, and the bastards in both places. What is most important is that this intonation—this intonation of refusal—preceded experience for Tsvetaeva. "To your insane world/But one reply—I refuse." Here it's not so much a matter even of the "insane world" (a single misfortune is all it takes to feel that), but of a howling sound, which acted as common denominator for this line. You could say that life's events only confirmed Tsvetaeva's original insight. However, life experience doesn't confirm anything. In *belles lettres,* as in music, experience is a secondary matter. The material at the disposal of a given branch of art has its own irrefutable, linear dynamic. That is why the explosive charge flies, if I can express myself metaphorically, as far as the material—not experience—dictates. Everyone has more or less the same experience. There have doubtless been people with experience even harder than Tsvetaeva's, but there have not been people with her mastery, her command of the material. Experience, life, the body, biography—at best, they absorb the recoil. The charge is sent far into the distance by the dynamic of the material. In any event, I do not look for parallels to my own life experience in Tsvetaeva's verse, and I don't feel anything beyond being absolutely dumbstruck in the face of her poetic power.

Volkov. What do you have to say about the relations between Tsvetaeva and the émigré press?

Brodsky. Riffraff. Such a petty crowd. We have to bear in mind the politicized nature of this expatriate audience. Plus—or rather, minus—the paucity of their means.

Volkov. Over the course of eleven years, Tsvetaeva was unable to publish a single book once she emigrated. Publishers wouldn't risk publishing her—and she very much wanted to publish. I'm surprised at the humiliations, the censor's changes, she was prepared to accept for this.

Brodsky. This is truly shocking. On the other hand, though, when you've already said what's most important to you, then you can excise bits and pieces.

Volkov. Has there ever been a situation in your life when you were forced to make changes in your poetry or prose because of outside pressure?

Brodsky. Never.

Volkov. Never?

Brodsky. Never.

Volkov. It is easy to be disenchanted by Tsvetaeva—because of her "Calvinism." I attended your lectures on Tsvetaeva and read your articles on her. All this, plus our conversations about Tsvetaeva, have taught me to read her poetry more closely and her prose much more attentively than I had before. Before, I must admit, I preferred Akhmatova to Tsvetaeva. Akhmatova herself always said that the premier poet of the twentieth century was Mandelstam. Do you agree?

Brodsky. Well, if we have to get into these kinds of discussions at all, then no, I don't agree. I consider Tsvetaeva the premier poet of the twentieth century. Certainly, Tsvetaeva.

Spring 1980–Fall 1990

BRODSKY AT HIS HOME ON MORTON STREET,
GREENWICH VILLAGE, NEW YORK, 1978

3

ARRESTS, ASYLUMS,
AND A TRIAL

Volkov. I've wanted to ask you about your trial in 1964, about your arrests and confinements in Soviet asylums. I know you don't like to discuss this, and usually you refuse to answer questions related to it, but if you have no objections right now . . .

Brodsky. You know, I don't, but I never really took my trial seriously. Not while it was going on and not after.

Volkov. Why was this whole machine suddenly set in motion? Why Leningrad, and why you? After all, it had been quite a while since the Soviet authorities had concocted anything as scandalous as the Pasternak campaign in 1958.

Brodsky. To tell you the truth, I've never gone into this. I haven't given it the slightest thought. If we're going to talk about it, though, then there's always a specific person standing behind any case like this. It's people who put machines in motion. That's how it was in my case, which was put into motion by someone by the name of Lerner, may he rest in peace, inasmuch as he's dead, I believe.

Volkov. Is this the Lerner who published that broadside against you, "A Quasi-Literary Drone," in a Leningrad newspaper in November 1963?

Brodsky. Yes, he had had long-standing "literary" interests, but at that moment his main occupation was supervising a people's volunteer patrol. Do you know what people's volunteer patrols were? It was a cheap way to make fascists out of the population, young men especially.

Volkov. I knew someone who was in one of those patrols, an idiot.

Brodsky. This particular patrol's main area of activity was the Hotel Europa, where many foreigners stayed. As you know, it's located on Isaak

Brodsky Street, so maybe that's why this gentleman developed an interest in me. They were mainly out for black marketeers, and meanwhile, whenever these patrols frisked any black marketeers, plenty stuck to their fingers—money and icons. But that's not important.

Volkov. Your arrest in 1964, it wasn't your first, was it?

Brodsky. No, the first time they took me in was when *Sintaksis* came out. Do you know that effort of Alexander Ginzburg's?

Volkov. It was a typewritten poetry journal put out in Moscow, right? In the late 1950s, I think. Who took you in then, the police or the KGB?

Brodsky. The KGB. That really was time immemorial.

Volkov. What did they want from you then?

Brodsky. I have absolutely no idea what those people usually want. I think that office, the KGB, like everything else in the world, is a victim of statistics. That is, the peasant gets to the field, and there's one strip left to harvest. The worker arrives at his factory, and there's an order waiting for him. But the KGB people get to their office and there's nothing there but a portrait of their leader, but they have to do something after all, to justify their existence somehow, don't they? This is very often where all these fabrications originate. All this came about largely not because Soviet power was so bad or, I don't know, Lenin and Stalin were so evil, or some other devil was whirling around somewhere, right? No, it's just the bureaucracy, a purely bureaucratic phenomenon, which, given the total absence of any checks and balances, grows like a weed and gets up to God knows what.

I think that in principle the idea of the KGB, that is, the idea of defending the revolution against its foreign and domestic enemies, that an idea like that is more or less natural. If, of course, one accepts the naturalness of revolution, which is really very unnatural. With time, though, this unnatural creation begins to look natural, that is, it conquers a definite space. When you go to sleep at night, you're supposed to lock your door, right? It's perfectly natural. The KGB is the kind of lock you need. You put a man on guard and he stands there. But this man has to have some kind of commander, and this commander has to have someone else supervising him, and so forth. In the case of the KGB, everything came about in exactly the opposite way. That is, you look over this guard's shoulder and there's no one there. He could have fallen asleep or he could have stuck you with his bayonet. And that's when all the fuss began! I think that ninety percent of the business of state security is simply fabricating cases. You must have run across people who dream up occupations only to have something to do. So here you have the KGB personnel, precisely the kind of people who go around dreaming up occupations for themselves because they don't have anything they're supposed to be doing. Who in Russia is really trying to overthrow the state? No one, of course!

Volkov. Not in our memory in any event.

Brodsky. Maybe prior to 1937 it did occur to people that they might put someone else in charge, but after 1937 such ideas scarcely flickered, and there could be no question of the population having any kind of weapon. Maybe by way of an exception, and such cases could easily have been dealt with by the militia. But no such luck! Since these guys from state security do already exist, they organize a system of denunciations, on the basis of which they gather information. Once they have something, they could finally do something. It's especially handy if you're dealing with a writer. If you're a writer, your dossier grows much faster—because all your manuscripts go in there, whether they're poems or novels, right?

Volkov. You dutifully produce the material for your own KGB dossier!

Brodsky. And eventually your case starts taking up an unseemly amount of space on the KGB's shelf. Then this character has to be picked up and something done with him. That's how it happens. When an excess of information comes in, they have to take whoever it is in and start leaning on him, according to their standard bill of fare. It's all very simple.

Volkov. You mean, your troubles with the KGB began the moment your poetry appeared in *Sintaksis?*

Brodsky. Yes, and later there was the so-called Umansky affair.

Volkov. I remember the authorities kept trotting out the Umansky affair at your trial. What specifically did it involve?

Brodsky. Actually, it didn't involve anything either. It all began when I was eighteen and my friend Alexander Umansky was probably about twenty. We met a man by the name of Oleg. He was older than us. He'd already done his military service. He'd been a pilot there. He knocked around the country but could never find a place for himself, and then somehow he hooked up with Umansky and got a job in Leningrad—I think it was at the Voeikov Geophysical Observatory. What interested Umansky most in the world was philosophy, yoga, and such matters, and at home he had the appropriate library. So Oleg started reading all these books. Can you imagine what goes through the mind of an officer of the Soviet army, a military pilot to boot, when he picks up Hegel, ancient Indian philosophers, Bertrand Russell, and Karl Marx for the first time?

Volkov. No, I can't.

Brodsky. What goes through his mind is a total catastrophe! Meanwhile, Oleg was an exceptional man. He had tremendous musical ability, he played the guitar, really a very talented fellow, and very interesting to spend time with. Then this happened: he pissed into his boots and threw them into the soup in the communal kitchen of his girlfriend's dorm to protest the fact that his girlfriend wouldn't let him into her room after midnight. They picked Oleg up for this and gave him a year for vandalism. He was jailed, released, and went back to Leningrad. I was favorably disposed toward him because I found him so fascinating. When you're twenty, everything's fascinating, and here was this colorful life story, a real pilot.

Later Oleg went away again and turned up in Samarkand, where he started studying the guitar at the local conservatory and living with his teacher, a rather remarkable lady, an Armenian. At the same time he was teaching music at the local Officers House. That's when he started summoning me to pay him a visit—you know, those outlandish letters from Central Asia?

And I wanted so much to go! So I saved up some money working in television, with photography, and went to Samarkand. Oleg and I were extremely unlucky there. We didn't even have a roof over our heads. Not a thing. God only knows where we ended up spending our nights. The whole story was pure epic. In short, one fine day, when Oleg was complaining to me for the umpteenth time about his utter misfortune (and he felt that he had suffered a great deal from Soviet authorities), an idea came to us—I don't remember which one of us . . . more than likely it was me . . . . In short, I say to him, "Oleg, if I were you, I'd just get into one of those little airplanes, like a YaK-12, and light out for Afghanistan. After all, you're a pilot! In Afghanistan you could go as far as your fuel lasted, and then you could just walk to the nearest city—Kabul, I don't know."

Volkov. How did Oleg react to the idea?

Brodsky. He suggested we run away to Afghanistan together. This was the plan. We would buy tickets for one of those small planes. Oleg would sit next to the pilot and I would sit behind him, with a rock. Bop the pilot on the head. I tie him up, and Oleg takes the controls. We ascend to a great height, level off, and cross the border, so that no radar cuts us off.

Volkov. An escapade right out of Kipling!

Brodsky. I don't know how realistic the plan was, but we certainly discussed it in earnest. Oleg was ten years older than me after all, and a pilot to boot. He ought to have known what he was talking about.

Volkov. As far as I know, escape, as such, did not figure at your trial, just the preparations for it. What stopped you?

Brodsky. The thing is that originally this was after all my idea. I behaved like a scoundrel. Because after we'd bought the tickets for this plane, all three seats, like we were supposed to—I suddenly had second thoughts.

Volkov. You got scared?

Brodsky. No, everything changed. An hour before takeoff I bought some walnuts with some change I had—I had a ruble left. So I'm sitting there and smashing them with the same stone I'd picked up to bop the pilot on the head. But in those days, I'd read my fill of Saint-Exupéry, and I idolized all pilots. I still do. Flying is a kind of ultimate idea for me. When I came to the States, I even took flying lessons for the first three or four months. I even flew—landed and took off! Well, that's beside the point . . . So I'm smashing these walnuts and suddenly I realize that the inside of the nut looks like . . .

Volkov. The human brain!

Brodsky. Exactly. And I think, Hey, what business do I have hitting him on the head? What did he ever do to me? And the main thing is, I'd already seen the pilot . . . And really, who needed all this, this Afghanistan? Homeland or no—I wasn't thinking in those categories, of course—but I suddenly remembered the girl I'd been going out with in Leningrad. Even though she was already married. I realized I'd never see her again. I thought about the other people I wouldn't see either—friends and acquaintances— and that got to me. Basically, I wanted to go home. So I told Oleg I couldn't go along with the game. We took different routes back to the European part of the Soviet Union. Later I saw Oleg in Moscow, where he was more or less impoverished. A year later they picked him up with a revolver in Krasnoyarsk.

Volkov. And that was the beginning of the Umansky affair?

Brodsky. Yes, because Oleg evidently got scared they'd give him another sentence, and he said he'd explain his possession of the revolver only to a representative of state security, one of which was immediately presented to him because there's nothing simpler than that in Russia. It's their equivalent of the quick coin laundry.

Volkov. In the trial materials, your idea of escape was described as a "plan to betray the homeland," or something like that. That is, the authorities knew all about it, right?

Brodsky. Yes. They started bringing us all in. About twenty people were called in as witnesses. I was called in as a witness, too, but I became a suspect. What do you expect?

Volkov. How did you manage to wiggle out then?

Brodsky. They held me and let me go, since it turned out that after interrogating twenty people there was testimony against me from only one person, and even for the Soviet legal system, this was not quite *comme il faut*.

Volkov. The thread that led to the Brodsky trial stretched directly from the Umansky affair?

Brodsky. I think that in fact it was all even more interesting and complicated, but I have no desire now to sort it out. The reasons don't interest me at all. I'm always interested in the consequences, which are always much crazier. For the viewer at least, they are much more intriguing.

Volkov. This jack-in-the-box, Lerner, where did he ever get the idea to write a broadside? After all, he certainly was not a professional journalist.

Brodsky. Evidently, it wasn't Lerner's own idea. Evidently state security sicced him on it, inasmuch as my dossier kept growing and growing. I think the time had come to take measures. As for Lerner, he was really a nobody. As I recall, he had seen action in state security. Well maybe not very active action, I don't know. Basically, he was a retired rheumy-eyed amateur. I think one of his eyes was actually fake. It was all just like you'd expect. A total disaster! And naturally, he felt like asserting himself, which coincided with the KGB's interest. And so it began! By the time they had picked me up a third time, they were already bringing up everything—*Sintaksis*, Umansky, Shakhmatov, Samarkand, and everyone we had met there.

Volkov. When all this was heaped on you—the third arrest, the trial— how did you perceive it all? As a calamity? As single combat? As an opportunity to confront the authorities?

Brodsky. This question is very hard to answer because it's so tempting to interpret the past from the standpoint of today. On the other hand, I have reason to think that in this respect there is no particular difference between my feelings then and now. That is, I personally don't notice any. And I can say that I didn't perceive all these events as a tragedy or as my confrontation with the authorities.

Volkov. Weren't you frightened?

Brodsky. You know, when they arrested me the first time, I was terribly frightened. After all, they usually take you in pretty early, around six in the morning, when you've just got out of your bed, you're all warm, and your defensive reflex is at its lowest. So of course, I was very scared. Well, imagine: they take you to the Big House [the headquarters of the Leningrad KGB], they interrogate you, and after the interrogation they take you to a cell. Just a moment, Solomon, I'm going to have a cigarette.

Volkov. You mean the cells are located right there, in the Big House?

Brodsky. You didn't know? The Big House is a rather interesting enterprise. It is constructed like a square within a square. And the inner square communicates with the outer square via the Bridge of Sighs.

Volkov. Like in Venice?

Brodsky. Exactly. This bridge is at the third-floor level—a kind of corridor that runs between the third and fourth floors. And they lead you across it from the outer building to the inner, which is the actual prison. The scariest moment comes after the interrogation, actually, when you're hoping they're just about to let you go, and you think, one more minute and I'll be outside! Hurry up! And then suddenly you realize that they're leading you in the exact opposite direction!

Volkov. What is the prison ritual after that?

Brodsky. After that they say: "Hands behind your back!" And they lead you. And doors start opening suddenly in front of you. No one tells you anything. You understand everything yourself. What's the point of talking? It's not a matter of interpretation.

Finally, the one who had led you to the end of the corridor, over this Bridge of Sighs, hands you over to the guard at the door to the inner prison. This guard and his assistant search you, after which they remove the laces from your boots. And they lead you on—farther. For example, I was taken to the fourth floor. By the way, my cell was right over Lenin's cell, if I'm not mistaken. When they were leading me, they told me not to look to the sides. I wondered why, and they explained that Lenin himself sat in that cell, and I, in my role as an enemy, was absolutely not supposed to look at it.

Volkov. Is the Big House really such an old building that Lenin could have served time there?

Brodsky. The inner building existed previously, before the revolution. The outer building was constructed under the Bolsheviks. Sometime in the 1920s, I think. When you'd think there could have been no question yet of a Stalinist terror. That is, these guys already knew what they were after. However, you're led to your cell. And when they took me to my cell for the first time in my life, I actually liked it pretty well. It's true, I liked it! Because it was a one-man cell.

Volkov. Do they really slam the cell door shut with that beastly clang the way they do in prison movies?

Brodsky. Yes, with that exact same clang.

Volkov. Here you are in a one-man cell in the Big House. Describe it for me.

Brodsky. Well, the walls are brick but smeared with oil paint—a kind of steely green color. A white ceiling, or maybe even gray, I don't remember. They lock you in and there you are, tête-à-tête with your cot, sink, and toilet.

Volkov. What size is the cell?

Brodsky. Eight or ten paces long. Approximately like my room here in New York, but twice as narrow. What was in it? A bedside table, a sink, and an *ochko*. What else?

Volkov. What's an *ochko*?

Brodsky. An *ochko*? It's a hole in the floor, it's the toilet. I don't understand. Where were you?

Volkov. At the time I was living in the same city as you, in Leningrad, in the boarding house of the music school attached to the conservatory. And I never heard a word like *ochko*.

Brodsky. What else? A window you couldn't see anything through because besides the bars you expect there was also a muzzle on the outside. It's a kind of wooden casement so you can't poke your head out and turn your face toward someone, or wave. And in general, to make life as unpleasant for you as possible.

Volkov. Is there a lamp on the bedside table?

Brodsky. No, the lamp hangs from the ceiling, also encased in bars, so you don't get any ideas about breaking it. The door, naturally, has a peephole and a food slot. But the fact is that in all the time I was there I never saw the food slot open. They kept me in interrogation for twelve hours at a stretch. When I came back to my cell my food was already on the bedside table, which was rather nice on their part.

Volkov. What kind of food was it?

Brodsky. Uninteresting. I remember, once I got a cutlet, which made me very happy. Well, what can I say about prison food? You don't know whether to laugh or cry. During the investigation they really feed you more or less decently compared with how they feed you in a real prison.

Volkov. When they arrested you during the Umansky affair, did they take you back to the Big House?

Brodsky. Yes, but the third time I bypassed it. They picked me up on the street and took me to a police station, where they held me for about a week, I think. After which they sent me to the asylum on Pryazhka for so-called forensic psychiatric assessment. They held me a few weeks. That was the bleakest time in my life.

Volkov. I understand that bringing this up is hard on you, but I would like to learn about your stay in the asylums in somewhat greater detail. How many times were you there?

Brodsky. Well . . . twice.

Volkov. When exactly?

Brodsky. The first time was in December 1963. The second . . . What month was that? February and March of 1964. I described it all in verse. Do you know "Gorbunov and Gorchakov"?

Volkov. I know the poem. Now describe how it was in fact. I'm especially interested in the second time, when the authorities sent you for mandatory forensic psychiatric assessment.

Brodsky. Well, it was an ordinary mental institution. Mixed wards where they kept the violent and the nonviolent, since both were under suspicion.

Volkov. Of faking?

Brodsky. Yes, of faking. And the very first night the man in the cot next to mine committed suicide. He slit his veins. I remember waking up at three in the morning to confusion everywhere and people running around—and the man lying in a pool of blood. Where did he get a razor? It's wild.

Volkov. Quite a first impression!

Brodsky. No, my first impression was different, and it almost drove me mad, as soon as I walked in there, into that ward. What struck me was the way space was organized there. To this day I don't know what was wrong. Either the windows were slightly smaller than usual, or else the ceilings were too low. Or else the beds were too big. But the beds there were those iron soldier's cots, very old, practically from the days of Nicholas II. Basically, what I was looking at was a tremendous violation of proportions, as if you had landed in some sixteenth-century peasant hut or some ancient chamber, but with modern furniture. This violation of proportions drove me crazy. In addition, the windows don't open, and you can't go outside. They let everyone but me have visits from their family.

Volkov. Why?

Brodsky. I don't know. They probably considered me the most inveterate one in there.

Volkov. I well understand that feeling of total isolation, but after all, was it any sweeter in solitary confinement?

Brodsky. In your prison cell you could call the guard if you had a heart attack or something like that. You could call—there was a kind of handle they had that you pulled. The problem was that if you pulled the handle a second time, the bell wouldn't ring. In the asylum it's much worse because they inject you with all kinds of crap and force various pills down your throat.

Volkov. What about the shots—were they painful?

Brodsky. As a rule, no. Except when they injected sulfur. Then even moving your pinky causes excruciating physical pain. This is done to slow you down, to stop you, so that you can do absolutely nothing, you can't move. Usually they injected sulfur in the violent patients, when they started getting agitated and outrageous, but apart from that, the women attendants and male nurses just got their kicks that way. I remember, there were young guys in this asylum with crazy ideas, imbeciles really, and the attendants would start ragging them. That is, they taunted them in an erotic way, so to speak, and as soon as these guys started to get an erection, the male nurses immediately showed up and started tying them up and injecting them with sulfur. Well, everyone gets their kicks however they can. In an asylum, the work is boring, ultimately.

Volkov. Did the attendants plague you very badly there?

Brodsky. Well, just imagine. You're lying there reading—oh, I don't know, Louis Boussenard—and suddenly in walk two male nurses who pull you off your cot, wind you up in a sheet, and start dunking you in a bathtub. Then they pull you out of the bathtub, but they don't unwind the sheet. And these sheets start drying on you. It's called the "wrap." A nasty piece of work. Very nasty . . . The Russian makes a terrible mistake thinking that the asylum is preferable to prison. Well, that was another time.

Volkov. Why do you think the Russian assumes that the asylum is still better than prison?

Brodsky. What makes him think that—and this is normal—is that the food is better, which, in fact, it is. Sometimes they give you white bread, butter, even meat.

Volkov. But you still insist it's better in prison?

Brodsky. Yes, because in prison at least you know where you stand. You have a sentence—till the whistle blows. Of course, they can always tack on another sentence, but they don't have to, and in principle you know that sooner or later they're going to let you out, right? Whereas in a mental institution you're totally dependent on the will of the doctors.

Volkov. I understand you couldn't trust these doctors . . .

Brodsky. I think that the level of psychiatry in Russia—as throughout the world—is extremely low. The means they use are extremely approximate. In fact, people have no idea of the true processes at work in the brain and nervous system. For example, I know that an airplane flies, but how specifically it does that I can only dimly imagine. The situation in psychiatry is similar. Therefore they subject you to utterly monstrous experiments. It's no different from opening a clock with a hatchet, right? That is, they really could damage you irrevocably. Whereas prison—well, what is it, really? A shortage of space compensated for by an excess of time. That's all.

Volkov. I see that you were able to adapt yourself to prison, which cannot be said of the asylum.

Brodsky. Because you can endure prison more or less. Nothing in particular happens to you there. They don't teach you to hate anyone, they don't give you injections. Of course, in prison they can smash you in the face or stick you in the *shizo*.

Volkov. What's the *shizo?*

Brodsky. The penalty isolator! Basically, prison is okay. Whereas the asylum . . . I remember when I crossed the threshold of that building, the first thing they told me was, "The main symptom of health is normal sound sleep." I considered myself absolutely normal, but I simply could not fall asleep! You start watching yourself, thinking about yourself, and the result is complexes that have absolutely no business coming up.

Volkov. Tell me about the Crosses. After all, the very title is part of the Petersburg–Leningrad folklore, just like the Big House.

Brodsky. Purely visually, the Crosses are a tremendous spectacle. I don't mean the inner courtyard, because that's rather banal, and I saw that when I was working in the morgue. But the view from inside! Because this prison was built sometime in the late nineteenth century. It's not really art nouveau, but still: all those galleries, springs, and wires.

Volkov. Like Piranesi?

Brodsky. Pure Piranesi! You know, *à la russe*. Not even *à la russe* but Germanic. It looks like the Putilov arms factory. Red brick everywhere you look. All in all, it's rather pleasant, but afterward it was less interesting because they put me in a common cell where there were four of us. That's more complicated, because you get interaction. It's always much better in solitary.

Volkov. How did your emotions change between your first and third incarcerations?

Brodsky. Well, when they took me to the Crosses the first time, I was in a panic. Close to hysterics, but I don't think I let this panic show at all, I didn't give myself away. The second time I had no particular emotions, I simply recognized familiar places. By the third time, it was absolute inertia. The most unpleasant part, after all, is the arrest. Or rather, the process of the arrest, when they pick you up, while they're searching you, beause you're still neither here nor there. You think there's a chance you might still break away, but by the time you're inside the prison, none of that seems very important. Ultimately, it's the same system as in freedom.

Volkov. What do you mean?

Brodsky. I once attempted to explain to my pals that prison isn't such an unfamiliar reality that you have to be afraid of it. You live quietly, you keep your thoughts to yourself—and all this because you're scared of prison? There was nothing special to be afraid of. We were a different generation. Maybe our threshold of terror was a little higher. The younger you are, the less afraid you are. You think you can stand more, so the prospect of losing your freedom doesn't make you so crazy.

Volkov. What kind of relationship did you have with your investigators?

Brodsky. Well, I simply wouldn't agree to any interaction or any discussion. I just kept my own counsel. That drove them crazy. They would beat you with their fists, smack you in the face . . .

Volkov. They beat you?

Brodsky. Yes. And rather severely, by the way.

Volkov. But those were relatively vegetarian times, as people liked to say. Wasn't there some legal way to protest those beatings?

Brodsky. Like what? You know, this was before the dawn of the human rights movement.

Volkov. Many who were not at the Brodsky trial are familiar with the proceedings from the transcripts made in the courtroom by the journalist Frida Vigdorova. That transcript was widely distributed in Russian *samizdat*. Do they accurately reflect the courtroom proceedings?

Brodsky. What's there is accurate, but that isn't everything, after all, maybe one-sixth of the trial, because they ejected her from the room pretty quickly. The more dramatic and remarkable episodes came later.

Volkov. I consider this transcript an outstanding document.

Brodsky. Maybe you do, but I don't. To say nothing of the fact that this document has been published a thousand times since then.

Volkov. Well, testifying to the interest in this document is the fact that it's been published all over the world and since then quoted innumerable times.

Brodsky. I was lucky in every respect. Other people had to go through much more and had a much harder time of it than I did.

Volkov. The peculiarity of this trial was that they were judging a poet. In

Russia, the poet is a symbolic figure, and no other Russian poet of your rank was treated as harshly by the authorities during that period.

Brodsky. Well, at the time I wasn't a poet of any rank.

Volkov. The trial against you came at a historical moment of great importance for Russia. During that period, many people had hopes that Russia was set on the road to greater freedom. Khrushchev allowed the publication of Solzhenitsyn's *One Day in the Life of Ivan Denisovich.* People started organizing art exhibits and playing modern music.

Brodsky. Well, that was already the end of the Khrushchev period. He was overthrown right in October of 1964.

Volkov. When one rereads Vigdorova's transcript of your trial, one realizes that all these hopes were naive.

Brodsky. You see, it was clear to me from the very outset of the trial that they were running the show. Therefore they had the right to put pressure on us. For them, the moment you become an alien body, all the applicable physical laws automatically go into operation—isolation, squeezing, crowding out. There's nothing extraordinary about it.

Volkov. You're judging all this so calmly now, in retrospect. Are you trivializing an important and dramatic event?

Brodsky. No, I'm not making anything up! I'm saying exactly what I really think about this! I thought the same then as well. And I refuse to dramatize all this!

Volkov. I understand this as a part of your aesthetic, but Vigdorova's transcript does not dramatize what was happening either, really. She doesn't reach for effects. The worst thing for me in these notes is the reaction of the courtroom, the so-called ordinary people.

Brodsky. Well, half the courtroom was KGB and police. I've never seen that many uniforms even in the documentary on the Nuremberg trial. The only thing they weren't wearing was helmets! My trial, well, that was a movie, too, by the way! A comedy! And a much more entertaining comedy than what Vigdorova described. The funniest part was that two lieutenants were sitting behind me and once a minute, if not more often, first one, then the other would say: "Brodsky, sit properly!" "Brodsky, sit right!" "Brodsky, sit the way you're supposed to!" "Brodsky, sit properly." I clearly remember this name, "Brodsky," after I'd heard it countless times—from the guards, from the judge, from the chairman, from the lawyer, from the witnesses— became meaningless for me. Like in Zen Buddhism, you know? If you repeat a name, it disappears. This idea even has a practical application. If, say, you want to wipe out the thought of George Washington, you repeat, "George Washington, George Washington, George Washington . . ." The seventeenth time—maybe even before, because for me, this is a foreign name—the idea of George Washington becomes totally absurd. The trial became just as absurd for me very quickly. The only thing that made an impression on me then, I remember, were the statements by the witnesses for the defense—Admoni and Etkind—because they said certain positive things about me, and I must admit, I had not heard many good things about myself in my life. So I was actually rather touched by it all. In every other respect it was a total zoo. And believe me, it made absolutely no impression on me whatsoever. Really, none whatsoever!

Volkov. In the trial there was mention of the diary you kept as a youth, in which you allegedly "reviled Marx and Lenin." Did you keep a diary in Russia?

Brodsky. No. What was the point? What Russian could allow himself to keep a diary? As a boy, when I was fourteen and fifteen, I did attempt to keep something like a diary, in which I recorded just my own remarks on the subject of the Soviet state that seemed witty to me. Now all this is in the KGB archives. There was no other diary.

Volkov. Here, in the West, have you never tried to keep a diary?

Brodsky. You know, I have. Quite recently, even. But I decided that if I was going to keep one, then it would be *à la* our sovereign emperor, in English. That is, like Nicholas II. And I did start writing something down, but in general, no, I'm not going to keep a diary. I don't have the requisite peace. To keep a diary you need a life *à la* Leo Tolstoy, right?

Volkov. At Yasnaya Polyana?

Brodsky. Yes, on your own estate. Where life flows evenly. To keep a diary, you need some kind of daily routine. That's something I don't have.

Winter 1982–Spring 1989

BRODSKY AT HIS HOME ON MORTON STREET,
GREENWICH VILLAGE, NEW YORK, 1986

4

EXILE TO THE NORTH

Volkov. Let's talk about your exile to the Russian North.

Brodsky. Well, this wasn't quite the same Russian North they usually talk about in literature and art. And that cultured Russians are so fond of. Although it was the real thing.

Volkov. How did you wind up there? How did events unfold after your trial?

Brodsky. After the trial they sent me back to the police station, and from the police station to the Crosses. From the Crosses I traveled by stages via Vologda to Arkhangelsk, where they put me on a train. Where they were taking me I had no idea. Nor did anyone else on the train.

Volkov. There was a whole crew of you?

Brodsky. Yes, and it included all kinds. The majority were criminals. I never did run across any so-called intellectuals there, although I did run into one person who, I must say, crossed the whole problem of the human rights movement off my agenda single-handedly. He was in the same compartment with me.

Volkov. You mean you rode in ordinary trains, in a compartment?

Brodsky. No! What ordinary trains! We rode in a "Stolypin," a prisoner train, what's called a *vagonzak*. There used to be two models: before and after modernization. We had a very old Stolypin. The compartment windows were barred, boarded, and shuttered. The compartment was intended to hold the usual four, but this four-man compartment held sixteen, right? That is, the upper berth was thrown across and used like a solid ledge. They really crammed you in there, like sardines in a can. And that's how they transport you.

Volkov. How did you survive?

Brodsky. It was a kind of hell on wheels. Something straight out of Fyodor Dostoevsky or Dante. They don't let you out to relieve yourself. When the people on top piss it all dribbles down, there's nothing to breathe, and the crowd is mainly thugs. Men not on their first sentence or their second or third but, oh, say, their sixteenth.

Sitting there in this train car across from me is this old Russian man, the kind Kramskoy used to paint. Exactly like that—the same callused hands, the same beard, everything just like it's supposed to be. He'd stolen some pathetic sack of grain from the livestock yard on the collective farm and they'd given him six years for it, and he was already an old man. It was perfectly obvious that he was going to die either during the transfer or in prison. He was never going to last until his release date, but not one intellectual in Russia or the West was going to rise up in his defense. Never! Simply because no one would ever find out about him!

This was before the Sinyavsky and Daniel trial, but still, there had already been some human rights stirrings. No one was going to speak out for this unlucky old man, though, not the BBC or the Voice of America. No one! When you see this—well, that's really all you need. Because all these young people— I used to call them black market dissidents—they knew what they were doing, what they were letting themselves in for, and why. It may really have been for the sake of certain changes, or it may have been for the sake of feeling good about themselves, because they always had a certain audience, their pals in Moscow. This old man didn't have an audience, though. Maybe he had his old lady and his sons back home, but his old lady and sons were never going to say, "You've acted nobly stealing the sack of grain from the collective farm yard because we had nothing to eat." When you see something like that, you see all this human rights lyricism in a somewhat different light.

Volkov. Where did they take you?

Brodsky. To Konusha, which is a station between Vologda and Nyandoma, in the southern sector of the Arkhangelsk region. They detached me from the convoy in Konusha. The chief of police there was a Major Odintsov, as I recall, the only decent person I think I ever met in that system. He's probably retired or dead now, because I don't think you last long in that life. He was an absolutely terrific man. He sent me out, like all the other exiles, to find work in the neighboring villages.

Volkov. What do you mean, find work? Didn't they send you to a specific place?

Brodsky. No, they said, "Hey, go out there and there and there and talk to people. If they hire you on, we'll support you, as they say." So I found myself in the village of Norenskaya in Konusha District. It was a fine village.

Volkov. It was a collective farm?

Brodsky. No, a state farm.

Volkov. What kind of work was it?

Brodsky. Well, what kind of work was there—farm work! That didn't frighten me in the least, though. On the contrary, I loved it because it was pure

Robert Frost on our poet Klyuev: the North, the cold, the village, the earth. This abstract rural landscape. More abstract than anything I've ever seen.

Volkov. What do you mean?

Brodsky. I don't know how to explain it. I don't have any particular theories on this subject. I can only speak of my own feelings. Above all, there's a very specific vegetation. Basically, it's unattractive, all those firs and marshes. There's nothing to do there, either as a moving body in the landscape or as a spectator, because what are you going to see there? As a result, this tremendous monotony communicates something to you about the world and life.

Volkov. And the white nights?

Brodsky. Splendid! They introduced an element of total absurdity because they shed too much light on what absolutely did not merit illumination. You saw what in principle you would do just as well not to and for longer than recommended.

Volkov. I'm familiar with that sensation, too, an even white light illuminating a flat gray surface.

Brodsky. And the structures there follow suit. I'm not talking about the types of houses, just about their color. The houses are wooden, and this wood is—well, it seems bleached out.

Volkov. What color are the people there?

Brodsky. As a rule, they are light-haired. That is, they're the same color. And they wear the same color. Consequently, the color scale there is absolutely monochromatic. I always say that if you imagined the color of time, it would probably be gray. That is the chief visual impression and sensation you get from the North.

Volkov. How did you withstand the cold?

Brodsky. When the temperature starts to drop in the winter, first to fifteen degrees below Celsius, then to twenty, then to twenty-five, you keep noticing that the frost is getting harder, that it's getting colder and colder, but the temperature continues to drop even farther, and then you stop noticing its changes as qualitative. You cease to react to them. That is, the temperature seems to have no more reason to fall. Nonetheless, it does. Something similar, but with the reverse sign, occurs at the equator. There, it's the hideous heat, which keeps increasing, although you don't perceive it anymore. There's a certain sense to this escalation of heat, though, because the heat allows certain additional life forms to poke through to the light, whereas in the cold this doesn't happen. It's as if you acquire a prehistoric memory—of the Ice Age and such things. But I found all this extremely pleasing, this impractical quality to nature.

Volkov. Tell me in more detail what kind of land this was.

Brodsky. These were the so-called Suvorov *dachas:* land that Catherine the

Great had given to Field Marshal Suvorov after certain victories of his. But he never went there, so there were never any landowners living on this land and the only quit-rent the peasants paid was a tithe to the monasteries.

Volkov. You mean these were strong farms?

Brodsky. Yes, fairly prosperous—insofar as the climate allowed. What's most amazing, really, is that up until 1917 in Arkhangelsk, as is quite apparent from many accounts, the water literally boiled from all the steamers hauling the grain produced on these lands. Whereas now it boils from all the foreign grain being brought in. I don't mean that I feel any nostalgia for prerevolutionary times, because I wasn't alive then, and really I don't care, but it is a fact that before the revolution the peasants there, in the North, did not know much misery.

Volkov. And after the revolution?

Brodsky. Let me say just one thing. With the coming of state farms and mechanization, the topsoil layer, which is very shallow there, since it all rests on stone, on granite, was scraped off by tractors. After all, what actually is the charm of the patriarchal method of working the soil? Not that the horse is a living being you can talk to and hold onto by the mane, but that the plow doesn't go that deep, it doesn't destroy the topsoil.

Volkov. How did the peasants there run things?

Brodsky. I arrived in the spring, it was March or April, and the sowing had begun. It was snowing, but that's the least of it, because they still had to dig out these incredible boulders from the fields. The populace spent half their sowing time digging up stones and boulders from the fields before anything could grow there. It's funny and sad to say, because if anything in the world really makes me angry or upset it's what is happening in Russia with its land, with the peasants. That literally makes me crazy! We intellectuals, we read a book and we forget about everything else, right? But these people have to live on the land. They don't have anything else. And for them this is a real sorrow. Not just a sorrow—they have no other solution. They aren't allowed to go to the city, and even if they were, what would they do there? So what's left for them? They drink, and turn into complete drunks, and fight, and knife each other. That is, the individual is in the process of being destroyed because the land has been ruined. It's simply been taken away.

Volkov. Are these people believers?

Brodsky. No, in fact, the people there aren't churchgoers at all. First of all, the church in the village there was destroyed back in 1918. The peasants told me what the Soviet authorities had done to their church. In my day, a few people still had icons hanging in corners, according to the custom, but this was more an observance of the old ways and an attempt to preserve some of the culture rather than any genuine belief in God. That is, just based on how they behaved there and how they sinned, there could be no question of any faith. Sometimes you'd sense a kind of sigh, that life's hard here and it really might be a good thing to pray, but it was quite a trek to the nearest church. So the subject never came up. Sometimes they got together to blather a little, but as a rule it all spilled over into drinking and brawling. A few times they went for their knives, but mainly these were fistfights, with face-smashing and blood. Your basic rural life.

Volkov. How did you ever manage there?

Brodsky. Wonderfully! It's a sin to say so, of course, and maybe it's not even true, but it was much easier for me to deal with the population of this village than with most of my friends and acquaintances in my native city. To say nothing of the authorities. Or so it seemed to me at the time.

Volkov. Where did you room there, in the village?

Brodsky. At first with Anisya Pestereva. What was her patronymic? Good God, I've completely forgotten! Then with Konstantin Borisovich Pesterev and his wife Afanasya Mikhailovna. They lived in two huts, a summer one and a winter one. Since I didn't need very much room anyway, I rented their summer hut in winter and their winter hut in summer.

Volkov. How much did you pay them for this?

Brodsky. Oh, a pittance: a hundred rubles, that is, ten new rubles. Pesterev took the money from me in advance anyway—for a bottle. He was a marvelous man. Really, the entire village, with the exception of one degenerate brigade leader, was absolutely marvelous, and the brigade leader didn't actually live in this village.

Volkov. Was it a big village?

Brodsky. No, only fourteen households. When I used to get up with the dawn there and early in the morning, at six or so, walk to the office for my duty detail, I realized that at that very hour all across what's called the great Russian land the same thing was happening, people were going to work, and I really did feel like I was a part of this nation. And this was a tremendous sensation! If you take a bird's eye view of the picture, it leaves you breathless. Textbook Russia! Well, it's hard work, and no one likes to work, but the people there, in the village, are tremendously good and smart. That is, not smart but clever.

Volkov. How did they treat you?

Brodsky. Absolutely marvelously! You see, they didn't have a medic or anything there, and I had a few medicines with me, so I could treat them a little, because of my old medical ambitions. I would give them analgesics, aspirin. They didn't have any of that. Or else you had to travel thirty kilometers for the stuff, which you weren't going to do just any day because the roads were horrendous. They didn't have electricity there, after all, no "little Lenin lamps."

Volkov. You used kerosene lamps?

Brodsky. Kerosene, candles . . . It was very pretty . . . Especially in the winter, at night.

Volkov. Did the peasants know why you'd been exiled? Did they know you wrote poetry?

Brodsky. Yes. At first they thought I was a spy because someone had heard a broadcast over the BBC—you could get it on a Motherland receiver, which ran on batteries. So a rumor went around that I was a spy. Later, though, they realized that no, I wasn't a spy at all. Then they decided that I was suffering for my faith. I explained to them that this was not entirely true. Then they simply got used to me, rather quickly. They would invite me over. When I was leaving after my release, their parting with me, I have to say, was rather touching.

Volkov. What did you eat there in exile?

Brodsky. They had a store there, where they sold bread, vodka, and soap, when it came in. Sometimes you'd see flour, and sometimes some horrible canned fish which I tried once and no matter how hungry I was just couldn't eat. This store was under repair for as long as I was there. What I remember is absolutely empty counters and shelves, all new, and in just one corner—you know, like the icons in the red corner?—they crammed the loaves of bread and bottles of vodka. And nothing else!

Volkov. But what else did you eat? Was there ever meat?

Brodsky. You know, it was a state livestock farm, after all, and they fattened calves there, but they never saw that meat. Only if a calf broke its leg, then the people taking care of it would slaughter it and an official act would be drawn up, and the calf's hide removed, and the meat distributed to the populace. That's how they live.

Volkov. Did letters reach you in exile?

Brodsky. Yes, quite a few. I wrote a number myself, too.

Volkov. Did they come straight to you?

Brodsky. More or less. They were vetted first, of course, but somehow I just didn't care. Well, several times I beat around the bush, but that was actually nice because that accelerates the development of metaphorical systems. Those kinds of things are always beneficial for the language, especially for a writer.

Volkov. Did the mailman bring you your letters or did you have to go somewhere to pick them up?

Brodsky. No, the letters came right to me in the village, the same as for everyone else.

Volkov. Where did you send your letters from?

Brodsky. Usually from the post office, but sometimes, if the opportunity arose, I would give them to a driver, who would mail them at the train station. This seemed to increase the likelihood of the letter reaching its proper destination. Those districts—Konusha, Nyandoma, Yertsevo—are traditionally prison camp districts, though, so all correspondence there is under some degree or another of surveillance.

Volkov. Were you yourself under surveillance?

Brodsky. A couple of times a month they came from the local office to see me and conduct a search.

Volkov. The local office of the KGB or the police?

Brodsky. There it's exactly the same thing. Two men would ride over on a motorcycle and come into my hut. The attitudes were utterly patriarchal. I understood why they had come. They would say, "Here, Joseph Alexandrovich, you have guests," and I would say, "Yes, I'm very glad to see you." They: "Well, how are you supposed to greet guests?" So I would realize I needed to go out for a bottle. I would come back with a bottle forty or fifty minutes later, when the deed had already been done. They usually sat there very pleased with themselves and waited for me. What could they possibly understand from all those books lying about there anyway? So we sat down and handed the bottle around, after which they left. It's so remarkable, this universal alcoholism, which all state programs and undertakings in Russia come up against eventually. This is sad, of course, and horrendous, but, on the other hand, at least there is something human left in people, thanks to this.

Volkov. Thanks to this drinking?

Brodsky. Yes, thanks to this drinking. So in principle I would prefer the bosses—there, on top—to be drunks rather than teetotalers.

Volkov. So you think they aren't drunks?

Brodsky. If they were drunks, they wouldn't be there. But I don't want to think about them. It's not all that interesting a subject for contemplation, and my health doesn't permit it anymore.

Volkov. Did you drink there, too?

Brodsky. You know, not much. The vodka there was a horrendous Nyandoma manufacture—pure rotgut, since they made it out of wood alcohol. If you shook it up, it turned white, like milk. That's the awful vodka the people there drank.

Volkov. What about a sex life?

Brodsky. None whatsoever.

Volkov. What, you were celibate the entire year and a half?

Brodsky. More or less, yes. My hands went into action, of course, but for the most part, celibacy. Sometimes my landlord would come to me and say, "Joseph Alexandrovich, go to Konusha!" At the time I was only allowed to go there if I'd gotten special permission from the police. So I would answer,

"And why would I go there, Konstantin Borisovich?" "There's a club there, and girls . . . Go, go! You'll feel better!" There at the club there really was a kind of sexual movement going on among the locals. Drivers would come and all those abandoned women would find a use for themselves. In general, though, there was a tremendous amount of incest going on there, inbreeding, because there were only a few families there, and everyone was some kind of relative to everyone else. Well, while a woman's man is in the field, the chairman of the village council runs over to see her. Everyone knows about it, but the decencies are observed, more or less. A man doesn't just go to the field, for instance; he goes there to convey a telephone message. Even though there is no regular telephone in the village, just an old crank phone.

Volkov. How did you live there without water?

Brodsky. Why without water? There were wells.

Volkov. No, that's not what I mean. Remember, you were telling me about your enchantment with Petersburg's views? In Petersburg, after all, they are linked to the water, the horizon. Was there some great river nearby you in exile?

Brodsky. No, just a little stream, the Norezhka. The house where I lived most of the time was at the very edge of the village, a little ways off. It was the closest to the stream, which was about the width of this room, maybe even narrower. The only thing they had was a little bridge. You're right, of course, the lack of a horizon drove me crazy, because all they had there were hills, endless hills. Not even hills really, but these knolls. And you're in the middle of them. There's good reason to go crazy. To get back to our recent conversation, our native city is especially pleasant in this regard. You stand on Liteiny Bridge and everything that happens past the Troitsky Bridge is the end of the world. Or, the opposite, a way out to a new world. And of course, the sun goes down over the horizon, and you go nuts over that. But there is the danger of a banal interpretation. You look at the sunset and you see a sign in it. It never occurs to you that all these incredible colors are connected with the expanse, with the refraction of light. This is a tremendously interesting phenomenon.

Volkov. Did books reach you in exile?

Brodsky. People did send me books, quite a few. The book situation was fine. When I was released, I brought a little over a hundred kilos of books back with me to Leningrad.

Volkov. Did you write poetry there?

Brodsky. A fair amount. After all, there wasn't anything else to do there. All in all, as I now think back, that was one of the best periods in my life. There have been no worse, but I don't think there have been better.

Spring 1986

BRODSKY READING HIS POETRY,
NEW YORK, 1990

5

ROBERT FROST

Volkov. I know you consider Frost one of the preeminent poets of the twentieth century, but for the Russian—and even more broadly, the European—reader, as a rule, Frost is not all that imposing a figure. Let's talk about Frost and about English-language poetry. Why should a Russian reader pick up Frost?

Brodsky. You can't explain Frost to the Russian. It's absolutely impossible.

Volkov. Let's try. Perhaps at least some parallels can be found with Russian poetry.

Brodsky. The only Russian parallel to Frost that occurs to me right now is Akhmatova's blank verse, her "Northern Elegies." To a certain extent, there is a common trait inherent to both Akhmatova and Frost—the monotone of their meter, the monotone of their sound.

Volkov. The pseudoneutrality of their attitude?

Brodsky. Yes, pseudoneutrality. A kind of muted note. In the "Northern Elegies," no one cries out, no one gasps for breath. We hear the sound of time itself. That's why we all love iambic pentameter so much. That's why Frost loved iambic pentameter so much. Frost has tremendous restraint: no exclamation points, no raising of the voice. Nevertheless, the "Northern Elegies" were written by an urbanite. Whereas Frost is, in theory, a pastoral poet. Of course, these are dark pastorals, but as far as the genre goes, it's still pastoral poetry. When a nightmarish situation arises between people in the open air, and the suspicion creeps up on the participants that nature is on their opponent's side. That they're not arguing with "him" or "her" but with the natural order of things, which makes you feel much worse than if all this were taking place indoors or on the street.

Volkov. What about the Russian peasant poets of the twentieth century: Klyuev, Klychkov, Oreshin?

Brodsky. No, that parallel doesn't work. It's a different pathos, a completely different orientation of the imagination, consciousness, thinking.

Volkov. How did you first come across Frost's poetry?

Brodsky. This is a funny story. A long time ago, when I was still living in my native city, someone gave me a typescript, various translations of English-language poetry done by Andrei Sergeyev. I remember, there was a translation there from Joyce, his ballad from *Finnegans Wake,* and various other things that I found incredibly exciting. Then I set out in search of the rest, if such a thing existed, and in this way got a hold of Frost's poetry in Sergeyev's translation. At the time they were still in typescript; the book only came out later. I read a poem that is called "A Hundred Collars," terribly interesting, and you know, I simply couldn't believe that there was such an American poet named Frost. I decided that this was some brilliant person in Moscow responsible for all these things, creating a kind of apocrypha. But it all became clear to me when I found "A Hundred Collars" in English. That was in 1962, I think.

Volkov. Don't Sergeyev's translations of Frost seem a little dry?

Brodsky. Lushness brings with it beauties that overshadow the essence of the original. They force the reader to focus on the language itself, in this instance, Russian, and this steals the reader away from the original. Or vice versa. It's easier to translate from English into Russian than the reverse. It's just simpler. If only because grammatically Russian is much more flexible. In Russian you can always make up for what's been omitted, say just about anything you like. Its power is in its subordinate clauses, in all those participial phrases and other grammatical turns of speech that the devil himself could break his leg on. All of this simply does not exist in English. In English translation, preserving this charm is, well, if not impossible, then at least incredibly difficult. So much is lost. Translation from Russian into English is one of the most horrendous mindbenders. There aren't all that many minds equal to this. Even a good, talented, brilliant poet who intuitively understands the task is incapable of restoring a Russian poem in English. The English language simply doesn't have those moves. The translator is tied grammatically, structurally. This is why translation from Russian into English always involves straightening out the text.

Volkov. What about from English into Russian?

Brodsky. Here you can do all kinds of things. You can even shove this English straightforwardness into some more or less edible turn of phrase so that you don't lose anything. The main difficulty in translating from English into Russian is the reader's lack of cultural preparation. For instance, what in English is called "reticence" can be restored in Russian, too, but the Russian reader is incapable of evaluating this reticence on its merits. He is not reared in a culture of restraint, of muffled irony.

Volkov. As I understand it, you don't think that the English-language poetic tradition has ever been truly mastered by Russian culture.

Brodsky. I think that only one person has been lucky in Russian translation—Frost. All the rest—well, not very, not even those Sergeyev translated.

Volkov. I remember an anthology of new twentieth-century American poetry put out in 1939. It was compiled by Kashkin and Zenkevich. The book was given to me, by way of a special favor, by my school librarian, who pulled it out from somewhere, from some dusty stack. This anthology introduced me to Vachel Lindsay and Edgar Lee Masters.

Brodsky. Both of them remarkable poets. But for Masters his *Spoon River Anthology* is more an interesting device. It's secondary, right after Edwin Arlington Robinson.

Volkov. Robinson was in this anthology, too, and that was the first time I'd ever come across him.

Brodsky. Once again, the translations in that anthology were not very good. If we're going to generalize about this, then there is no such phenomenon as English-language poetry in the Russian reader's consciousness. German and French literature are much closer to him. French poetry has its tradition of twisting, of piling on, its tradition of pathos, of urgent statements. Hugo, Baudelaire (for me these are the same poet with two different names)—their gaudiness, their eloquence—are understandable to a Russian, whereas the English-language poetic tradition, if one tries to define it in a few words (which is an absolutely idiotic occupation and doomed to failure), is an abstract poetic tone. I remember back in Russia I was amazed by a line from a poem by the rather mediocre American poet Anne Sexton. She's standing on a little bridge over a brook and sees small fish swimming there, "like silver spoons," she adds. This is an image that would never occur to a Russian poet because in the Russian consciousness fish and spoons are strongly dissociated. If a Russian poet did combine one with the other, he would make a big deal of it.

Volkov. A shocking image in the manner of the early Mayakovsky?

Brodsky. If not shocking then at least an image that demands emphasis. The poet would consider it a find and would have no compunctions about laying it on thick, whereas in Sexton all this slips by very quietly. This is natural for the Anglo-Saxon eye, which is trained to it. Visually, it's the cocked eyebrow, right?

Volkov. What about the Byronesque tradition in Russian literature?

Brodsky. My impression of the Russian Byron is an incredible surfeit of words.

Volkov. Doesn't it correspond to the original source?

Brodsky. No. Byron is an extremely witty gentleman, but in Russian translations a completely different tone takes over. Basically, we perceive Byron through the prism of Pushkin, so for the Russian reader Byron is much more continental than any other English poet. When I used to read Byron in Russian, the echo of Pushkin was with me constantly. In the best sense, this was Pushkin; in the worst, Lermontov. I couldn't read *Childe Harold's Pilgrimage* at all in Russian due to the heavy-handedness of the translation. In English, I read Byron with pleasure, and without any allusions whatsoever to Pushkin or any other Russian poets. Generally speaking, I could read English-language poetry in Russian only before I knew English. Now, it gets harder and harder for me to look on the problem of mutual influences from the Russian perspective. When I read an English-language text, I can still remember how it looked in Russian. On the whole, though, my view is now from *inside* English-language poetry. And that's why it's hard for me to sort out what's going on. Here is another significant distinction of English-language poetry: a poem in English is verse with mainly male endings, therefore Dante, who seems possible in Russian translations, is impossible in English. English doesn't have those sounds. Because of its male endings, the snottiest English-language poet comes across to the Russian ear as the voice of restraint, as a voice that is, if not severe, then replete with dignity.

Volkov. But to focus on American literature: aren't its most outstanding figures represented adequately in Russian translations?

Brodsky. If we're talking about prose writers, then yes, basically, but poets as a rule are more important than prose writers, both as individuals and as literature. If we are speaking seriously, the difference between prose and *belles lettres* is the difference between the infantry and the air force.

Volkov. And what about Walt Whitman?

Brodsky. A strange thing is happening now with Whitman's poetry in Russia. What made Whitman's verse possible? What does it rest on? Biblical verse, the Puritan Bible. That is, today the Russian reader could assess Whitman much better if—

Volkov. —if he knew the Bible better.

Brodsky. Yes, if the Bible were more commonplace in Russia, because the length of the Whitman verse, its cadence, rests on the biblical intonation, in precisely the same way as the other pole of American poetry, Emily Dickinson, rests on the Psalter. And here's the paradox: Whitman is well known in Russia, and Dickinson is unknown, although it would be much more natural to translate her.

Volkov. Did your experience in the rural North make it easier for you to understand Frost's "farmer" poetry?

Brodsky. Life in the North didn't give me anything, in the sense that nature gave Frost something. Frost exhausted the symbolic imagery that nature suggested to him. It would be almost impossible to delve more deeply into these matters than he did. But in the North it was easier for me to identify with Frost. I spent basically three years in the Soviet Union strongly under the mark of Frost. First came Sergeyev's translations, then getting to know Sergeyev, then Frost's book in Russian. Then I was imprisoned. Evidently I was more susceptible then than I am today. Frost made an incredible impression on me. Only a few poets have been so cardinally distinct for me, such unique spirits. These are Frost, Tsvetaeva, Cavafy, and Auden. Of course, there are other marvelous poets as well, but for uniqueness of soul—it's these four. This is what you look for in poetry.

Volkov. Frost, Tsvetaeva, Cavafy, and Auden make for rather strange company.

Brodsky. They are very diverse, certainly. If you look at them from the Russian point of view, then Frost is closer to Cavafy.

Volkov. What if you compare Tsvetaeva and Cavafy?

Brodsky. That would be impossible. Whereas Tsvetaeva and Frost—those you can. They share a common conception of horror. The fact is that Frost is a scary poet, a poet of existential horror, and an extremely restrained horror at that, as we have already discussed. The horror in Frost is only stated rather than amplified. This is not romanticism or its modern offspring, expressionism. Frost is a poet of horror or terror, but not of tragedy or drama. Tragedy is what we call a *fait accompli,* a done deal, right? Whereas horror or fear always implies a supposition, the imagination, if you like. What might just yet happen.

Volkov. What about horror in the poems by Mandelstam from the 1930s?

Brodsky. Horror, true, but basically, there's no way you can compare Frost and Mandelstam. Mandelstam's poetry is much more urban. Also, in Mandelstam this is an open text, a cry: "Petersburg, I don't want to die yet . . ." Or this: "You are not dead, you're not alone,/ So long as you and your beggar-girl/ Delight in the grandeur of the plains,/ And the haze, and the cold, and the blizzard."

Volkov. In English, unfortunately, this comes across as tasteless.

Brodsky. It's not a matter of being tasteless. In Frost it comes out like this: "Good fences make good neighbors." That is, it is a statement replete with unresolved horror. Once again we are dealing with the understatement of the English language, but this understatement rather directly serves its own purpose. The distance between what ought to have been said and what actually was said is reduced to a minimum, which, however, is expressed with maximum restraint. By the way, if you forget about particular devices and purposes, you can find a general similarity between Frost and Pushkin's *Little Tragedies.*

Volkov. A surprising comparison.

Brodsky. What is most interesting in Frost are the narrative poems written between 1911 and 1926. The main power of Frost's narration is not so much his description as his dialogue. As a result, the action in Frost takes place within four walls. Two people talking (and the whole horror is what they *don't* say to each other!). Frost's dialogue includes all the essential playwright's remarks, all the stage directions. The set is described, as well as the movements. It is a tragedy in the Greek sense, a ballet almost. Frost was an extremely well-educated man.

Volkov. Don't you find the same kind of narrative motifs of country life in the poetry of our Afanasy Fet?

Brodsky. I see what you're hinting at, but no, that's not right. Frost's New England is a farmer's world that doesn't exist. Frost invented it. It was simply his nod in the direction of pastoral poetry. Frost was often called the last of the Lake Poets, that is, he was linked with Coleridge and Wordsworth. This comparison grew mainly out of Frost's abuse of blank verse, and also because his poetry is narrative, but it isn't true! It isn't true that this is the farm. It isn't true that these conversations are being carried on by farmers. These are masks, dialogues between masks. Whereas Fet really was a landowner. There is a very subtle difference here.

Frost was infused with classical culture. His poetry is extremely terse, a compressed version of Aeschylus (these are my own heretical notions). Of course, Frost took a great deal from the Lake Poets. The Frost idiom is blank verse, iambic pentameter, but you have to remember that English iambic pentameter is the bread and butter of English poetry, just as iambic tetrameter is for Russian poetry. Frost has everyone behind him—from

Shakespeare, whose dramas were written in the same verse, to Keats. What interests me much more, though, is what Frost learned from the Greeks, who taught him how to use dialogue. Although Frost's art is unquestionably of the twentieth century. There's this forest, this colonnade, this perspective—and its violation. The forest as a source of death or a synonym for life. All this is not simply deeply felt, it is a cultured man's view of nature. Only a highly cultured man could invest this kind of semantic burden in this stage set: a forest, a fence, and firewood . . . In European literatures, this kind of existential horror in the description of nature is totally absent. I must admit that in a certain sense Frost was, of course, a limited man. He was interested in specific things—the forest, say—and he sensed the horror the forest emits, radiates, like no one else. It would be impossible to give a deeper interpretation of this sylvan absurd, but nothing of the kind ever occurred to him about, say, grass. This is a very interesting topic—what Frost chose from nature for his metaphors and what he rejected.

Volkov. You have rejected a parallel between Frost and Klyuev, as well as the other Russian peasant poets. Why?

Brodsky. The civic element is very strong in Klyuev: "There is in Lenin a Kerzhen spirit." With him, as with any Russian, you're constantly aware of his desire to pronounce sentence on the world. Also, the lyricism and musicality of Klyuev's line are completely different. It's a sectarian lyricism. In my opinion, almost all Russian poets (whether or not they are believers) abuse ecclesiastical terminology. You're always getting the "God and I" situation in their poetry, which, in my opinion, is immodest. This kind of disposition seems to assume that God must know about me, too, must read my poems, and so forth. Meanwhile, what I've just said refers strongly to young Russian poets. There isn't a poem where the author doesn't beat his brow in prayer. Well, they've smashed their foreheads in the process. In and of itself the rebirth of religious consciousness can only be welcomed, but literature has its own laws, and from the literary standpoint, these kinds of close relationships with the Lord come across as bad taste. You get a kind of religious-literary inflation.

Volkov. Igor Stravinsky insisted that only a believer could write music in religious forms—masses, vespers, and so forth. Moreover, a believer not simply in the "symbolic images" but, as Stravinsky put it, "in the person of the Lord, the person of the Devil, and the miracles of the Church."

Brodsky. I remember what Auden said, that Johann Sebastian Bach found himself very much in a winning situation. When Bach felt like praising the

Lord, he simply wrote a cantata or a passion. Whereas today, if you want to do the same thing, you have to resort to oblique speech. That's marvelously stated, I think.

Volkov. Stravinsky, by the way, despite his expressed opinion, was not entirely consistent on this issue. He rejected spontaneous addresses to the Lord, firmly believing that only formalized prayer was effective. However, according to his biographer Robert Craft, he attended church only rarely, and not even once between 1952 and his death in 1971. How did Akhmatova's religiosity manifest itself in her daily life?

Brodsky. Akhmatova never flaunted her religiosity in public.

Volkov. Did Akhmatova go to church on Sundays?

Brodsky. No, there was nothing like that. It would have been physically impossible for her. In the days when I knew Akhmatova, she was extremely sluggish. Moreover, there were no icons in Akhmatova's apartment.

Volkov. Stravinsky was dissatisfied with Auden's "literary" approach to religion. He said that all Auden's intellect and gift took from Christianity was its form, its uniform even.

Brodsky. Auden was quite conversant with the ritual aspect of religion. He belonged to the Anglican Church, and his greatest ambition was to conduct a service in the capacity of priest, which was arranged for him twice in England. Auden used to tell me that when he was living here, in New York, he often attended the Armenian and Russian churches. Auden used to say how terribly pleasant it was to be in a church and listen to the service without understanding the language because then you're not distracted from the main thing, which, all in all, is an extremely sensible justification for performing the service in Latin.

Volkov. In her poems, especially her early poems, Akhmatova often addressed God.

Brodsky. Well, Akhmatova does have poems that are simply prayers, but after all, any art is essentially prayer. Any art is directed to the ear of the Almighty. Herein, actually, lies the essence of art. That's for certain. A poem, if it's not a prayer, then it's at least put in motion by the same mechanism as prayer. On the purely terminological level, this is expressed most candidly in Akhmatova. As a rule, though, a decent person involved in *belles lettres* will remember one commandment: thou shalt not take My name in vain. Take Frost again. He had absolutely no such inclination. Nor did Shakespeare. I remember, Akhmatova and I were discussing the possibility of recasting the Bible in verse. Here, in America, no poet would ever think to do this. Edwin Arlington Robinson was the last person who might

have been able to take this on. In Protestant art, there is no tendency to ec-
clesiasticize imagery, no inclination toward ritual, whereas in Russian the
tradition is different. This is why it's so hard to put Frost in the context of
Russian literature in any way at all and why Frost's world view (and in the
wake of his world view, his verse as well) is so much the alternative to the
Russian. It's completely different.

Volkov. After all, from the formal standpoint Frost is very traditional.
Shouldn't he really be close to Russian verse culture, which is also traditional?

Brodsky. True. Metrically, Frost is close to Russian poetry because formally, Frost is not that varied or interesting, but in spirit it would be hard
to find anything more opposite. Frost is the representative of an art that
simply doesn't exist in Russian. A Russian poet uses verse to express himself, to pour out his soul. Even the most abstract, the coldest, the most formal of Russian poets. Unlike Russian poets, Frost never splashes himself
out on the piano. You know, in poetry we look for a world view that is unfamiliar to us, and if we look at those we more or less know, then we find
no particular surprises. What's there to say about our compatriots? We
know them inside and out. "Great God of love, great God of detail"—so,
nothing special. Rilke? All right, an aesthete. Paul Valéry? The same, to a
certain extent. Where are the qualitatively new world views in twentieth-
century literature, though? In Russia, the most interesting phenomenon is,
of course, Tsvetaeva, and outside Russian culture—Frost.

Almost all modern poetry owes its existence to some degree or another
to the romantic lineage. Frost has absolutely no connection to romanticism. He is located as far outside the European tradition as the national
American experience is from the European. This is why Frost cannot be
called a tragic poet. When Frost sees a house standing on a hill, for him this
is not just a house but a usurpation of space. When he looks at the boards
the house is nailed together from, he understands that the tree originally
had definitely not been expecting this. Take, for example, Frost's poem,
"The Wood-Pile." This kind of vision of the world has never found adequate expression in Russian culture.

Volkov. Where else do you see Frost's uniqueness as a voice of the American national consciousness?

Brodsky. Frost senses the utter isolation of his own existence. He has no
one and nothing for his helper. Incredible individualism, right? But individualism not in its romantic, European version, not the repudiation of society.

Volkov. The individualism of Tsvetaeva.

Brodsky. If you like, yes. Frost's individualism is different. It is the awareness that he has no one to rely on but himself. Frost has a marvelous phrase that I often recall, in one of his poems, "A Servant to Servants," the monologue of an insane woman who has been locked up several times in an insane asylum. She's explaining that her husband, Len, always says, "the best way out is always through." This means that the only solution to any situation is to scrape through it, right? Or like "The Wood-Pile." This poem of Frost's ends with the man coming upon a cord of wood and realizing that only someone with other things to do could leave his work. So the firewood lies there "to warm the frozen swamp as best it could/ With the slow smokeless burning of decay." Here we have a formula for creativity. Or a poet's legacy. An abandoned cord of wood, right? Here we can see a parallel with the quatrain, with the abandoned poem.

Volkov. What do you see in this that is specifically American?

Brodsky. The tremendous restraint and the absence of emotion. The absence of pathos. Everything is called by its proper name.

Volkov. But what is there specific about Frost's use of plot or narration?

Brodsky. In Frost this goes back to Lake poetry, but it does in fact have much deeper roots. Frost is a marvelous storyteller and gets this from a close reading of the authors of antiquity. I've already spoken of the possible parallel to Pushkin's *Little Tragedies,* but Frost's "plays" are much more horrible and simple. After all, our sense of tragedy is linked to the notion that something went wrong, and the result is a tragic situation. According to Frost, everything is as it should be, everything is in its proper place. Frost shows the horror of everyday situations, simple words, undemanding landscapes. Herein lies his uniqueness.

Volkov. Auden once said that Frost's favorite image was that of the abandoned house. Auden emphasizes the uniqueness of this image in Frost. In European poetic thinking, a ruin is associated with war, or else the ruin is used as an image of pillaged nature—say, a description of an abandoned mine. In Frost (according to Auden) a ruin becomes a metaphor for courage, an image of man's hopeless struggle for survival.

Brodsky. Auden is the only person who realized what Frost was about. I think that Auden as a poet was more influenced by Frost than, say, Eliot, although people usually believe just the opposite.

Volkov. Why do people who knew Frost well speak so malevolently of him? Take the famous three-volume biography by Thompson, in which Frost looms as a two-faced, petty, often spiteful man. Even someone as unsympathetic as Ezra Pound does not provoke such biased assessments.

Brodsky. I think there is a simple explanation for this. Frost won enormous popularity in America. Every possible honor that a writer might attain here was heaped on Frost. If you take the honorary degrees, Pulitzers, and other prizes that Frost accumulated and transform them into medals, then Frost would have as many awards as Marshal Zhukov. All this was topped off by the invitation to read a poem at John Kennedy's inauguration. Many poets felt overlooked. They perceived Frost as a kind of usurper, especially since as he got older Frost wrote rather distinctive but still less interesting poetry than he had in the first half of his career. (Not that his later work doesn't include several mind-boggling pieces.)

Volkov. Are we really dealing here with simple envy?

Brodsky. No, the problem is more complicated. Frost is an incredibly tragic figure. Recall Frost's biography: his first son died of cholera in infancy; his other son committed suicide; one of his daughters died; and the other landed in a mental hospital. His wife died suddenly. Horrible, true? Frost was very attached to his wife. They had lived together for more than forty years, yet there was no real love there, which is also tragic. I think that Frost had a huge guilt complex in his soul. In this kind of situation, people behave differently. You can snivel at every turn, or you can bury your disasters deep down, that is, behave as Frost did. The people who attacked Frost for his hypocrisy were simply beneath him as individuals. Their souls were less complex, if you like. When people talk about Frost's "dual personality," they often cite the following instance. Frost was supposed to appear somewhere in New England, before a group of elderly ladies, the Daughters of the American Revolution. You know, old ladies with blue hair. In the wings, shortly before going out on stage, Frost reviled everything in the world, including these old ladies, in the strongest possible language, but when he came out to the audience, he was calm and smiling, like the Russian Santa Claus.

Volkov. Grandfather Frost.

Brodsky. Precisely. And he calmly read his poems. In my opinion, this is absolutely natural behavior. You can think whatever you like about people. You can have any kind of attitude toward them you like. But when you climb up on stage, you're not supposed to give them a hard time. Once he was standing in front of them, he was not about to pour salt on their open wounds. Rather, he would try to create the sensation that the world was still under man's control. Many of Frost's colleagues do not agree with that point of view, and herein lies yet another reason for the latent ill will toward him.

Volkov. Frost insisted that he was not "reading" his poems to the audience but "telling" them. In the blank for "profession," he wrote "teacher." Or "farmer."

Brodsky. What drove Frost the craziest was that people did not understand him. That as a poet they didn't accept him for who he was. If you read Frost's poems closely, then of course you can give him the Pulitzer Prize, but you have to look on him with horror, not applaud him. That is, when Frost read, people ought to have fled screaming, not flocked. Such is the role of the poet in society, though. He tries to meet society halfway, but society doesn't, right? The poet tells the audience about *what* man is, but no one listens, no one.

Volkov. Frost liked to say, "I don't like obscurity in poetry. I don't think a thing ought to be obvious before it is said, but it ought to be obvious when it is said. I like to read Eliot because it is fun seeing the way he does things, but I'm always glad it is his way and not mine."

Brodsky. Frost is a more profound poet than Eliot. Ultimately Eliot can be shrugged off. When Eliot says, "I will show you fear in a handful of dust," this is still fairly comfortable, whereas Frost irritates the reader. Outwardly, Frost is simple, he gets along without contrivances. He doesn't cram his poems with the sophomore's mandatory verbiage: he doesn't refer to yoga or allude to classical mythology. He doesn't have all those quotations and recitations from Dante. Eliot is outwardly obscure, so he obviates the reader's need to think. Frost seems more accessible, which makes the reader tense. Ultimately, it provokes reader dissatisfaction because man's chief aspiration is to turn away, to hide from the truth of the world in which he lives. Any time the truth is served up to you, you either wave it off or else you start to hate the poet doing the serving. Or else, which is even worse, you heap on him a golden shower of awards and do your best to forget him. In modern society, the poet is supposed to be either persecuted or recognized. It's easier to be persecuted, that is, much easier to create a situation in which you're going to be persecuted, because genuine recognition requires understanding. Society offers a poet like Frost, for example, mere recognition without understanding.

Volkov. Auden, who admired Frost, nonetheless spoke of his miserable personality. He said that Frost envied other poets, especially younger poets.

Brodsky. I don't know which younger poets you're talking about, but Frost helped the young Lowell and Wilbur, for example. In conversations Lowell invariably spoke of Frost with tremendous liking—much more than he did of Auden, for instance.

Volkov. Why is it in the modern literary world of the United States that if someone praises Auden, then he is more reserved in his opinion of Frost? And the reverse: for admirers of Frost, Auden might just as well not exist.

Brodsky. Well, that's perfect nonsense. All these camps arise as a result of notions that bear a very distant relationship to literature. It is another matter that Auden himself harbored a certain prejudice toward Frost the man, but Auden harbored the same prejudice toward Yeats and Bertolt Brecht. Poetically, Auden and Frost do not comprise two poles. If we were to talk about polar opposite poets, that would be Auden and Yeats. Generally, the people who make the so-called literary weather as a rule have little personal connection to *belles lettres.* This is politics pure and simple. Certain connections, certain friendships. Affairs of the past, literary platforms. All those "isms." In these situations I use the English expression, "an ism is an isn't."

Volkov. I wanted to talk with you about one episode in Frost's life that here, in America, was once invested with great importance: the trip the nearly ninety-year-old Frost made to the Soviet Union. This was 1962, the world was on the brink of many dramatic events, and Frost went to Russia at the request of President Kennedy. In those days, Frost used to repeat the story of how in the early nineteenth century a certain American sailor set out for St. Petersburg. This sailor brought the tsar a present, an acorn from an oak that grew next to the home of George Washington, and apparently he even managed to plant this American acorn in Russian soil. Frost cherished the idea that he would bring a similar symbolic acorn to Khrushchev. And that perhaps in historical perspective his visit would bring significant benefit. I have always believed that the course of the historical process largely depended on the individual. Do you remember how Solzhenitsyn called Khrushchev the "peasant tsar" and said that Khrushchev—alone of all the Soviet rulers—possessed a glimmer of something akin to unconscious Christianity? The "Christian" poet Frost went to talk with the "peasant tsar" Khrushchev. His idea was that a poet can speak with a tyrant but not with a democracy. A tyrant can be convinced of something, whereas a poet is powerless in the face of a democratic system.

Brodsky. A poet really does have a lot in common with a tyrant, starting with the fact that both wish to be potentates—one of men's bodies, the other of men's minds. The poet and the tyrant are bound up together. Uniting them, in part, is the idea of a cultural center where they both preside, an idea that goes back to ancient Rome, a small city. The poet and the Maecenas, right? Poets have always fed in courts. This is perfectly natural, really, but if we're talking about Frost, then I don't think he had any particular illusions on this score. Including that he was seriously counting on convincing Khrushchev to make friends with America. Frost, of course, was a republican—not by party affiliation, but in spirit. It might occur to him that he might influence Khrushchev, but not for long, I think. To say nothing of the fact that Frost may have been many things, but he was not a "peasant" poet. This is a universal aberration, what Anna Akhmatova used to call "popular hopes."

Volkov. Auden, who in his youth was quite active politically, finally took a pessimistic view of the possibility of a poet influencing political events. He used to say, "Political and social history would be no different if Dante, Michelangelo, Byron had never lived. Nothing I wrote against Hitler prevented one Jew from being killed." On the contrary, to the end of his days Frost firmly believed that a poet can change history. Can a poet influence a society's political development?

Brodsky. Yes. Here I agree with Frost. But it is not a matter of instantaneous changes. A poet's influence stretches beyond the limits of his worldly term, so to speak. The poet changes society indirectly. He changes its language, its diction. He affects society's self-awareness. How does this come about? People read the poet and, if the poet's labor has been accomplished in a sensible way, what he has done begins to settle to some degree in people's consciousness. A poet has only one obligation to society: to write well. That is, his obligation is to the language. He is language's servant, guardian, and motive force. When what the poet has done is accepted, then people speak the language of the poet and not of the state. For instance, today Italians speak a language of the poet and not of the state. For instance, today Italians speak a language that is more indebted to Dante than to all those Guelphs and Ghibellines and their programs.

Volkov. The Russian literary language is more the language of Pushkin and Nekrasov than of Benkendorf and Dubelt.

Brodsky. In Russia, the situation is even more telling because there the contrast between the state language and the language of educated people is so great. The language used by the state is in many respects not Russian but a language strongly Germanicized, befouled by the jargon of turn-of-the-century Marxist tracts, the polemics between Lenin and Kautsky, and so on. It is the jargon of polemical Social Democratic programs, which suddenly became the language of the people who had come to power. It was touching to observe the Soviet press attempting to Russify this language. This makes it clear why literature filled such a noteworthy role in Soviet society. This is also the source for all the conflicts between authority and literature. The writer uses a language that does not coincide with the jargon of the central organ, so those who run this central organ begin to regard anyone who knows this other lexicon with prejudice and suspicion, demanding proofs that he is not a camel. Some have the time and desire to try to prove this; some don't. Hence all the consequences. Today, though, the Russian does not speak in the language of editorials, and I don't think he will. Soviet power triumphed in all spheres except one—speech.

Volkov. Frost went to Russia at the invitation of Alexander Tvardovsky, who did have a real influence on Khrushchev, and this, in turn, left its mark on Russia's destiny. We have only to recall one historical milestone: the appearance of Solzhenitsyn's *One Day in the Life of Ivan Denisovich* in the magazine *Novy Mir,* of which Tvardovsky was editor-in-chief.

Brodsky. That may be. I give the enthusiasm and energy Tvardovsky manifested in publishing *Ivan Denisovich* their due, as I do the effect that the appearance of *Ivan Denisovich* produced. However, I do not think that the rise of free thinking in the Soviet Union, the emancipation of consciousness in general, dates from *Ivan Denisovich.*

Volkov. What do you think it all does begin with then?

Brodsky. For my generation, *Tarzan.* This was the first movie in which we saw natural life. And long hair. And that marvelous cry of Tarzan, which, as you remember, hung over every Russian city. We were so eager to imitate Tarzan. That's what started it all. And the state fought this much harder than it did Solzhenitsyn later.

Volkov. I think of Tvardovsky-the-editor quite often here, in the West, when I read the works of Russian émigré writers, because they all need an editor.

Brodsky. What's true is true. The writer who is outside Russia instantly starts to feel like Caesar's wife. The editor's scissors are the last thing he can allow. It's absolutely true that there is no writer who doesn't need an editor. Especially major writers—they need them urgently. Without exception. As for Tvardovsky as an editor, I had one meeting with him. The consequences of which were most favorable. Someone, I don't remember who, set it up so that I could go to see him at *Novy Mir* and bring my poems. He and I talked. It was an extremely brief audience, fifteen minutes at most. It was very much like a meeting in the office of a factory director, which, by the way, is just what Tvardovsky looked like. Shortly thereafter I received an envelope from him with my poems and his rather civil comments. Tvardovsky was an unhappy and ruined man. I don't think it was the system that destroyed him, though. He destroyed himself. Really, the system can only destroy you physically. If the system puts the brakes on you as an individual, it's testimony to your own fragility. The meaning of this system may in fact be that it brings out this fragility, and the person's basic essence in general, in the fullest possible way. If, of course, it doesn't wipe him out physically.

Volkov. When Frost went to Russia, he met with Akhmatova. What did Akhmatova tell you about this meeting?

Brodsky. It all turned out rather comically. Frost asked to meet with Akhmatova because he knew that both of them had been nominated for the Nobel Prize that year. Naturally, the Writers Union's administration knew this, too. When the idea of a meeting came up, it became perfectly obvious to the organizers that Frost could not be invited to Akhmatova's. What would Frost say when he saw Akhmatova's kennel? What would the press who were accompanying Frost say? Therefore it was decided to arrange a meeting at the *dacha* of Academician Alekseyev. They brought Akhmatova. It was babel there, full of all kinds of idiots, stool pigeons, and Writers Union rabble. Akhmatova used to say, "Here, on one side, sits Frost, decorated with all the honors and medals and prizes ever possible or imaginable. And on the other side there I sit, I, decorated with all the dogs in existence. The conversation proceeds as if everything were perfectly normal. Until he asks me, 'And what, madame, do you do with the trees on your land? I, for example, make pencils out of my trees.' Well, at this point I could not restrain myself and I said, 'Tell Mr. Frost that if I were to chop down a tree on my land, I would have to pay the state a six-thousand-ruble fine.'"

Volkov. Why did Akhmatova speak with Frost through an interpreter? After all, she knew English.

Brodsky. The authorities would have been highly displeased, to say nothing of the fact that Frost's English was American English, so there was potential for misunderstanding. There was an American interpreter there who later wrote a book about this, a stupid book—Frank Reeves, whose sole merit consists of the fact that he is the father of an actor who successfully played Superman in the movies. Doesn't that sound marvelous—"Superman's father"? Well, as a rule, Slavists don't understand one or the other or both. Really, it's astonishing how many dull people have studied Akhmatova and Frost.

Volkov. How did it happen that at the meeting with Frost Akhmatova read two poems of hers, "The Last Rose" and "Of my own I'll cry no more . . ." and both are dedicated to you?

Brodsky. I don't know. I think it was by accident. As for the second poem, I'm not certain it refers to me.

Volkov. Akhmatova never did anything by accident.

Brodsky. That's very true. Maybe the point is that I was the first to show her Frost's poems. I was trying to pump her up about what a great poet he was. More than likely, though, the poems Akhmatova read were just her most recent.

Volkov. At their meeting, Frost gave Akhmatova a book with an inscription. In a message to Chukovsky, she subsequently spoke very guardedly about this book: "Clearly he knows nature." Faint praise indeed coming from her.

Brodsky. I remember when I brought her Frost's book in Sergeyev's translation, her response was, "I don't understand this poet. He keeps talking about what you can buy and what you can sell. What kinds of conversations are those?" She also told me, pointing to Frost's photograph, "A great-grandfather on his way to becoming a great-grandmother." But, of course, Akhmatova realized whom she was talking to. Just as Frost, I think, realized whom he was dealing with.

Volkov. Steinbeck got the Nobel Prize that year.

Brodsky. Not a bad writer. Actually, that's not important.

Volkov. Neither Tsvetaeva nor Auden was awarded a Nobel, and Auden wanted one so badly.

Brodsky. Where did you get that information? I can say one thing: he wanted it less than Pasternak. That I know for certain.

Volkov. When you tell your American students about Frost, what is their reaction? It's assumed that everyone here knows Frost. They're constantly quoting him, the same way Mayakovsky was once quoted in Soviet schools and colleges.

Brodsky. American youth have a tremendous bias regarding Frost's poems. They've always been told that Frost is a poet of rural life, a kind of pastoralist. A model American. Then you show them that Frost really is an American, only of a completely different variety than they had assumed, that Frost is not a textbook poet but a phenomenon much more profound and scary. That this is genuinely tragic and authentic American consciousness that masks itself with balanced speech and circumspection and hides behind the ordinariness of the phenomena being described. When the students finally understand this, they're ecstatic.

Fall 1979–Winter 1982

BRODSKY AT COLUMBIA UNIVERSITY, NEW YORK, 1978

6

PERSECUTION AND EXPULSION

Volkov. The trial against you became a major event in Russian intellectual life of the 1960s. Speaking in your defense were many prominent figures of Russian culture. Akhmatova, of course, to whose circle you belonged during that period, but also Chukovsky, Paustovsky, and Marshak. Several of the reigning personalities of the period refused to be drawn into this affair. They tell the story that Solzhenitsyn, when they went to him for support, replied that he was not going to get involved, since persecution had never hurt a Russian writer. I am particularly interested in Dmitri Shostakovich's position in this affair, inasmuch as we worked together on his memoirs. Did Shostakovich sign the statement or letter to the authorities in your defense?

Brodsky. You know, I have no idea what Shostakovich did or didn't sign, but he certainly did stand up for me in a very active way. I don't know exactly how many times and in what form, but this was definitely the case.

Volkov. I remember, back in Moscow, Nayman told me about going to see Shostakovich in connection with your case. Nayman came with Akhmatova. Shostakovich's first question was, "Did he meet with foreigners?" When Nayman confirmed that fact, Shostakovich became very gloomy. For him, during that period, contact with foreigners that was not sanctioned by the authorities was a serious infraction of the rules of the game. Later his views changed, but at that point Shostakovich proceeded from a presumption of guilt in a situation like that.

Brodsky. Lord! That we should be discussing these categories now—what Shostakovich did or didn't proceed from. This is all absolute drivel. The trouble with the state of morals in our homeland is precisely this endless analysis of all the nuances of virtue or the lack thereof. In my opinion, everything has to be either-or. Yes or no. I realize that circumstances have to be taken into account, and so on and so forth, but all this is utter nonsense because when you start taking circumstances into account, it's already too late to talk about virtue and just the right time to talk about the lack thereof. I think the individual should ignore circumstances. He should proceed from more or less timeless categories. When you start editing your ethics, your morality—according to what is or isn't allowed today—then you're already courting disaster.

Volkov. You're assuming a strictly determined scheme of development for events whereby one thing flows with inexorable logic from another, but rarely do people develop according to such laws. Their development is much more chaotic.

Brodsky. Weren't we taught this all our lives, that everything develops in a logical progression?

Volkov. Formally, yes. In fact, though, the history they taught us was so riddled with black holes that it lost all logical, to say nothing of actual, consistency. For me, one of the proofs of this was the simple fact that in Soviet libraries by the late 1960s the ordinary reader could not get Soviet newspapers published before 1964, that is, the year of Khrushchev's fall. That's how much the official position had changed in that period of time.

Brodsky. This is all very interesting, but it just confirms my point of view. All this changed precisely because of the authorities' consistency, as a result of their consistency.

Volkov. I remember ordering a certain number of photographs of Shostakovich from various years at the state photography archive. I paid for them in advance, just like you're supposed to, but they were handed over to me by an iron lady who only lacked the epaulettes showing through her suit. Naturally, she checked every shot before giving it to me, and the photographs of Shostakovich and Khrushchev—she wouldn't give them to me! She would drop them in the dust bin. One! Two! Three! She didn't even bother to explain. I was supposed to understand just like that, without added explanation, that Shostakovich was not supposed to be standing next to Khrushchev, because at the time Khrushchev was persona non grata.

Brodsky. So you see how it all works out. Shostakovich and Khrushchev no longer possible, Shostakovich and Stalin still not possible, Shostakovich and Lenin never possible. I think that may even be for the better. For Shostakovich, at any rate.

Volkov. Well, with Shostakovich—it's a complicated matter.

Brodsky. What's so complicated about it? He could have done perfectly well without all that, to be blunt.

Volkov. To be blunt, yes, but you can try being less blunt, too. After all, Shostakovich's work attracted the authorities' attention almost from the very beginning, when the times were far from vegetarian, and he could simply have lost his life. Whereas personal acquaintance with the leaders could serve, at least for a while, as a kind of safe conduct. Shostakovich saved more than just his own life, after all. He also saved his talent, his work. Although to this day I can't understand one of his acts, in 1973, when he signed one of the anti-Sakharov letters published at the time in *Pravda.* I was told that his wife later called the higher offices and warned them not to bring Shostakovich letters of that kind for his signature any more because he could die of a heart attack! Why did he sign to begin with, though? By then the authorities were long past the point of being able to do him any particular harm.

Brodsky. All this has its own device, its own method, because the catastrophe we're talking about is exactly of this sort. It destroys the individual. It transforms the individual into ruins: the roof is gone, but the chimney, for example, might still be standing.

Volkov. As far as I know, the authorities also made an attempt to domesticate and play cat and mouse with you. I think they even offered to let you publish in the magazine *Yunost* [Youth].

Brodsky. Perfectly true.

Volkov. When was that?

Brodsky. Right after my release, when intellectuals were carrying me around on their shield, as they say. Yevtushenko even expressed his readiness to facilitate my publication in *Yunost,* which at that moment was like giving a poet the green light. Yevtushenko asked me to bring him my poems, so I brought him fifteen or twenty poems, from which he ended up selecting six or seven, I think. However, since I was already in Leningrad at the time, I didn't know precisely which ones. Suddenly I get a call from Moscow from the poetry editor at *Yunost.* What was his name? Oh, to hell with him! It's not important because I'd still have to say he was scum, so why bother calling anyone by his name? Well, anyway, he calls and says that Yevtushenko has chosen six poems for them, and he lists them. I reply, "You know, that's all very nice, but I don't like that selection because I come out looking like a shorn sheep." I asked him to put in at least one more poem—as I remember it now, this was "Prophecy." He started waffling, "Oh, we can't, it's Yevtushenko's selection." And I say, "Well, these are my poems, not Yevtushenko's!" But he digs his heels in. Then I tell him, "You and Yevtushenko can go . . . you know where." That was the end of it.

Volkov. Nonetheless, a few of your poems did appear in two Leningrad miscellanies. Apparently there was discussion about a first volume of your poems as well—the first in the homeland, because in the West by this time you had already had books published, both in Russian and in translation.

Brodsky. Yes, and in this instance the authorities' ploys were subtler and more entertaining. Out of the blue, the publishing house Sovetsky Pisatel [Soviet Writer] in Leningrad expressed its readiness to bring out my book. Which made me extremely happy. Although, on the other hand, the poems weren't very good. Well, they asked me to show them a manuscript, so I selected some poems and showed them their manuscript. They approved it, tossing out a few poems, but basically everything was going absolutely wonderfully. They assigned me to an editor, and work was proceeding without disruption. Once again, I've forgotten the editor's name. Suddenly they call me up. "Joseph Alexandrovich, come in on such and such a day at such and such a time and we'll have a contract for you to sign." I didn't get too excited since I didn't really believe in all this, but still, it was pleasant. So I hustle on down to the publisher to sign a contract.

Volkov. Where was the Leningrad office of Sovetsky Pisatel?

Brodsky. At the House of Books, on Nevsky Prospect. I go up to the fourth floor, I think it was, and walk into the office of the editor-in-chief, and suddenly I remember that he only has a year to go until his pension. I think, How can this be? How can he take on such a responsibility, deciding the matter of the contract? It meant his pension, after all. That was when I finally realized that I'd been somewhat hasty, inasmuch as I was dealing with this man in 1967, I think it was.

Volkov. In connection with the publication of the collection named *Young Leningrad?*

Brodsky. Exactly. They had asked me for two or three poems. At first I'd given them "In the Village God" and "New Stanzas to Augusta." So the editor-in-chief himself calls me in. He sits there, pondering and coughing. "Here in this 'New Stanzas to Augusta' you have this line, 'in the swamp where the guard has been lifted.' That word, 'guard,' has to go." I object, especially since in this instance it was utterly inoffensive. He digs his heels in. "Oh no, 'guard' is impossible!" I show my surprise. "Why impossible? Isn't there such a Russian word?" He keeps insisting. "Yes, well, Joseph Alexandrovich, you have to understand . . ." Then I simply suggest he choose a different poem, "Verses on the Death of T. S. Eliot." I wanted them to print a long poem because they paid more for long ones, and since there wasn't any "guard" or anything like it there, they did take the poem and publish it!

Which I actually found quite touching because, if I'm not mistaken, this was the first mention of Eliot in the Soviet press in a positive light.

Volkov. I can imagine the trouble they got into for that.

Brodsky. So here I am sitting in the office of this same man. He is taking his time, smiling at me with his gold crowns and carrying on this completely incomprehensible conversation, which I finally interrupt. "You invited me in to discuss a contract. So what, are you planning to sign a contract with me or not?" In reply he dispatches me to the office of the director of the publishing house, with whom I now have the following dialogue: "I don't understand. What's going on?"

"What's the matter?" he inquires.

"Your editor-in-chief called me and told me to come in about a contract. I come, and there's no mention of a contract. What's really the matter?"

"You see . . . There are complicated circumstances involved."

"You know, I could tell you a thing or two about complicated circumstances myself. What interests me at this moment is whether or not Sovetsky Pisatel intends to sign a contract with me for my book of poems. I'm asking you frankly, man to man. What interests me is 'yes' or 'no.' As for the nuances, and why it's 'yes' or 'no,' that doesn't interest me at all. Yes or no?"

"Well, if you put it that way . . ."

"That's exactly the way I put it!"

"Well, in that case, no."

"Fine. Thank you. Good luck."

That was it. I left. Around 1970 the discussions of a book were revived. Evidently, they had received some signal from on high.

Volkov. How did it turn out this time?

Brodsky. I had an appointment to see Oleg Shestinsky, who at that time was the head of the Leningrad Union of Writers. He was, to a certain extent, a perfectly dear man. What was I planning to talk with him about? I don't remember, but that's not terribly important. Naturally, I was acting in the role of petitioner. What else could I be? I come to Shestinsky's reception area, and there's some kind of delay. These two guys are darting in and out, looking at me in a totally unambiguous way. It's not that I knew everyone by face in the Leningrad Writers Union, but those two simply reeked . . .

Volkov. Of the organs?

Brodsky. Yes! They smelled like bars. Iron bars. I turn around and those guys are gone. Then Oleg sticks his head out of his office, crooks his finger at me, and says, "Listen, Joseph, there are two men here from the KGB wanting to see you. Have you been up to something?" I reply, "Me? Up to something? I have no idea what I've been up to! I had an appointment to see you." But if people from the KGB want to see me—fine, the law's the law. I cross the reception room, walk into the office of Shestinsky's deputy, where those kinds of deals are played out, and these two guys are there.

Volkov. Describe them. It's interesting!

Brodsky. One of them is older, that is, he's old-guard secret policeman. The other is young, with a university pin. A sympathetic lad to look at. I've forgotten his name.

Volkov. You mean they introduced themselves?

Brodsky. Yes. They showed me their IDs.

Volkov. Well, in their IDs, as far as I remember, they're all Ivan Ivanovich Ivanov!

Brodsky. No, they had their titles there and I think their real names. We shook hands and they started talking about the weather, their health, and so on.

Volkov. A worldly chat.

Brodsky. Yes, a real worldly chat, the fucks. Then they start playing a perfectly marvelous piece of good cop–bad cop music. The good cop sings that an abnormal situation has arisen around your biography, Joseph Alexandrovich, and especially your—how can I put it—literary activity. "Your books are coming out in the West, and I think that both you and we are equally interested in bringing clarity to all this. We would like to put everything to rights so that you can be a perfectly normal published author in the Soviet Union."

I reply, "Lord! This is music to my ears!"

But then the bad cop sings out, "You have foreigners coming to see you constantly. Some of them are true friends of the Soviet Union, but some of them, as you understand, are working for hostile intelligence services. As you yourself realize, on the one hand, they do not have an interest, but on the other hand, quite the reverse, they do have an interest . . ." And so on and so forth.

"Well," I say, "you know best. I don't know."

They say, "You know, Joseph Alexandrovich, we do of course know best, but you're an educated man"—this is me, who didn't finish high school!—"so we value your opinion very highly."

Then the good cop sings, "It's time! It's time for you to put out a book!"

And all this is going on in tandem! On the one hand, "From time to time we would be extremely interested in your assessment, your impressions, of one person or another. You understand that among them . . ." And on the other hand, "You need to publish a book. You need to!" A real Punch-and-Judy show, and this conversation, you know, is proceeding—how can I put it?—on a perfectly natural level:

"If I understand correctly what's happening right now, you're offering to publish a book of my poems if I agree to collaborate with you, right?"

"Must you put the matter so bluntly?"

"No, I would simply like to know what we're talking about."

"We feel that an abnormal situation has arisen around your book, and we would gladly help you—publish it without any censorship, and on good Finnish paper." But on the other hand, "Various professors are coming to visit you from the West."

I tell them, "All this is marvelous, of course. The fact that the book will come out—that's all fine, that goes without saying. But I can agree to all this on one condition only."

"What?"

"That you make me a major and pay me accordingly."

They were flabbergasted: "Well, we never expected to hear that from you!"

Volkov. They're all so thin-skinned!

Brodsky. You have to bear one thing more in mind, Solomon. You see, at moments like these your consciousness is split in a way. You remember the situation of that period. We were always being shown spy films—about Richard Sorge or somebody—on television, in the newspapers, always the same thing. Eventually, you really do start to think that maybe it's true, maybe some of those Western pricks who come over really are spies. I still tell them, though, "That's your department, not mine. I'm in no position to deal with that, even if I wanted to."

They reply, "After all, you're a loyal Soviet person!"

"As loyal as they come! But there is still a definite difference between you and me, and not only in salary."

"What?"

At that moment I realize I can talk rings around them. And talk rings around myself, too. Since the conversation is proceeding on such a worldly level, no one is jingling handcuffs in his pocket, and basically at that moment

I have nothing in particular against the KGB, since they haven't leaned on me in quite some time. But then I suddenly remember my friend Efim Slavinsky, who at that moment is in prison, and I think, "Fuck your mother. Slavinsky's in prison, and I'm having a conversation with these guys. Maybe one of them put him inside." Then I say, "Well, Lord! It's absolutely not a matter of loyalty. Here's what the matter is. I'm sitting here with you right now and behind me there's what, my room, my typewriter, and nothing else, right? Behind you there's an enormous system. We're not talking as equals, so this conversation is in fact absurd, because there's a total incongruity at play."

Volkov. How did they round out the conversation after that?

Brodsky. They tell me, "Well, we were thinking you'd be *smarter* than this, Joseph Alexandrovich." Meaning by that, you Jews are supposed to be smart.

I answer back, "Well, I guess you were wrong, and I'm probably wrong, too. Nonetheless, let's leave it at that—at the level of a mistake."

"Still, take our telephone number, just in case."

"Well Lord! Thank you for the telephone number, but we have absolutely nothing to talk about."

Well, I had no fear of them whatsoever. If you've been three times in prison, there's nothing they can scare you with. What, a fourth, fifth, sixth time?

Volkov. Did this whole remarkable conversation last very long?

Brodsky. For about three hours. After which I left.

Volkov. And it ended at that?

Brodsky. By no means! A few days later, a professor comes to see me from some American university and brings me galleys for my book, *A Halt in the Wilderness.* He'd been asked to get me these pages for proofreading. This was terribly pleasant for me, by the way, holding my book in my hands. What could be better! Simultaneously, he gives me an offprint of his essay from some Slavic journal, about some classic of Russian literature, and suddenly I realize that it was this professor the KGB guys had in mind when they were making fools of themselves! It was this man I was supposed to snitch on! I calculated that when this professor arrived in Moscow from the States, they opened his suitcase and saw *A Halt in the Wilderness.* So because of this I worry a little about this American and try to explain to him on paper what's happening. You're being tailed, I write. Be extremely cautious. After which he and I blather on about classical Russian literature.

Later I walk him out to make sure there isn't a tail, and I see him to the Metro. That same evening there was someone at the door. There on the threshold is this same KGB guy with his university pin. I tell him, "As long as you're here, you might as well come in." He comes in, sits in my armchair, and starts praising my library, especially my dictionaries.

"Here's a dictionary I don't have."

"I only got a hold of it recently."

"Was there some professor here to see you?"

"Yes, imagine, there was!"

"And he didn't leave you anything?" "Here." I handed him the essay on the classic of Russian literature with the professor's inscription.

"Nothing else?"

I look at him totally innocently and think, Fuck your mother!

"No, nothing. Would you like some coffee?"

"Yes, with pleasure."

Then I go out into the kitchen and take about fifteen minutes making coffee there, to give him time to do his little search. I come back, pour his coffee, and we blather on again about dictionaries, after which he leaves. And that's it.

Volkov. That's it?

Brodsky. No, there was an epilogue, too. This American fool sent me a postcard from somewhere in Italy, which he'd obviously composed under the influence. He says, "Thanks very much for warning me about the KGB tail." An open text!

Volkov. How did that fateful conversation at the KGB go when they finally suggested you leave the confines of the Soviet Union?

Brodsky. That wasn't the KGB, that was Visas and Registration. On the morning of May 10, 1972, the telephone rings at our house. I don't answer the phone because there's been another round of talks at the military commissariat about drafting me. Well, there was no chance of them driving me into that, with my service record. Still . . .

Volkov. Slight solace.

Brodsky. Very slight. My mother picks up, they ask for Brodsky, and she asks, "Alexander Ivanovich or Joseph Alexandrovich?" They clarify, Joseph Alexandrovich. I think, All right, I'm going to talk my way out of this right now. I pick up the receiver and say, "Yes, I'm listening."

"Joseph Alexandrovich, I'm calling from Visas and Registration."

"Really? How interesting."

"Could you stop by to see us today?"

Civility! I reply, "You know, I would stop by, but the thing is that today I have so many things to do, and I won't be free before six o'clock."

"Well come by at six, when you're free. We'll be waiting for you."

And remember, Visas and Registration closes at four or five!

Volkov. How obliging!

Brodsky. And that day—it happened to coincide—American publisher Carl Proffer came to see me.

Volkov. How did you and he meet, by the way?

Brodsky. Nadezhda Mandelstam introduced us. One fine evening, I remember, I get a telephone call from her from Moscow. "Joseph, a friend of mine is going to stop by to see you, a very fine man." Carlusha appeared, and he and I became friends. Instantly. And here he turned up in Leningrad that banner day. He stopped by with his children. That day, I really did have a lot of things to attend to. I remember, I was supposed to send some translations to Moscow—from some Yugoslav poet—and something else, and something else. My last appointment was at Lenfilm.

Volkov. You were writing screenplays for them?

Brodsky. No, they were setting my poem to some animated film—I don't remember whether it was Hungarian or Armenian. At about five, Lenfilm closes. I walk out with the woman who had gotten me this job there (quite a fabulous girl she was), and she says, "Where are you going now? You're practically on my way home!" I explain, "I can't because today I had a phone call in the morning—imagine!—from Visas and Registration, for me to stop by. But they didn't explain what about. I don't get it. Maybe some American granddad of mine died and left me an inheritance." Because what thoughts could the ordinary person have about this, right?

So I get to Visas and Registration. A policeman opens the door. I walk in. No one's there, naturally. I come to an office where there's a colonel sitting, so all's well. He launches into this highly intellectual discussion about current affairs and the weather until I say, "Surely you didn't call me in here to talk about the weather?"

The colonel says, "Joseph Alexandrovich, have you received an invitation to go to Israel?"

"Yes, I have. More than one, actually, a whole two. What of it?"

"Why haven't you used these invitations?"

"What point would there be to me using them? First of all, I don't know whom they're from, and then . . . you didn't let me go to Czechoslovakia or Italy, even when I was invited."

"So you didn't submit a visa application because you assumed we wouldn't let you go to Israel?"

"Well, as long as you're asking . . . Yes, I assumed you wouldn't let me go, but that was definitely neither the first nor the last reason."

The colonel keeps up this dance, though, around and about, and asks me this question, "Well, then tell me your first reason."

"Well, Lord—any! Above all, what am I supposed to do in Israel, ultimately? I wouldn't mind going for a visit, but forever? I have my own affairs here."

Suddenly the conversation turns around very quickly and the colonel says, leaving all those "Joseph Alexandroviches" behind, "Well, here's the deal, Brodsky! We're going to give you the applications now. You fill them in. In the shortest possible time we will consider your case, and we'll inform you of the outcome."

This is happening, by the way, on a Friday, if I'm not mistaken. A lady appears with the forms.

I say, "You know, I'd do better to take these forms with me and fill them out at home."

"No, you will fill them in now. Here."

I start filling in these forms, and at that moment I suddenly understand. I understand what's happening. I stare out at the street for a while and then I say, "What if I refuse to fill in these forms?"

The colonel replies, "Then, Brodsky, in the extremely foreseeable future you will be having a very hot time."

This is exactly what he said! I'm thinking, Well, this means either the asylum or prison again . . . I wasn't afraid in the least, just painfully bored. They put an invitation from Israel in front of me. I look. It's from Ivry Yakov, which probably means Jacob the Jew, right? I ask, "What degree relation should I write?" The colonel says, "Write, 'grand-nephew.'" I write "grand-nephew."

He says, "We'll help you out with money if need be."

I decline, fill out the forms, and go. This is, as I said, Friday, five or six in the evening. On Monday morning, the telephone rings.

"Joseph Alexandrovich, we have examined your application to go to Israel. A favorable decision has been taken on it. Come in to draw up the documents for your departure and bring your passport."

Volkov. Why were they in such a hurry to get rid of you?

Brodsky. There were two or three considerations. The main thing was that Nixon was supposed to be coming to Moscow then, and by that time

I already had a reputation in the West. I mean, what reputation! Nonetheless, to a certain extent . . .

Volkov. Surely they couldn't have managed to put you out before Nixon's visit, though?

Brodsky. Yes, although they wanted to very much. They phoned me on Monday, and by Wednesday I had been given all the papers. I was supposed to present my visas and get the hell out, but at that point I dug my heels in. "No, I can't, I have a lot of things to do. Look, I have to put my archive in order."

"What archive?"

"I understand that you have my entire archive, but still . . . Anyway, May 24 is my birthday, and I want to celebrate it with my parents."

"What's your date?"

"Oh, sometime in late August or the second half of September . . ."

"No, that's out of the question!"

"Well, mid-July at least! I can't possibly go before that."

They reply, "June 4 is the last possible date."

And this, imagine, was the fifteenth or sixteenth of May!

I say, "And otherwise?"

"Don't forget that you have already turned in your passport. Without a passport, your life could get very difficult."

Volkov. Still, expulsion, and such an urgent expulsion, was a rather unusual step for that time. Did you ever attempt to figure out what was behind it?

Brodsky. You know, I never gave it much thought. I have no desire to try imagining their line of thinking, because directing my imagination down that channel is just not very fruitful. In addition, there's a lot I didn't know. I did manage to clear up a few things when I went to Moscow to submit those visas. You'd be interested in this.

Volkov. I'm all attention.

Brodsky. So I arrive in Moscow to submit these visas and when I've finished up with everything the phone rings. It's a friend who says, "Listen, Yevtushenko wants to see you very much. He knows everything that's happened."

I have a few hours to kill in Moscow, so I think, All right, I'll call. I call Yevtukh, and he says, "Joseph, I know everything. Couldn't you come see me right away?"

I get in a taxi and go to his place on the Kotelnicheskaya Embankment, and he tells me, "Joseph, listen closely. I got back from the United States at the end of April."

(I should tell you that right at that time I'd been in Armenia. Remember, that was the year when they celebrated the fiftieth anniversary of the creation of the Soviet Union. Every month they made a special presentation for one of the republics, right? So, at the request of Lev Loseff, I was collecting Armenian folklore for the journal *Kostyor* [Flame] and translating it into Russian. That was quite a remarkable time.)

So here is what Yevtukh says: "On such and such a date in late April I got back from my trip to the States and Canada, and at Sheremetievo airport the customs officers confiscated my luggage!"

I say, "Okay."

"And in Canada some Ukrainian nationalists had thrown rotten eggs at me!"

Well, this was all just what you'd expect—pure opera!

I say, "Okay."

"And at Sheremetievo they confiscated my luggage! All this made me furious and I called my friend . . ."

Those Muscovites, they all have friends, right?

Yevtukh continues. "I called a friend I knew a long time ago, back at the Helsinki Youth Festival."

Mentally I calculate that this is Yuri Andropov, naturally. I don't say this out loud but ask, "What's your friend's name?"

"I can't tell you that!"

"Well, all right, go on."

Yevtushenko goes on. "I tell this person that in Canada some Ukrainian nationalists threw me off the stage! I come home, and my luggage gets confiscated! I'm a poet! I'm a vulnerable being, impressionable! I could write something that would give you no end of trouble! Really . . . we need to get together! And this person says to me, 'Well then, come!' I go to see him and say that I'm a vulnerable being and so on, and this person promises me that my luggage will be released. In his office, I thought, since I'm already talking to him about my own problems, why not talk to him about other people's?"

Yevtushenko says he tells this person, "Really, just look at how you're treating the poets!"

"What about it? What's the matter?"

"Well, Brodsky, for example."

"What's this?"

"In the States they asked me what was happening with him."

"Why are you so upset? Brodsky submitted an application to go to Israel a long time ago and we granted him permission. Right now he's either in Israel or en route. In any case, he's already outside our jurisdiction."

Hearing these words, Yevtushenko allegedly exclaimed, "Fuck your mother!" Which is a lie, because no matter what, he would never swear in the office of a big boss. Well, I could care less about that, too. Now listen closely, Solomon, since what is kindly called an inconsistency comes next. Yevtushenko allegedly says to Andropov, "If you've already taken that decision, then I beg of you, since he's a poet and, consequently, a vulnerable, impressionable being—and I know how you deal with the poor Jews . . ."

Which is a total lie! That is, he could not have said that!

". . . I beg of you—try to cut the red tape for Brodsky and all the unpleasant parts that go along with leaving."

And allegedly this person promises him he'll see to it, which is really absolute, total drivel! If Andropov told Yevtukh that I was en route to Israel or already in Israel and consequently not within their jurisdiction, this meant that the deed had already been done and the time for petitions had passed. And there was no need to give Andropov any kind of advice. It was too late, right? Nonetheless, I listen to all this without flinching, and I say, "Well, Zhenya, thank you."

To which Yevtushenko says, "Joseph, they understand that you're not going to Israel. You'll probably go to England or to the States, but if you do go to the states, don't bury yourself in the provinces. Settle somewhere on the East Coast. And for appearances you should ask for this much . . ."

I say, "Thank you for the advice and information, Zhenya. But now, goodbye."

Yevtukh says, "Look on it as an extended trip . . ."

Well, he sounds like bad Hemingway.

"All right, I'll see how this affects me."

He walks up to me and gets ready to embrace me, at which point I say, "No, Zhenya. Thank you for the information, but you know, we can get along without that. It's not necessary."

I leave. But what do I understand? That when Yevtushenko came back from his trip to the States, the KGB called him in as a consultant on the issue of me and he set forth his ideas. I hope with all my heart that he really did advise them to simplify the procedure, and I hope that my expulsion did not come about at his initiative. I hope that this never occurred to him, because as far as being a consultant there, he certainly was.* Here's what I don't understand, though. That is, I understand it but I don't understand it from the human standpoint. Why didn't Yevtushenko let me know about all this right away? He could have told me about all this at the end of April. Evidently, though, they asked him not to discuss this with me. Although in Moscow, when I arrived for the visas, this was already more or less known.

Volkov. Why do you think that?

Brodsky. Because of this other story. I'm trying to catch a taxi near the telegraph office when suddenly the poet Vinokurov dives out from around some corner.

"Hey, Joseph!"

"Hello, Evgeny Mikhailovich."

"I heard you're going to America."

"Who did you hear that from?"

"Oh, that's not important! I have a relative living in America by the name of Navrozov. When you get there, say hello to him from me!"

At this I allowed myself for the first and last time in my life something like civic indignation. I told Vinokurov, "Evgeny Mikhailovich, you should be ashamed to say such a thing!"

At that point a taxi appeared and I got in. Or he got in, I don't remember anymore. That's what happened. And that is why I think they knew all about it at the Writers Union. Those kinds of actions usually came about with the knowledge and encouragement of the Writers Union.

Volkov. I think this is all recorded in the appropriate documents and protocols, and sooner or later they'll come to light. On the other hand, in these kinds of ticklish situations, a lot never finds its way onto paper and it's lost forever.

Brodsky. Actually, I've never told this story about Yevtushenko before, so this is for the record, so to speak.

Volkov. How did your relationship with Yevtushenko unfold after that?

Brodsky. The fact of the matter is that this story did have a few more repercussions. When I arrived in America, I was invited to appear at Queens College. Moreover, the initiative came not from the Slavic Department but from the Department of Comparative Literature, whose chair was the poet Paul Zweig, who had read me in French translation.

*Yevtushenko has denied being a consultant to the KGB. His version of his conversation at the KGB and subsequent meetings with Brodsky is widely thought to be told in his novel *Don't Die Before You're Dead.*—S.V.

And the Slavic Department, well, what could they do . . . So we arrive, my interpreter George Kline and I, and we're sitting on stage, and Bert Todd, the chair of the Slavic Department, is introducing us to the honorable audience. Todd was Yevtukh's best friend, a kind of American alter ego for Yevtukh. In all respects. So here Bert Todd is talking about me. "See, in some strange fashion this man came to be in the United States . . ." and other such rubbish. I think, well, all right. Then I read my poems. All's well. Then Bert Todd comes up to me at the cocktail party:

"I'm a great friend of Zhenya Yevtushenko."

"Well, you know, Bert, your friend is a shit, and you stink, too!"

I relate to him briefly the whole Moscow story, and then I forget all about it.

A little while passes. I'm living in New York, teaching, by the way, at Queens College. One morning, the phone rings and a man says, "Joseph, hello!"

"Who is this?"

"Have you already forgotten the sound of my voice? It's Yevtushenko! I'd like to have a word with you!"

I say, "You know, Zhenya, I can't in the next few days. I'm flying to Boston. And when I return . . ."

Three days later Yevtushenko calls and we agree to meet at his hotel, somewhere near Columbus Circle. I drive up in a taxi, and I see Yevtukh walking toward the hotel. A remarkable spectacle really. A one-man theater! He has on a sort of purplish-pink denim jacket, a camera hanging around his neck, a big sky-blue cap on his head, and a package in each hand. A boy come to the big city from somewhere in the state of Georgia! Well, the main thing is this is all for the benefit of the public! We walk into the elevator and I help him with his packages. In his room I ask, "Well, why did you want to see me?"

"Here's the thing, Joseph. The people here who used to work on my image are now starting to work against my image. What do you think about Robert Conquest's article in the *New York Times?*"

I say, "I didn't read it. I have no idea."

But Yevtushenko keeps complaining. "I'm in a terribly complicated situation. In Moscow, Maximov asks me whether I'm a lieutenant colonel in the KGB yet, and the Stalinists declare they'll see me yet with an ace of diamonds between my shoulder blades."

To which I reply, "Well, Zhenya, ultimately these problems are your problems. It's your own fault. You're like a submarine: one hole gets smashed through and . . ."

Well, these subtleties don't reach him. He harps on about how in Moscow they've conceived of publishing a magazine, *The Studio* or *The Staircase*, I don't remember what it was going to be called, and Brezhnev himself had already given the go-ahead, and now everything had come to a screeching halt.

I tell him, "These secrets from the court of Madrid had absolutely no interest for me, Zhenya, since it's all so unreal for me, as you yourself must understand."

At this, Yevtukh changes his tune. "You remember, Joseph, how in Moscow, when you and I said goodbye, you came up to me and embraced me?"

"Well, Zhenya, I do remember it all very well, but if we're going to talk about who was planning to embrace whom—"

At this he jumps up, flaps his arms, and a scene straight out of Fyodor Dostoevsky ensues.

"What! How can you say that! Who was planning to embrace whom! I fear for your soul!"

"Well, Zhenya, I will take care of my soul somehow. Or God will. And now give me a break . . ."

Whereupon Yevtushenko says, "Listen, you told Bert Todd about our Moscow conversation. I assure you, you misunderstood me!"

"Well, if I did misunderstand you, then tell me the name of the man you talked about me with in April 1972?"

"I can't tell you that!"

"You want to go outside? Will you tell me outside?"

"No, I can't."

"So just how did I misunderstand you? All right, Zhenya, let's drop the subject."

"Listen, Joseph. Bert is going to come by now and we're going to have dinner at a Chinese restaurant. My friends are going to be there, and for the sake of your soul I want you to tell Bert that you misunderstood me!"

"You know, Zhenya, not so much for the sake of my soul, but for there to be less shit in the world, why not? Especially since I really don't care."

We all go down to the restaurant, get seated, and Yevtushenko starts nudging me.

"Well, begin!"

This is total theater now!

I say, "Well, Zhenya, how am I supposed to begin? You get me started!"

"I don't know how to get you started!"

All right then. I clink my fork on my glass and say, "Ladies and gentlemen! Bert, remember our conversation about Zhenya's part in my leaving?"

He says, "What conversation?"

Well, here I have to retell it all in brief. And I add, "It's entirely possible that there was some misunderstanding. That I misunderstood Zhenya then in Moscow. And now, ladies and gentlemen, *bon appétit,* but unfortunately, I must take a leave." (A friend of mine really was expecting me.) I stand up and get ready to leave.

At this Yevtukh takes my by the arms.

"Joseph, I hear you've been trying to invite your parents for a visit."

"Yes. Imagine. How did you know that?"

"Well, it's not important how I know. I'll see what I can do to help."

"I would be very grateful."

And I leave. But the story doesn't end here! A year or a year and a half passes, and conversations reach me from Moscow about how Koma Ivanov punched Yevtukh in the eye in public because in Moscow Yevtukh complained about how that scum Brodsky ran to see him at his hotel in New York and begged him to help his parents come to the States. But he, Yevtushenko, does not help traitors to the homeland. Something to that effect. For which he got socked in the eye!

Fall 1981–Summer 1983

BRODSKY READING HIS POETRY AT THE
RUSSIAN HOUSE, NEW YORK, 1992

7

W. H. AUDEN

Volkov. The foreword to your second book of poetry, which came out in English translation in 1973, was written by Auden. I started reading his poetry and prose after attending your lectures at Columbia University. Could you describe Auden's face for me?

Brodsky. It's often compared to a map. In fact, it did resemble a map, with the eyes in the middle. That's how creased it was, with wrinkles fanning out in all directions. Auden's face reminded me of the surface of a lizard or a tortoise.

Volkov. Stravinsky complained that to see how Auden actually looked, you would have to iron out his face. Henry Moore went into raptures over the "monumental ruggedness of his face, its deep furrows like plow marks crossing a field." Auden himself jokingly compared his face to a wedding cake after a rain.

Brodsky. It was a striking face. If I could choose a face for myself, I'd choose either Auden's or Beckett's. More likely Auden's.

Volkov. When Auden got to talking, did his face move? Did it come alive?

Brodsky. Yes, it was very expressive. Anyway, you can't speak English without moving your face—unless you're Irish. That is, if you barely open your mouth when you speak.

Volkov. Did Auden speak quickly?

Brodsky. Very quickly. It was "New York English." Not that he used slang, but his accents got mixed up. It was "British English," if you like, but with a trans-Atlantic tinge. Especially at first, I found it extremely difficult to follow Auden; I'd never heard anything like it.

I think that encountering a strange language is something a Russian basically can but would rather not understand. The circumstances of his life haven't prepared him for it. You know what a pleasure it is to hear, say, a Petersburg accent. It was just as pleasurable for me—more than that, gripping, stunning—to hear Oxford English. The phenomenal nobility of the sound!

That is what happened when Auden and I arrived in London and I heard English from the mouth of Auden's good friend, the poet Stephen Spender. I remember my reaction: I nearly fainted. I was simply staggered! Few things have ever made that kind of impression on me. Well, maybe the view of the planet from the air. I immediately understood why English is an imperial language. All empires have existed not because of their political structures but because of the linguistic bond. Because what unifies people more than anything else is language.

Volkov. Was Auden's conversation like his prose? That is, simple, logical, witty?

Brodsky. It's impossible to speak illogically in English.

Volkov. Why not? It's perfectly possible to speak pompously, irrationally . . .

Brodsky. I don't think so. What makes English different from other languages? In Russian, Italian, or German you can write a sentence—and you'll like it. Right? That is, the first thing you'll notice is how attractive the sentence is, how intricate, how elegant. Whether or not it makes sense is less important. In fact, it's clearly secondary. Whereas in the English language it's immediately obvious whether what you've written makes sense. Meaning is the first thing that interests anyone speaking or writing in this language. The difference between English and other languages is like the difference between tennis and chess.

Volkov. What were your conversations with Auden like?

Brodsky. He soliloquized. He spoke very quickly. It was utterly impossible to interrupt him—not that I had any wish to do so. Perhaps one of the bitterest pills for me in my life is that during the years I knew Auden my English was useless. That is, I could make out everything he said, but just like the dog, I couldn't really say anything. I did try—I did attempt to express certain thoughts—but I think it all came out fairly hideously. Nonetheless, Auden never winced.

The point is that real—I mean self-actualized—people have a special wisdom. Call it a third eye or a sixth sense. When you *understand* who or what you're dealing with, and it doesn't really matter what the person sitting in front of you is actually saying. Without any discussion whatsoever. This instinct, this principal, ultimate instinct, has to do with self-actualization and, strange though it may seem, age. To acquire this knowledge, you have to live long enough—as you do to acquire gray hair and wrinkles.

Volkov. We have both seen plenty of old people who are perfectly stupid.

Brodsky. Quite true. This is why I emphasize the importance of self-actualization. There are certain accelerators, and literature is one of them. That is, *belles lettres* facilitates this process.

Volkov. If you participate in it.

Brodsky. Yes, quite true, specifically if you participate in it. I think that a reader, lamentable though it may be, always lags severely behind. No matter how highly he thinks of himself, no matter how well he understands a given poet, nonetheless, sad though it is, he is always just a reader. I don't want to say that the author is a being of a higher order, but still, the psychological processes . . .

Volkov. Are happening at different levels.

Brodsky. Mainly—at different speeds. For example, I took up *belles lettres* for one simple reason: it gives you extraordinary speed. When you compose a line, things occur to you that in principle shouldn't. This is why you should be involved in literature. Why, ideally, *everyone* should be involved in literature. It is a species-specific, biological necessity. The individual's duty to himself, to his own DNA.

In any event, we should be talking about society's debt to the poet or writer, not the poet's duty to society. That is, society should simply accept what the poet says and try to emulate him. Not follow him, but emulate him. For example, not repeat what has already been said once. In the good old days, that's how it was. Literature set certain standards for society, and society bowed to them, at least those involving speech. Today—and I really don't know how it happened—literature is supposed to submit to society's standards.

Volkov. That's not quite true. Even now, society very often accepts the rules of the game proposed by literature or, more broadly, by culture as a whole.

Brodsky. You have a rather narrow notion of society.

Volkov. Look at what's going on around us. Sometimes it seems as if now as never before society is imitating the images that are offered up, sometimes even foisted upon it, by art.

Brodsky. Do you mean television?

Volkov. Which, don't forget, employs a lot of writers. Dickens published his early novels in weekly installments. Today he would probably be working for television. High-brow and mass cultures are both parts of a single process.

Brodsky. Solomon, you're living in an ivory tower. As Lenin would have said, You're terribly removed from the masses.

Volkov. Whom would you compare Auden the man with?

Brodsky. Outwardly, his habits reminded me a great deal of Anna Akhmatova. That is, there was something majestic about him, a patrician element. I think Akhmatova and Auden were approximately the same height; Auden perhaps a little shorter.

Volkov. Akhmatova never seemed particularly tall to me.

Brodsky. Oh, she was grandiose! When she and I walked together, I always tried to stretch. To keep from getting a complex.

Volkov. Did you and Akhmatova ever discuss Auden?

Brodsky. Never. I doubt she ever guessed at his existence.

Volkov. What were Akhmatova's tastes in modern English poetry?

Brodsky. Akhmatova didn't know it properly. It wasn't that she couldn't have—she could, her English was pretty good. She read Shakespeare in the original.

Volkov. When did you first hear of Auden? When did you read him?

Brodsky. I probably heard of him at about twenty-five, when I first became truly interested in literature. Then Auden for me was just one name among many. The first person to talk about Auden seriously with me was my friend Andrei Sergeyev, the English translator who introduced Frost (among other poets) to the Russian reader. If there has ever existed any kind of higher court for me on matters of poetry, then it was Sergeyev's opinion. At that time, however, I didn't think of Sergeyev in that way. He and I had only just met. After I was released from exile, I brought him some of my poems. He said to me, "Very much like Auden." I think this was in connection with "Two Hours in an Empty Tank." At the time, I liked this poem a lot. Even now I can't judge it objectively. That's why I took an interest in Auden. Especially since I knew that Sergeyev had done the Russian Frost.

Volkov. Apparently Sergeyev met Frost when he went to the Soviet Union in 1962.

Brodsky. Yes. Sergeyev was deep into Anglo-American poetry, and that's why I value his opinion so highly. I would even say that Sergeyev's opinion about my poems was always the most important in the world. For me, Sergeyev was not just a translator. He didn't so much translate as recreate English-language literature for the reader using the means of Russian linguistic culture. Because the English-language and Russian-language cultures are absolute polar opposites. Which is what makes the translations interesting, by the way. Therein lies their metaphysical essence, if you like.

So here I naturally took an interest in Auden and set about reading anything I could get my hands on. And what I could get my hands on was an anthology of new English poetry published in 1937 and compiled by Mikhail Gutner. So far as I know, all the translators in that anthology were either shot or imprisoned. Hardly any of them survived. I only knew one who did, Ivan Likhachev, a remarkable gentlemen.

It was this anthology that became the main source for my opinions on Auden at that time. As far as the quality of the translations goes, they're ridiculous, of course, but I didn't know English then. I was just beginning to figure things out. So my impression of Auden was approximate, just like the translations. I picked up on a thing or two, but not especially well. The further I went, though, the more I got. Beginning in about 1964, I would read Auden when I came across him, deciphering him line by line. At some point in the late 1960s I was already beginning to understand things. I couldn't help but understand him—not so much his poetics as his metrics. That is, this is what poetics are. What in Russia is called a *dolnik,* or accentual verse—disciplined and very well organized. With a marvelous internal caesura, in a hexametrical manner. And this aftertaste of irony. I don't even know where it comes from. This ironical element is more the achievement of the English language than of Auden. That whole English technique of understatement.

Well, I liked Auden more and more. I even composed a few poems that seemed to me to be under his influence: "The End of a Beautiful Era," "Song of Innocence," and then also "Letter to General Z" (to a certain extent) and a few other poems. With that slightly loose-jointed rhythm. In those days I especially liked two poets, Auden and Louis MacNeice.

By the end of my existence in the Soviet Union—the late 1960s and early 1970s—I knew Auden more or less decently. That is, for a Russian, I knew him better than anyone, I think. Especially one of Auden's works, his "Letter to Lord Byron," which I labored over mightily, translating it. For me, "Letter to Lord Byron" became an antidote for every kind of demagoguery. Whenever I was pushed over the edge, I would read this poem by Auden.

The Russian reader may also delight in Auden because he is outwardly traditional. That is, Auden employs formal stanza structures and all that other paraphernalia. Stanza doesn't bother him at all. No one after him ever wrote better sestinas, I think. One of Auden's contemporaries, a remarkable critic and writer, Cyril Connolly, said that Auden was the last poet whom the generation of the 1930s could learn by heart. Indeed, he was easy to memorize, the way our Griboedov is, for example. With the exception of Tsvetaeva, Auden is more precious to me than any other poet.

Volkov. How did you get in touch with Auden?

Brodsky. When my translator George Kline came to the Soviet Union, he told me that the British publisher Penguin was planning to put out my book. I don't remember anymore when that was. In a previous incarnation. Kline asked, "Joseph, whom would you ask to write the foreword?" I said, "Lord! Auden, naturally! But that's highly unlikely." My surprise was very great indeed when I learned that Auden had actually agreed to do the foreword. From that point on we were in a kind of correspondence (while I was still living in the Soviet Union). He would send me books and cards. In reply, I would send him cards in my broken English.

Volkov. How did you and Auden meet?

Brodsky. It was in June of 1972. When I landed in Vienna, I was met there by my friend Carl Proffer. I knew that Auden spent his summers in Austria, so I asked Proffer if we couldn't search him out.

I flew into Vienna on the fourth of June, and on the sixth or seventh we got into a car and set out in search of Kirchstetten in northern Austria, where Auden was living (there are three of these Kirchstettens in Austria). Finally we found the right Kirchstetten, and we drove up to the house. The housekeeper tried to shoo us away, saying that Auden wasn't home (actually, she shooed Carl, because I didn't know a damn thing about German). We were just about to leave when suddenly I saw a stocky man wearing a red shirt and suspenders climbing the slope of the hill. He had a bundle of books under one arm and a jacket in hand. He was coming home from the train—he was back from Vienna, where he'd bought the books.

Volkov. How did you and Auden find a common language?

Brodsky. On the first day, when he and I sat down in Kirchstetten and began our conversation, I started to ask him questions. It was a long interview about what he thought of various English-language poets. In reply, Auden gave me (somewhat reluctantly) rather precise formulations which to this day are for me—well, not exactly law, but something to bear in mind nonetheless. All this took place over several sessions. Auden was objective. He judged poets regardless of his personal sympathies or antipathies or whether or not the given idiom was close to him.

I remember he valued Robert Lowell highly as a poet, although as a person he was greatly prejudiced against him. At that time he had claims of a moral order against Lowell. Auden was of a very high opinion of Frost; he spoke rather well of Anthony Hecht. You have to understand, this wasn't the kind of man who would say, "Oh! How marvelous!"

Volkov. Did Auden ask you anything?

Brodsky. His first question was this: "I heard that in Moscow when someone parks his car somewhere he removes the wipers, pockets them, and walks away. Why?" Typical Wystan. I tried to explain: wipers are in short supply because spare parts are manufactured sporadically, so you can never get anything. Despite my explanations, though, this remained for Auden one of the Russian mysteries.

Volkov. Did Auden discuss Russian literature with you?

Brodsky. Yes. He asked me about the Russian poets he knew. He said that the only Russian writer he could relate to was Chekhov. Also, I remember, Auden commented that he couldn't live under the same roof with Dostoevsky. Such a typical English expression, right? By the way, Auden wrote quite a favorable review of a volume of Konstantin Leontiev that had been translated into English.

Volkov. Stephen Spender used to talk about how early Soviet cinema had such an enormous influence on all of them. Spender recalled how in the 1930s, when he and Christopher Isherwood were living in Berlin, they would search through the papers to see whether a Soviet film was playing anywhere, and when they found one they had to go see it. This circle's ideas about Soviet reality were probably shaped by *Road to Life* and other Soviet films of that ilk.

Brodsky. I think not so much *Road to Life* as Eisenstein. My sense is that Eisenstein influenced Auden more or less directly. After all, what is Eisenstein and Russian cinematography of that period in general? It is the remarkable use of montage, which Eisenstein took, in turn, from poetry. If you look at how Auden differs from other poets, you find it is specifically his montage technique. Auden is montage, whereas Pablo Neruda is collage.

Volkov. Discussing the Soviet cinema, Spender pointed out especially what he termed the "poetic symbolism": the depiction of tractors, steamers, factory smokestacks. Didn't Auden's leftist views surprise you?

Brodsky. At the time he and I met not the slightest trace remained of those views. I understand what happened in the minds of Western liberals then, in the 1930s, though. Ultimately, it's impossible to view existence, human life, and be content with what you see. In any circumstance. And when it seems to you that a means exists—

Volkov. An alternative—

Brodsky. Yes, an alternative—you seize upon it, especially the younger you are. Simply because your conscience gives you no rest: "What can I do?" But the poet rejects political solutions of any kind of problem more readily than others. So, too, Auden abandoned Marxism fairly quickly. I think he was serious about Marxism for two or three years.

Volkov. Akhmatova once spoke rather ironically on the topic of Western intellectuals' flirtation with communism.

Brodsky. Yes, once Anatoly Nayman and I were discussing in her presence how marvelous American writers were, how well they understood life and existence, what firmness they displayed, what restraint and depth. Meanwhile all of them, when they brought out a hero with leftist sympathies, demonstrated tremendous weakness, right?

Volkov. Hemingway in *The Fifth Column.*

Brodsky. Well, Hemingway is hopeless, but even Faulkner, who's the most decent of the lot . . .

Volkov. Right, he has that Linda Snopes, too.

Brodsky. At which point Akhmatova commented: "Only someone who lives in Russia and listens to the radio every day can understand what communism is."

Volkov. Did Auden ask you about your Soviet experience: the trial, your northern exile, and the rest?

Brodsky. He did ask me a few questions on the subject, but as a polite man (or perhaps I have the wrong idea of politeness?), I prefer not to go into that subject especially. A person should not allow himself to make anything that hints at the exclusiveness of his existence the topic of conversation.

Volkov. Describe Auden's house in Kirchstetten.

Brodsky. It was a two-story house. Auden lived there with his friend, Chester Kallman, and their Austrian housekeeper. The house had a stunning kitchen—huge and fitted out with spices in tiny bottles. A real library of a kitchen.

Volkov. People talk about the incredible disarray there—dirty linen scattered about, old newspapers, remains of food.

Brodsky. No, that's all a fiction. There was a certain chaos, but there wasn't any dirty linen scattered about. Actually, I didn't go upstairs, having absolutely no call to go into the bedroom. In the living room there were numerous books, and there were pictures on the walls, including a very good portrait of Stravinsky.

Volkov. If I'm not mistaken, Auden helped you a great deal during your first days in the West.

Brodsky. He attempted to put all my affairs in order. He got me a thousand dollars from the Academy of American Poets, so that I had money at the start. In some absolutely inexplicable way telegrams started arriving for me "c/o Auden." He clucked over me like a mother hen over her chick. I had tremendous luck. It ended with us boarding a plane two weeks after my arrival in Austria and flying to London together for the Poetry International festival, where we appeared together—and even stayed together—with Stephen Spender. I spent five or six days there. Auden slept on the first floor; I was on the third.

Volkov. How did Spender and Auden get along?

Brodsky. The thing was, their relationship had formed long before, and Spender had always been in the junior position, if I can put it like that. Evidently, Spender himself had set things up that way from the very outset. It seemed clear that Wystan was the more important being. Right? Here, by the way, Spender should be given his due. Because recognizing anyone's superiority, refusing to compete, is an act of significant emotional generosity. Spender realized that Wystan was a gift to him.

Volkov. After Auden's death, everyone kept asking Spender about him. He was even forced to prove that Auden hadn't dragged him into his bed.

Brodsky. Yes, I know, in the *Times Literary Supplement.* I realize that Stephen is a little tired of this role that's been foisted on him—Auden's confidant, connoisseur, and commentator. Ultimately, Spender is a major poet in his own right.

Volkov. After Kirchstetten and London in the summer of 1972, when did you next see Auden?

Brodsky. I spent Christmas 1972 in Venice, and on the return trip to America I flew via Paris and London. While I was in London, I called Auden, who at the time was living in Oxford. I went to see him there, and we talked at length. After which I saw Auden only the following summer, at Poetry International 1973, in London. That fall he died. That was a tremendous shock for me.

Volkov. Did you look on Auden as a father figure?

Brodsky. Not at all. But the longer I live and the longer I practice my profession, the more real this poet keeps getting. I fall into a certain dependence on him. An ethical rather than stylistic dependence. I could compare Auden's influence with Akhmatova's. I was dependent to approximately the same extent on Akhmatova and her ethics. In those days I was a callow youth. And with Akhmatova, if you'd never heard anything about Christianity, then you found out about it from her, by associating with her. This was a human influence more than anything else.

If we wanted to talk about whom I found and whom I lost, then I would name three people: Akhmatova, Auden, and Robert Lowell. Lowell was in a somewhat different vein, of course, but the three do have something in common.

Volkov. I've been wanting to ask you about Lowell for a long time.

Brodsky. I knew him for a relatively long time. He and I met in 1972 at that same Poetry International Auden brought me to. Lowell volunteered to read my poems in English, which was an extraordinarily noble gesture on his part. Then he invited me to visit him in Kent, where he was vacationing that summer. A certain intuitive understanding arose between us instantaneously, but something got in the way of our meeting.

The thing is, by that point I was pretty well frazzled by all these relocations: Vienna, London, moving from one apartment to another. At first you're overcome by a feeling—well, it's greed and at the same time a kind of fear that all this is going to end. You try to understand and see everything at once nonetheless. Right? So everything gets mixed up in a kind of vinaigrette.

I remember arriving at Victoria to set out for Lowell's, and when I saw the train schedule, I suddenly lost it completely. I stopped being able to process information. It wasn't that I was frightened by the thought that here was somewhere else I had to go but . . . My retina was overworked, probably, and I thought with some horror about the notion of space unfolding before me right then. You can probably imagine what that's like.

Volkov. Oh yes! It's a sensation of horror and uncertainty about—

Brodsky. About what's happening just around the corner, right? Anyway, I called Lowell from the station and tried to explain why I couldn't come. I tried to set forth all these reasons, but then my money ran out and I was disconnected.

Later Lowell told me that he had decided Wystan had dissuaded me from going, since there was a certain tension between Lowell and Auden. Nothing of the kind! Wystan didn't even know I was planning to meet with Lowell. But this reaction of Lowell's sheds light on what kind of person he was. Not that he had an inferiority complex, but he wasn't very sure of himself. Of course, this only concerns the purely human side because as a poet Lowell well knew his own worth. On that account he had no misconceptions.

Not counting Auden, I've never met a more organic figure in the writing sense. Lowell could write poetry no matter what the weather. I don't think he had periods when it dried up. That is, he probably did, as everyone does from time to time. But I don't think it bothered Lowell the way it did most of his contemporaries—Dylan Thomas, John Berryman, Sylvia

Plath. In my opinion, it was these torments that led Berryman and Plath to suicide, not alcoholism or depression.

Lowell was an extraordinarily witty man and, moreover, one of the most remarkable people to talk to I ever knew. As I already said, Auden absolutely dominated a conversation. Whenever I think about Lowell, I remember his enormous attention. The expression on his face was extremely good-natured. You realized you weren't talking to a wall. You were face to face with a man who was listening rather than a set of specific idiosyncrasies.

Volkov. And you didn't have that feeling when you were with Auden?

Brodsky. The situation was somewhat different with Auden. When I arrived, my English was in an embryonic state, which was natural if you consider the odds then of a Russian ever using it. I even wonder somewhat at the patience Auden exhibited toward all my grammatical eccentricities. I was capable of asking a few questions and listening to the answers, but to formulate my own thought in such a way that I wasn't ashamed . . . In addition, you have to bear in mind the purely subordinate quality of Russian thinking, which at that time I simply was incapable of getting away from in conversation.

With Lowell things worked out differently. After meeting in 1972, he and I didn't see each other until 1975. There was friendly correspondence that bore more of a general nature. In 1975 I was teaching at Smith College, when suddenly there was a phone call from Lowell in Boston. He invited me to visit, at the same time showering me—right there, over the telephone—with compliments (I think he had picked up my book for the first time).

There was another comic episode, because I went to see Lowell a week earlier or later than we had agreed. I don't remember anymore. But my conversations with Lowell were earthshaking! For example, I hadn't had a chance to talk with anyone about Dante since my times with Akhmatova. He knew the *Divine Comedy* the way we know *Eugene Onegin.* For him it was like the Bible. Or *Mein Kampf,* by the way.

Volkov. An odd combination of favorite books.

Brodsky. It's a complicated story. The point is that when Lowell was drafted during World War II, he refused military service. He was a pacifist. And for this he was subject to some kind of nominal punishment; he served a certain amount of time. When the war was over, however, it became clear that having pacifist convictions was noble, but fascism was exactly the kind of evil you really *had* to fight. Evidently, for all his sense of principle, Lowell felt rather awkward. As far as I can make out, he decided to study fascism more closely, to get his information at first hand, so to speak. So he read *Mein Kampf.* I think it was the vulgarity of the consciousness inherent to Hitler that made an impression on Lowell. This vulgarity had its own poetics. That is what occurred to me. The point is that there is an element of truth in every crackpot theory. That's what makes it so catastrophic. Add to this Auden's statement, which he made in about 1935 or 1936, that it's not Hitler but the fact that there's a Hitler inside each one of us.

His study of *Mein Kampf* combined in Lowell with his tendency toward depression. He suffered from a form of manic-depressive psychosis that actually never took on fierce expression, but the attacks were quite regular. At least once a year he wound up in the hospital, and every time when these manic periods came on, he would show acquaintances *Mein Kampf* as if it were his favorite book. It was a signal that Lowell was losing it.

I think that when he was depressed Lowell identified—to a certain extent—with Hitler. The underpinning of this is extremely simple: the idea that I'm a bad person, a representative of evil. Right? In fact, this kind of mania is much more acceptable than when someone identifies with Christ or Napoleon. Hitler is much more plausible, I think.

Volkov. Don't you think this attests to a certain psychological and perhaps intellectual depravity?

Brodsky. Probably. Lowell possessed remarkable intuition. Intellectual depravity—when you don't pay attention to details but strive to generalize—is inherent, to some extent, in anyone connected to literature. Especially *belles lettres.* You're trying to formulate something, not get bogged down in detail. This is characteristic of me as well as others. Well, in my case, this may simply be the small-town Jew's tendency to generalize.

Lowell's formulations were remarkable. What I liked, too, was that he was one hundred percent American. What irritates me in educated Americans is their inferiority complex with respect to Europe. Ezra Pound or someone else runs off to Europe and starts shouting once he's there about how all Americans are scum. This makes just as bad an impression on me as vulgar manifestations of westernizing in Russia. As if to say, we're grunting like pigs and eating cabbage soup with our sandals, while in foreign lands there is Jean-Jacques Rousseau and . . .

Volkov. The Brooklyn Bridge.

Brodsky. Whatever. There was absolutely none of that about Lowell.

Volkov. Lowell obviously was not the easiest person to talk to. The same goes for Auden. I read that in the evenings Auden was so drunk he could not absorb any information. Spender said that as Auden got on in years he would often forget everything that had been said to him after six o'clock at night.

Brodsky. It may have been a matter of the quality of the information . . . The main thing is that Auden went to bed at nine o'clock. So at that time of night it made no sense to approach him. As far as I know, he observed a unique routine all his life. He got up quite early and I think drank his first martini at around noon. I remember him about this time—a glass in one hand and a cigarette in the other. After lunch, Auden took a nap. He would get up, if I'm not mistaken, at three or so. Then the evening round began.

Volkov. At the same time Auden was extremely productive: poetry, critical prose, plays . . .

Brodsky. I don't think any other poet has wasted less time. He even managed to get in an incredible amount of reading! That is, you could say that all Auden's life boiled down to writing and reading, punctuated by martinis. Every time I spoke with him, the first thing we started talking about was what I'd read and what he'd read.

Volkov. Was it a problem for you that Auden was a homosexual?

Brodsky. At the very beginning (despite everything I knew and had read about him), I didn't know that. When I did find out, it didn't make the slightest impression on me. Quite the reverse. I took this as additional grounds for the despair he had in him. The fact is that the poet is always being doomed to loneliness to one degree or another. This is a kind of activity that simply does not allow for assistants, and the further you take it, the more detached you become from everyone and everything.

By that time I knew the history of *belles lettres* well enough to realize that the poet is doomed to far from the most prosperous existence, especially in the personal sense. There have been exceptions, but very rarely do we hear about an author's happy family life, be he a Russian or an English-speaking poet.

Auden impressed me as an extremely lonely man. I think that the better the poet you are, the more terrible your loneliness. The more hopeless . . .

Volkov. Total.

Brodsky. Entirely true, a very accurate word. On course, Auden was totally alone. In the final analysis, all Auden's romantic attachments were the fruits of this loneliness.

Volkov. Did Auden himself ever broach this subject with you?

Brodsky. Oh, no. First of all, I think that if he had even started talking about this, my English at that time would have been so inadequate that we could not have had any kind of substantive conversation. Right? Secondly, Auden belonged—simply by virtue of his age—to a different school. This was homosexuality with a Victorian cast, a completely different sort.

Volkov. The English school.

Brodsky. If you like, yes. But here even more important is the principle that regardless of whether you're a homosexual, your personal affairs, your sex life, is not an object of public property or drum beating. It drives me crazy, for example, when literary scholars devote their life to proving that Proust's Albertine is actually Alfred. This is not literary scholarship but a process inimical to art. In particular, the art of a researched writer. It's unweaving the fabric. Imagine! The writer tatted that whole work, concealing a certain fact. Concealment is frequently the source of creativity. A form of creation, if you like. It is like the author throwing a veil over his face. The person who unravels this lace, who lays bare this entire complex fabric, is doing something directly contrary to the creative process. If you like, it is book burning, and not one whit better.

As for Auden, we know that eating any forbidden fruit is bound up with a sense of guilt. This ongoing sense of guilt—like the creativity we were just talking about—leads, paradoxically, to the incredible moral development of the individual. This is development leading to a higher degree of emotional subtlety. I think homosexuals are frequently more highly nuanced psychological beings than heterosexuals. You run into this quite often. When all this is interwoven with such a unique linguistic gift as Auden's, then you are truly dealing with someone who has realized all his possibilities in regard to emotional subtlety.

Volkov. Is it true that life and poetry are in no way connected? Beginning with the romantic period, it is often very difficult to draw a distinction between the poet's life and his poetry. Look at Byron, Novalis, and Lermontov. Can one really imagine a connoisseur of Pushkin's poetry not knowing the details of Pushkin's personal life? This life is Pushkin's creation to no less a degree than is his *Bronze Horseman*.

Brodsky. Romanticism is to blame for the delirious situation that it obviously makes no sense to discuss or analyze. Of course, when we say "romantic hero," this does not mean Childe Harold or Pechorin. In fact, it is the poet himself. It is Byron and Lermontov. It is marvelous, of course, that they lived this way, but after all, it takes so many things to support this tradition: going to war, dying young . . . damned if I know what else! For despite all the diversity of an author's life circumstances, despite all their complexity and so forth, these variations are much more limited than the product of his creativity. A life simply has fewer variations than art, for the material of the latter is much more flexible and inexhaustible. There is nothing duller than to look at an artist's work as the result of his life, of specific circumstances. The poet composes because of the language, not because "she left." The material the poet utilizes has its own history. It, the material, if you like, is the history, and frequently it absolutely does not coincide with the private life, because it has already outrun it. Even while striving perfectly consciously to be realistic, an author catches himself every minute, for instance, at "Stop. This has already been said." Biography, I repeat, does not explain a damn thing.

Volkov. But don't you think that the attitude of poets themselves toward this problem is at least ambivalent? Take Auden, who also often declared that reading biographies clarified nothing in the understanding of a given writer. He asked that no biography be written of him, and tried to talk his friends into destroying the letters he had addressed to them. On the other hand, though, this same Auden, in reviewing an English edition of Tchaikovsky's diaries, wrote that there was nothing more interesting than reading a friend's diary. And look at Auden the essayist! The obvious pleasure he takes in analyzing the biographies of great people! He delights in digging up some wholly private but telling detail. Isn't this really a natural impulse?

Brodsky. You know why Auden was against biographies? I've thought about this. Recently my American students and I were discussing it. Here's the problem: although knowledge of a poet's biography in and of itself can be a marvelous thing, especially for disciples of a given talent, nonetheless this knowledge very often by no means clarifies the content of the verse. It can even obscure it. Circumstances may recur—prison, persecution, exile—but the result, in the sense of art, is unrepeatable. Dante was not the only one, after all, to be exiled from Florence. Nor Ovid from Rome.

Volkov. Forgive me, but I see only one thing in this ambivalence of Auden's: his reluctance—

Brodsky. That someone might dig around in *his* life, right? Not at all! If you want to read biographies, go ahead and read them! Go write them, too. It's of no consequence. What interests me is the position of the writer himself. Basically, all of them see themselves when they're still alive in a posthumous light. We all have started with reading the biographies of great people. We've all thought that this is us. Right? The danger is that at a certain moment biography and art commingle in the consciousness of the poet himself. A kind of self-mythologizing comes about. This is what was totally absent in Auden.

Another example is Czeslaw Milosz. Recently he appeared in New York reading his poems, and someone in the auditorium asked him, "How do you think events will develop in Poland?" Milosz answered: "You're in the thrall of a romantic misconception. You identify the poet and the prophet, but these are two different things."

Of course, the poet may predict something and it may come true . . .

Volkov. Andrei Bely predicted the appearance of the atom bomb.

Brodsky. Still, predictions of this type are not the poet's business. Auden spoke well about this: you can write, "It will rain tomorrow." There's even a chance that it will. But in fact the poet simply needed to rhyme "tomorrow" and "sorrow."

Volkov. I can agree with that. What I can't agree with is this desire on the part of the author to fence off his biography from his art. It would be another matter if modern art were anonymous, as in antiquity. We don't know anything about Homer's personal life. Romanticism made such a thing impossible, once and for all. The poet's life is one of his most important compositions. Sometimes you can't differentiate which is more important for the reader, the poet's life or his poetry. It's paradoxical, but something similar is happening right now with Auden. He asked that people not write about him; in response, Auden biographies are coming out in quick succession. One critic commented that before long more readers would be deriving their satisfaction from Auden's stories than from his poetry.

Brodsky. It's likely for it's so philistine . . . In fact, it is a natural situation. And it arose for one simple reason: Auden was a remarkable aphoristic thinker. I don't think there are any more like that. So the opinions that Auden expressed (and frequently simply dropped) possess, in my view, no less value than his poetic work.

Volkov. Of course! We are coming to the conclusion that Auden's life, his persona, obviously possesses an aesthetic value. Auden created the "Auden myth," which has him the Greek cynic, with his deep wrinkles, his alcoholism, his dirty fingernails . . .

Brodsky. I never noticed that about him!

Volkov. Well, that's the myth. Let's leave the readers of Auden biographies "their" Auden.

Brodsky. You know, the interest in biographies, and poets' biographies in particular, is based on two circumstances. First of all, biography is the last bastion of realism. Right? In modern prose, we are constantly running across complex devices: here is a stream of consciousness, and its duality, and so forth. The only genre in which the philistine—

Volkov. —the reader—

Brodsky. It's a synonym . . . in which he can still find a coherent narration from beginning to end—chapter one, chapter two, chapter three—is biography. Secondly, in our secularized society, where the church has lost all authority, where almost no one pays philosophers any heed, the poet is seen as a sort of prophet. The philistine views the poet as the sole possible approximation of the sacred. Society foists on the poet the role of saint, which he is utterly incapable of playing. Auden was an example for me, because he was constantly fighting this role.

Volkov. As a result, though, he played it brilliantly. As we see, perhaps even better than any of his contemporaries.

Brodsky. Absolutely true. But I think that it wasn't society that foisted this role on him and not the readers but the times. Therefore it doesn't matter ultimately whether or not he rejected the role.

Volkov. The times create out of an author a historical character, whether he wants it or not.

Brodsky. That's not quite how matters stand. One of the most grandiose opinions I ever read in my life I found in a certain minor poet from Alexandria, who said, "Try during your life to imitate time. That is, try to be restrained and calm and to avoid extremes. Don't be especially eloquent, but strive for a monotone." He went on. "But do not be upset if you cannot do this during your life. Because when you die, you will be like time anyway." Not bad? Two thousand years ago!

This is the sense in which time attempts to liken man to itself. The whole issue is whether the poet, the writer—man in general—realizes what he's dealing with. Some people turn out to be more receptive to what time wants of them, others less. That's the whole trick.

Volkov. I recall Pushkin's letter in which he replies to Prince Vyazemsky, who was distraught over the loss of Byron's notes. Pushkin became irritated: "The mob reads confessions and notes, etc. so avidly because in their baseness they rejoice at the humiliations of the high and the weaknesses of the mighty. Upon discovering any kind of vileness, they are delighted. *He's little, like us! He's vile, like us!* You lie, scoundrels: he is little and vile, but differently, not like you."

At the same time, Pushkin said of the poet: "Among the worthless children of the world, he may be the most worthless of all." Don't you think that what we have here is a contradiction, which is also in Auden's position? That is, on the one hand, Pushkin insists the poet *always,* in all his worldly manifestations, stands above the crowd, which would not dare stick its nose into his life. On the other hand, he attempts to secure the poet's right in his daily life to be the most worthless of the worthless—"until Apollo requires the poet for a holy sacrifice," as Pushkin wrote. Behind all this, it seems to me, stands one thing: a desire to delimit one's private life from public judgment while remaining a public figure, which is impossible. Ultimately, it's dishonest as well!

Brodsky. That's right and wrong both. Why, if a poet is vile, is he not like everyone else? Because the poet is constantly dealing with time. What is a poem, what is verse meter in general? Like any song, it is reorganized time. The bird sings. What's that? Reorganized rhythm. Where does the rhythm come from? Who is the father—or the mother— of this rhythm? There you are. The poet is constantly dealing with *this!* The more technically diverse the poet, the more immediate his contact with the source of rhythm. Right? Whether he likes it or not. If we are talking about Auden, then there is no more varied poet—in the rhythmic respect. So it's natural that Auden himself more or less becomes—well, I don't know, call it time.

Volkov. So, you feel that the poet's earthly existence is purified by his contact with rhythm, with time?

Brodsky. When we say "purification" we immediately introduce a qualitative category. In fact, we are not talking about purifying. Purifying from what—life? These days we often use the word "detachment." This is what is going on. Detachment from cliché. That is, why is Auden, for instance, such a great poet? Especially the later Auden, whom many do not like. Because he achieved a neutrality of sound, a neutrality of voice. This neutrality comes at a high price. It comes not when the poet is becoming objective, dry, and restrained. It comes when he merges with time. Because time is neutral. The substance of life is neutral.

Volkov. Let's try to imagine a Russian lover of poetry who has never seen Auden's poems. To make the figure of Auden more understandable and precious to such a reader, I would like you to draw a parallel between Auden and the Russian poets similar to him.

Brodsky. This is rather difficult. Any parallel is approximate.

Volkov. Let's agree that this parallel will not be the goal but the means, the instrument.

Brodsky. If it is only the instrument, then I would cite Alexei Konstantinovich Tolstoy or the late Zabolotsky.

Volkov. That's an unexpected comparison! But after all, it's true, Alexei Konstantinovich Tolstoy was among the forefathers of Russian absurdism!

Brodsky. Yes, quite true. He was a remarkable gentleman, but I remind you that this parallel is exclusively stylistic, just a hint at certain stylistic characteristics.

Volkov. Why, in speaking about Auden, do you recall specifically the late Zabolotsky?

Brodsky. I think that the late Zabolotsky is much more significant than the early Zabolotsky.

Volkov. I never would have expected such an assessment.

Brodsky. Generally speaking, Zabolotsky is an underappreciated figure. Here was a brilliant poet, and of course, his collection *Columns* and his long poem "A Celebration of Agriculture"—these are remarkable, these are interesting. But if we are speaking in earnest, they are interesting as a stage in the development of poetry. A stage, not a result. This stage is incredibly important, especially for those who write. When you read something like that, you realize you have to keep on working.

In fact, it's stupid to divide a poet's work into stages because all creativity is a linear process. Therefore, to say that the early Zabolotsky is remarkable and the later just the reverse is silly. When I read "A Celebration of Agriculture" or *Lodeinikov,* I realize that after this I should do this or that, but mainly I should look to see what Zabolotsky himself did after that! And when I saw what the later Zabolotsky did, it shook me even more powerfully than *Columns.* I think the most stunning Russian poem about the camps and the camp experience came from the pen of Zabolotsky. It is his "Somewhere in the field, down Magadan way. . . ." There's a line in there that beats out anything you could imagine in connection with this topic. It's a very simple sentence: "So they went walking in their peacoats— two old men, unlucky Russians." These are stunning words. This is that simplicity Boris Pasternak talked about and that he, with the exception of four poems from his novel and two from *When the Weather Clears,* was incapable of. Just look at how this Zabolotsky poem utilizes the experience of *Columns,* their surrealistic poetics:

> Around the men the blizzard whistles,
> Sweeping over frozen stumps.
> And on them, faces, eyes averted,
> Freezing cold, the old men slump.

Eyes averted! This is what all modernism strives for but never does achieve.

Volkov. But the later Zabolotsky, unlike the earlier, was capable of writing—and publishing—a disgracefully weak poem. I've been selecting for myself a little anthology of "Russian Poems of Venice," and I think that out of this whole set of poems, Zabolotsky's on Venice is the worst. You could have printed it in *Pravda:* Venice in the thrall of American tourists, the contrasts between rich and poor. Political propaganda in verse.

Brodsky. That's understandable. It seems to me personally that Zabolotsky's bad poems are a mark of his authenticity. It's worse when everything is wonderful. By the way, I don't know of any such instance. Maybe only Pasternak.

Volkov. What about Pasternak's war poems?

Brodsky. Yes . . . but his diction saves him. Mandelstam is full of failures. Tsvetaeva goes without saying, especially when it comes to bad taste. Although, of course, the most tasteless major Russian poet of all is Blok. No, they all have their failures, and thank God they do, because this creates a certain scale. Really, if a poet is developing, failures are inevitable. Fear of failure narrows a poet's potential. T. S. Eliot, for example.

By the way, I've noticed that Soviet poets are especially inclined to submit to the image created for them. Not by them, for them! Take Boris Slutsky, whom I've always considered better than all the rest. He has committed so many sad stupidities by subscribing to his image as a courageous poet and courageous political worker. For example, he stated that a courageous person should not write love lyrics. Proceeding from those same courageous considerations, he asserted that he published poems, according to his own words, "of the first and thirty-first sort." He'd do better not to compose the thirty-first sort at all! Evidently, though, this mix is inevitable—in a great poet in any case, and it is quite likely that Slutsky considered concealing it to be a form of posing.

Volkov. In his essay on Stravinsky, Auden says that it is evolution that distinguishes the great artist from the minor one. Looking at two poems by a minor poet, you can't say which one of them was written first. That is, having achieved a certain level of maturity, the minor artist ceases to develop. He has no more history. Whereas a great artist, not content with what he has achieved, attempts to capture even higher ground. Moreover (Auden adds) only in the light of the final works of a great artist can we evaluate his earlier opuses as we should.

Brodsky. Lord! But of course! It's absolutely true! You know how the Japanese used to do this? They really have a healthier attitude toward matters of creative evolution. When a Japanese artist achieves celebrity in one style, he simply changes his style, and along with it his name. Hokusai, I believe, had nearly thirty different periods.

Volkov. But then Hokusai lived almost a hundred years. What do you think of the later Auden versions of his early poems? In many instances, they differ radically from the originals.

Brodsky. I'm very sorry that Auden did this, but ultimately, these versions are not the final ones for us. These are revisions that remain just that—revisions. True, there are instances when Auden's intervention led to a significant improvement in the text. But, as a rule, I prefer his original versions.

Volkov. What do you think of the changes Pasternak made in his early works in his declining years?

Brodsky. Again, these changes are lamentable. The fact that he even did this is cause for every regret. Almost without exception.

Volkov. In his later years, Zabolotsky also radically reworked his *Columns* and other early poems. In addition, he compiled his "final" collected works. I see that you are not thrilled about revisions in other poets. Do you correct your own texts?

Brodsky. First of all, one needs to live to the age of a Pasternak or Zabolotsky. Secondly, I'm simply incapable of rereading my own poems. Physically, simply, I cannot bear what I wrote before, and in general I try not to touch on this. My eye is simply repelled. I'm not capable of reading a poem through to the end. Really! There are a few poems I like, but those are just the ones I don't reread. I have a certain memory of the fact that I like them. I think that in all my life I've reread my old poems less than once.

As for a "definitive" edition, I don't think I'll ever do that. For one simple reason: I have plenty to worry about as is. Moreover, when you see someone revising his early works, you always think, "Doesn't he feel like writing now?" When I don't feel like writing, I feel so bad that it would simply never occur to me to work on editing myself.

Volkov. Was Auden a witty man?

Brodsky. Oh, extremely so! It wasn't even humor but good sense concentrated into such precise formulas that when you heard them they make you laugh. In amazement! Suddenly you saw how much the generally accepted point of view did not coincide with the real state of affairs. Or what a stupidity you yourself just dished out.

Volkov. Freud often pops up—one way or another—in Auden's poems. Did you and he ever discuss Freud?

Brodsky. You know, we didn't. And thank God, because there would have been a scandal. As you know, Auden was very enthusiastic about

Freud. After all, Auden was a rationalist. For him, Freudianism was one of the possible languages. Ultimately, all human activity can be looked on as a kind of language, and Freudianism is one of the simplest. There's also the language of politics. Or, for instance, the language of money, which in my opinion is the most specific, the closest to metaphysics.

Volkov. Reading memoirs about Auden, you see how often people came to see him, to see the poet, to see a man who outwardly was highly eccentric, for mundane advice. Sometimes these were people who were very far removed from literature or art.

Brodsky. The same thing happened with Akhmatova, by the way. No matter where she went, what we used to call an *akhmatovka* would start. That is, people would come in droves. For the same reason.

Volkov. Auden moved to America from England when he was thirty-two and became an American citizen. He loved New York very much and in general felt a great tenderness for America, it seems to me. Do you still consider Auden a British poet?

Brodsky. Unquestionably. If we're talking about the texture of Auden's verse, it is of course British. But a remarkable transformation occurred in Auden; he is also a trans-Atlantic poet. Remember, I was telling you that Auden's conversational language was trans-Atlantic in a way. In fact, the tendency to trans-Atlanticism is evidently inherent to English itself. It is a more precise and therefore imperial language that seems to embrace the whole world.

Auden was extremely jealous of his language. A reason he came to the States was the linguistic gain he realized by doing so. He noticed that the English language was becoming Americanized. During the prewar and war years, Auden made an intensified effort to master American idioms and cram them into his poems.

Volkov. Isn't it odd that for all this Auden was constantly speaking out against the corruption of the language?

Brodsky. Not all Americanisms corrupt the language. Quite the contrary. Americanisms can be somewhat vulgar, but I think they're very expressive. After all, the poet is always interested in a more capacious form of expressiveness. For Auden, who was born in York and educated at Oxford, America was a true safari. He picked things up, as Akhmatova used to say, right and left: from the archaisms, from the dictionary, from professional jargon, from the jokes of assimilated ethnic minorities, from pop songs, and other things like that.

Volkov. Don't you think that the freer atmosphere of bohemian Greenwich Village, where Auden settled, facilitated this kind of linguistic emancipation?

Brodsky. I don't know. You might well say that. In the beginning there was Brooklyn.

Volkov. When Auden left New York at the end of his life and returned to Oxford, he saw—probably to his own surprise—that Oxford was absolutely unfit to live in. Don't you find this ironic?

Brodsky. In part, yes. Auden missed New York badly. You can't go home again and expect it to look the way you left it. Unfortunately, there's nothing about this in Ecclesiastes.

Volkov. He used to grumble. He was tired of life.

Brodsky. You may well be right. I can say this. When a person changes his place of residence, as a rule he is guided not by abstract considerations but by something extremely concrete. When Auden and Christopher Isherwood made their way to the States, there was a perfectly concrete reason for doing so. In turn, I well remember the reasons Auden advanced as a basis for his return to Oxford. Auden said that he was an old man, and although he was absolutely, ideally healthy—which was a tremendous exaggeration—nonetheless, he wanted tending. In Oxford, Auden was provided a servant. He lived in a fifteenth-century cottage—renovated, of course.

Auden's life at Oxford was different—a completely different rhythm, different surroundings. Indeed, Auden was bored in Oxford, but that's not the only reason why it was sad. It was sad to see how Auden's Oxford colleagues treated him. I remember, Auden and I went to lunch at the mess hall. It wasn't that his colleagues slighted Auden; they simply didn't give a damn about him.

Volkov. What do American young people think of Auden? Your students, for example?

Brodsky. As a rule, American students don't know Auden, at least not as things stand today. Or else they have the vaguest notions of him foisted on them by the dominant cliques or trends. The point is that Auden wielded incredible influence on modern American poetry. The so-called "confessional" school came from him. They are all a direct consequence of Auden, his children in the spiritual sense, and frequently even in the purely technical sense as well, but no one recognizes that! When you try to show your students who the father is of their present idols and then who Auden's father is, you are simply opening up a treasure trove for them.

When I came to the States, at first I suffered a severe loss of nerve. I thought, really, who do I think I am? How am I going to talk to Americans about their own literature? I felt like I was usurping someone else's place. I arrived with the notion that everyone here knew everything. At best, I could point out some odd nuance that had been revealed to me, as someone coming from Russia. That is, I could offer the Slavic perspective on English-language literature. I thought my point of view could offer merely a sidelight on the subject.

But I encountered a completely different situation. I'm not saying this to brag, but for the sake of observation as such. It became clear that I knew not one whit less about American literature, and American poetry in particular, than most American professors. You see, my knowledge of this subject is qualitatively different. It is an active knowledge, the knowledge of someone for whom all these texts are precious. More precious, if you like, than for most of them, because my life—to say nothing of my world view—was *changed* by these texts, and American students, as a rule, never come across that kind of approach to literature. At best, they are offered Auden within the framework of a survey course of twentieth-century English poetry, when a poet is brought in by way of illustration for a given "ism." Rather than the reverse, right? And this is extremely tragic, really. But such, by necessity, is any academic system.

Actually, the virtue of the local academic system lies in the fact that it is sufficiently flexible to include the nonacademic perspective as well. When the teacher is not an academic but someone like Auden, Lowell, or Frost. Even, forgive me, like your humble servant. That is, a person who is involved with poetry and is not making soup from it. Right? When the teacher is a character out of the chaos . . .

Volkov. You have studied the English metaphysical poets a great deal: John Donne and company. What was Auden's attitude toward them? What, in your opinion, did the metaphysical poets give to modern English-language poetry?

Brodsky. Auden and I did not talk a lot about this—we never got around to it. Nor would it ever have occurred to me to ask, for it's utterly obvious that Auden is flesh of their flesh. This is like asking someone how he feels about his own cells. What did the metaphysical poets give the new poetry? In essence, everything. Poetry is by definition a metaphysical art, for its very material—language—is metaphysical. The difference between metaphysical and nonmetaphysical poets is the difference between those who understand what language is (and where language gets its legs, so to speak) and those who really don't have a clue. The former, roughly speaking, are interested in the source of language and, thus, the source of *everything*. The latter are just chirping.

Volkov. Isn't that too strongly put?

Brodsky. Of course, of course. Plenty that's interesting slips through this chirping, too. After all, not only words as such are metaphysical. Or the thoughts and feelings they designate. Pauses and caesuras are also metaphysical, for they are also forms of time. I think I've already said that speech—and even chirping—is nothing but a reorganization of time.

Volkov. The English metaphysical poets are a relatively recent discovery for the Russian reader. What makes them unique, "special"?

Brodsky. Roughly speaking, the poetic trend that preceded the metaphysical poets could be called traditional and mannered. The poetry was not exactly jam-packed with content. All this goes back to Italian mellifluousness. I'm oversimplifying, naturally, but you could say that the metaphysical school created a poetics whose prime mover was the development of thought, thesis, content, whereas its predecessors were more interested in the pure plasticity—at most lightly soiled with meaning. Generally, it's like the reaction that came about in Russia at the turn of our century after the symbolists inflated the mellifluousness of late nineteenth-century poetry to the point of the totally absurd.

Volkov. Are you talking about the summons of the acmeists, who "vanquished symbolism" in the name of "splendid clarity"?

Brodsky. The acmeists, and the early futurists, and the young Pasternak. As for the English metaphysical poets, they arose as a result of the Renaissance, which (unlike the widely held point of view) was a time of tremendous spiritual disruption, uncertainty, the total compromise or loss of ideals.

Volkov. Your characterization of the era sounds painfully familiar.

Brodsky. Yes, similar to the atmosphere in Europe after World War I. Only during the Renaissance, the destabilizing factor was not war but scientific discoveries. Everything was shaken, faith in particular. Metaphysical poetry is the mirror of this disorder. This is why the poets of our century, people with war experience, found the metaphysical school so alluring. In short, the metaphysical poets gave English poetry a sense of infinity, which was more powerful than the religious notion of infinity. They may have been the first to understand that dissonance is not an end of art but just the reverse: dissonance is the moment when art is only just getting going in earnest. This is on the level of ideas.

Volkov. And in the sense of the poetic craft?

Brodsky. Oh, this was a tremendous qualitative breakthrough, a great leap forward! Incredible diversity of stanza construction, head-spinning use of metaphor. All this defined the stylistic independence of English poetry from continental poetic structures for a long time to come. Just look at the technical aspect of Auden's art. You'll see that in this century—with the possible exception of Thomas Hardy—there has never been a more diverse poet.

In Auden you'll find the Sapphic stanza, anacreontic verse, syllabic verse (absolutely phenomenal syllabic verse, as in "The Sea and the Mirror" or "In Praise of Limestone"); and the sestinas, villanelles, rondos, Horatian odes. In the formal sense Auden is simply the culmination of what we consider our civilization. In essence, he is the ultimate effort to animate it.

Volkov. The 1967 edition of the Soviet literary encyclopedia says that the English metaphysical school breaks with the realistic and humanistic traditions of the Renaissance lyric." In Soviet literary jargon this implies disapprobation. On the other hand, in the booklet for the scholarly series Literary Monuments, also published in Moscow in 1967, the metaphysical poets are characterized with great respect. The booklet announced plans for an edition of *Poetry of the English Baroque* in your translation with commentaries by Academician Zhirmunsky. How did this volume get started?

Brodsky. In an utterly banal way. In 1964, I came across John Donne, and then all the others—Herbert, Crashaw, and Vaughan—and I began translating them. At first for myself and my buddies, and later for some possible publication—in the future.

Volkov. Why did Donne attract your attention?

Brodsky. My enthusiasm for Donne began—as it did for everyone in Russia, I believe—with this famous quotation from Hemingway's *For Whom the Bell Tolls:* "No man is an island, entire of itself; every man is a piece of the Continent, a part of the main; if a clod be worked away by the Sea, Europe is the less, as well as if a Promontory were, as well as if a Manor of the friends or of thine own were; any man's death diminishes me, because I am involved in Mankind; And therefore never send to know for whom the bell tolls; It tolls for thee."

This epigraph made a major impression on me, and I attempted to find the quotation from Donne in the original (although I didn't know English very well at the time). Some foreign student—one of the grad students studying in Leningrad—brought me a book by Donne. I went through it all, but I never did find the quotation I was looking for. Only later did I get it that Hemingway wasn't using a Donne poem but an excerpt from a sermon.

By this time, though, it was rather late in the day to be studying Donne, because I'd been put in prison. Later, when I was already in the village, Lydia Chukovskaya sent me—evidently from her father's library—a book by Donne published by Sovremennaya Biblioteka. So there, in exile, I set about translating Donne little by little. I did this for my own pleasure for one and a half or two years. Through Akhmatova I met Viktor Zhirmunsky, who had evidently read my translations and suggested doing a volume for the Literary Monuments series. This idea pleased me greatly, but unfortunately my continued work on the translations was sporadic. I had to earn my living, after all, as well as write something of my own.

In 1971, Zhirmunsky died, but the idea of the edition did not die with him. I was summoned to Moscow, to the Nauka publishing house, where they said that the agreement remained in force. At this point I still didn't have enough translations. Consequently, publication of the volume was moved back a couple of years. But May 10, 1972, came, and there could be no question of any book then. Too bad. There would have been more than Donne there. We had planned an anthology of metaphysical poetry, that whole band. In parallel with me, Boris Tomashevsky was translating Donne.

Volkov. Who as a result did put out the Russian volume of Donne.

Brodsky. Yes, I've had a look at it. If you know Donne in the original, you can't read it. The translations are on the level of "a love perfidious and cruel." I have no love for this translator.

Volkov. Besides Donne and the other metaphysical poets, who are the English-language poets you have translated?

Brodsky. Frost, Dylan Thomas, Lowell. All kinds. I translated Eliot's *The Four Quartets,* but the result was rather mediocre. There was too much of my own devising. I tried to translate Auden, which is hardest of all. All in all, I've translated from every living or dead language: Czech, Polish, Arabic. I've even translated from Hindi.

Volkov. Do you remember we were talking about Auden's interest in "light" poetry? I know he liked the literary work of John Lennon. What do you think of the Beatles' poems? I believe you translated their "Yellow Submarine?"

Brodsky. Yes, at the request of the Leningrad magazine *Kostyor.* The lyrics written by John Lennon and Paul McCartney are perfectly marvelous.

Really, the best examples of the English and American light genre—and not all that light. To a certain extent, this is a scary genre. For instance, Noël Coward. Or the brilliant Cole Porter. And the blues! But it's extremely difficult to translate all this. You have to know the blues tradition, the traditions of the English ballad. In Russia, no one knows what the English ballad is, to say nothing of the Scottish ballad.

Volkov. What about Zhukovsky's translations?

Brodsky. Try combining Zhukovsky and the Beatles' poetry! All this is rather sad because the Russian cultural tradition is oriented mainly toward French and German literature. Which in comparison with what was happening at the same time in English literature is pure kindergarten.

Fall 1978–Spring 1983

BRODSKY AND THE AUTHOR ON MORTON STREET,
GREENWICH VILLAGE, NEW YORK, 1978

8

LIFE IN NEW YORK
AND THE DEFECTION OF
ALEXANDER GODUNOV

Volkov. For many years now you've been a resident of New York, having put down roots in a fashionable, vaguely bohemian neighborhood. Everyone here knows you and you know everyone. Your life, at least outwardly, is quite comfortable and your routine more or less established. Doesn't it seem to you that existence here, in comparison with the same in the Soviet Union, is more predictable, more stable?

Brodsky. Yes and no. More no, I think.

Volkov. Why is that?

Brodsky. The hell if I know. Probably because you don't live much of an outward life here. After all, what's bad about predictability? It manifests itself in your relations with the outside world—your place of work, your job, people. First of all, though, New York is too diverse for that kind of predictability. There's a physiognomical kaleidoscope constantly at play here. That sweeps aside the effect of predictability, at least in part. Besides, my inner life doesn't much depend on what's happening to me on the street, in the subway, at the university, or whatever. I don't want to say that I live some kind of especially diverse and rich inner life, but basically, everything that happens to me happens mainly not on the outside but on the inside, and here, in the West, even more so than in the Soviet Union. Maybe thanks to the fact that this is still a somewhat alien milieu.

Anyway, in my business, in literature, work gets projected onto life one

Most of the interviews with Joseph Brodsky on which this chapter is based took place in New York in the second half of the 1980s.

155

way or another, and your life starts being affected by what you're doing on paper. And if you can repeat certain situations in life, well, on paper you really can't, because in literature and art those kinds of repetitions would be called clichés, right? Just as you avoid clichés in literature, you try to avoid them—in some kind of natural way—in your normal, everyday existence. That is, there is a kind of inexorable, linear movement going on.

Volkov. You once told me that you don't divide your life up into periods, but what about your inner life?

Brodsky. I've never taken myself that seriously. And I am absolutely not being coy. It's impossible to detect inner changes, really, unless they take on a qualitative character. When something happens that you yourself never suspected.

Volkov. In life or on paper?

Brodsky. In the mind. But you notice it especially when you're composing, when suddenly your writing leads to something specific. When a certain phrase occurs to you that in a general way turns out to be the truth for your inner state. I remember one such moment very distinctly. It was in about 1962. I had written a poem, "The tenant finds his new house wholly strange." In fact, of course, it's not about a tenant, it's a kind of a metaphor. Suddenly I realized it wasn't that I'd become a new person but that another soul had taken up residence in the same body, and suddenly I understood that I was a different I. No changes of that order have happened to me since that time, but the intonation of what gets put down on paper, that intonation has changed. There's that common expression, "buried deep in the unconscious." This psychological state existed before, too, but it gradually began to manifest itself with increasing frequency, and in recent years I seem to have begun to find a form for it. For me this has been a relatively new sensation, but this shift is more noticeable on paper than inwardly. That is, when you no longer lose your temper, you no longer react, and the solutions on paper are no longer local but purely optical. Or deductive.

Volkov. What does it feel like to be a poet living in a foreign country but continuing to write in his native language?

Brodsky. It doesn't feel like anything in particular. It was Thomas Mann, I think, who said, after he moved to live here, to the United States: "German literature is wherever I am." That's it.

Volkov. Still, there is a difference between prose and poetry.

Brodsky. Verse is a more complicated business, of course, because prose—it gets going and . . . In prose there's that mechanical element, which evidently is very helpful. I don't know. I've never done much with prose. As for writing verse, that, of course, is somewhat more complicated. In order to write verse, you have to stew in the idiomatics of the language constantly. That is, you have to hear it all the time—at the grocery store, on the tram, at the beer stand, in line, and so forth. Or not hear it at all. The deal is that, living in New York, you find yourself in a half-and-half situation. On the one hand, the phone rings and it's as if it's all still happening. On the other, nothing is happening. It's this kind of fictitious situation. It would be better not to hear my native language at all. Or the reverse—to hear it much more often. But more often is impossible, right? Just so you don't create an artificial milieu for yourself. Of course, you meet with people from Russia and you talk with them, but as a rule, it's an artificial selection, an artificial use of the language. To say nothing of the fact that here you sometimes have to deal with people I wouldn't even speak to at home. Essentially, what is important is not which language a person speaks but what he says. In this respect, though, the situation here is not one whit better than back home.

Volkov. You once remarked that for a poet it's important when he goes outside to see signs in his native language. That is, for the poet not only the spoken language but also its visual forms have significance. Is that right?

Brodsky. To a certain degree. The hieroglyphics here are different. The color spectrum is completely different. I don't think there's any call to overemphasize this, though, because in principle, the color scale here is just what it should in fact be. Perhaps that's the way it was in Russia before the Revolution of 1917.

Volkov. What influence has the change in landscape had on the way you write verse, say, the New York for the Petersburg landscape?

Brodsky. Overall it hasn't made a major impression. No, of course, it has. It has made an impression. Only it's the change in the totality of my surroundings, not just the landscape, that's affected it. You're born in a city, you live in it, you'll die there. You know all there is to know about that city, to the end of time . . . Everything concerns you. You've gone through so many stages: curiosity, attachment, respect, passive interest, indifference, revulsion. When you live your entire life in one city, eventually the clouds start to interest you. The climate, the weather, the changes in the light. At first it seemed as if the same story ought to repeat itself here, too, in New York, but New York is radically different. I mean visually. It is, in essence, a different system. Just try to find a colonnade here. Right? Here you're not going to acquire that inertia of perception that helped you out so much at home, because it's not a matter of a change of palette or scenery so much as

simple inertia. An interrupted routine. I don't know how long it takes to re-
gain that sensation.

Volkov. Don't you feel that New York—and I mean New York, not New
England—is cautiously, gradually starting to demand its own place in your
poems? Or will it remain foreign in this sense?

Brodsky. The Petersburg landscape is so classical that somehow it becomes
adequate to a person's psychic state, his psychological reactions. At least it
seems that way to the author. It's a kind of rhythm, quite conscious. Maybe
even a natural biological rhythm. But what happens here is another dimension somehow, and to master it psychologically, that is, to make it your own
inner rhythm, I think, is simply impossible. At least, for me. I must say, no
one has ever managed to do it, and not just the person who has come virtually as a guest. Nor has a native managed to do it, either. The sole attempt to
digest New York in some way and stick it into *belles lettres* was accomplished
by Hart Crane in *The Bridge,* which is a terrific poem. It has so much of everything in it. Still, New York cannot be inscribed in verse by natural means. If
Superman started writing poetry, maybe he could describe New York.

Volkov. Haven't other poets tried their hand at it?

Brodsky. I remember only one other serious attempt, by Federico García
Lorca. But that didn't come to anything either, in my opinion. Except for
one remarkable metaphor, a "gray sponge," or something like that. When
you look at the New York panorama from a certain distance, with a certain
degree of detachment, it really does look like a sponge.

Volkov. Living here, I see Lorca's New York poems as terribly spiteful.

Brodsky. But he has terrific plays. Of course, the best Spanish poet is An-
tonio Machado, not Lorca. Unfortunately, Machado never spent any time
in New York. Too bad.

Volkov. Nonetheless, do you think the switchover to English-language
tracks is inevitable? Hasn't it already begun?

Brodsky. It has and it hasn't. When it comes to *belles lettres,* it definitely
hasn't. As for prose, that—Lord!—it's an absolute delight, of course, and
I'm terribly pleased. When you write in a foreign language . . . When you
have to write in a foreign language, this spurs you on. Maybe I'm overesti-
mating my part in Russian literature, but I really am sick of it. I didn't write
prose, essays, in Russia, and if I find I do have to write prose here, in the
West, then I at least need to entertain myself somehow. I know of no
greater entertainment than writing in a foreign language. Why "foreign,"
ultimately? I feel that two languages is proper. In Russia, by the way, that
was always the case, in the good old days. I realize, of course, that such a

thing is more appropriate to hear coming from a Russian nobleman than from a Russian Jew. It's impossible, though, to write verse in two languages, although I have tried.

Volkov. I remember, in the first issue of *Kenyon Review* after it resumed publication, they ran a translation you did of a poem by Vladimir Nabokov—from Russian into English. An interesting historical-linguistic situation. What was it like, translating the Nabokov poem?

Brodsky. My feelings were very mixed. First of all, there was pure revulsion at what I was doing because Nabokov's poem was of very poor quality. In my opinion, he is a failed poet. It's precisely because Nabokov is a failed poet, though, that he writes such marvelous prose. It's always that way. As a rule, a prose writer without active poetic experience is inclined to verbosity and magniloquence. When the publishers of *Kenyon Review* suggested I translate Nabokov's poem, I told them, "Are you crazy?" I was against the idea. They insisted, however—I don't even know what their reasoning was. (It would be interesting to trace the psychological source of this insistence.) Well, I decided, if that's how matters stand, I'll do what I can. For my part, it was and wasn't an act of mischief. By the way, I think now—that is, in English—this poem of Nabokov's sounds a little better than it does in Russian, a little less banal. And maybe it is better to translate second-rate poetry, like this poem of Nabokov's, because you feel . . . how can I put this . . . less accountable. It's easier to deal with these gentlemen. If they'd asked me to translate Marina Tsvetaeva, or Boris Pasternak, that would have given me serious pause. Although, who the hell knows! Ultimately, it's simply a matter of leisure. That is, if I were a little freer inwardly—and outwardly, actually—then perhaps I should have taken this up in earnest, but matters will never reach that point, I hope, because that would be a great disgrace.

Volkov. When you write poetry, are you addressing some assumed audience?

Brodsky. You know, how did Stravinsky answer a similar question? I believe Robert Craft asked Stravinsky, "Who do you compose for?" And he replied, "For myself and for my hypothetical alter ego." That's it.

Volkov. In your case, does this hypothetical alter ego speak Russian?

Brodsky. Probably. Or rather, I never gave any thought to what language he speaks.

Volkov. In that case, where does he live, this alter ego?

Brodsky. The hell if I know. That's his business.

Volkov. Do you remember Nabokov's arguments in connection with the translation he did of *Lolita* into Russian? He said he himself didn't understand what inner impulse had prompted him to do it. He said he couldn't even imagine a possible reader.

Brodsky. This is very much the psychology of the prose writer. A prose writer thinks seriously about these kinds of things, but a poet doesn't. The fact of the matter is that the difference between people involved in *belles lettres* and those involved in prose is very great. In general, dividing literature into prose and poetry began with the appearance of prose, for only in prose could such a division be expressed. By its nature, by its essence, art is hierarchical. The writer's consciousness is also hierarchical, automatically, and in this hierarchy, poetry stands above prose. If only because poetry is older. Poetry really is a very strange thing, because it belongs to a troglodyte as well as to a snob. It can be produced in the Stone Age and in the most modern salon, whereas prose requires a developed society, a developed structure, certain established classes, if you like. Here you could start reasoning like a Marxist without even being wrong. The poet works from the voice, from the sound. For him, content is not as important as is ordinarily believed. For a poet, there is almost no difference between phonetics and semantics. Therefore, only very rarely does the poet give any thought to who in fact comprises his audience. That is, he does so much more rarely than the prose writer.

Tsvetaeva once put it marvelously: "Reading is complicity in creativity." This is the remark of a poet. A prose writer would never say such a thing. Tolstoy would never say it. Because knowledge is in fact complicity. What is knowledge, that is, the solving of a crime? It is psychic complicity, complicity of the imagination. Therefore the poet—I don't want to start speaking in the name of poets . . . "I am a poet" . . . Robert Frost said, "To say I am a poet is to say I am a good person."

Very rarely have I ever encountered people of this profession who would give serious thought to whom they were writing for. It's mainly poets who are asked whom they're writing for, and depending on the answer, more or less trouble ensues.

Volkov. What do you feel about the paradox that many who could be called leaders of Russian culture are at the moment living outside the mother country, in the West? That's the situation in prose, poetry, music, ballet, and philosophy.

Brodsky. We tend to mistake a temporary situation for a permanent one. If we're talking about creativity, about the creation of new art, then I don't really think that anything is going on now that could be called that. The creation of a new Russian art and literature—there is no such thing today, in my opinion. Not anywhere, I don't think. Nowhere. Not in Russia or the West. If for this reason alone, it's hard to talk about leaders. I realize that I might be suspected here of false modesty. Maybe I do write better poetry than the rest. I totally agree. Otherwise I wouldn't do it. But I don't think that this entails any kind of leadership. If it's come to that, I would say this. It is true that a huge number of talented Russians are living in the West now. The point is, though, that Russians are always émigrés from Russia to some extent or another. They have always taken an active part in the cultural life of the West. Take Diaghilev, Bakst, Stravinsky, anyone you like. With literature this was somewhat different, but it happened with literature, too.

Volkov. Turgenev spent the last twenty years of his life abroad primarily, and he died in Bougival.

Brodsky. That's Turgenev, but what about Fyodor Mikhailovich Dostoevsky! And, forgive me, Gogol.

Volkov. Dead Souls was written in Rome, which—

Brodsky. —which everyone always forgets. Right? Lord, almost everyone went to the West! With the exception of poor Alexander Sergeyevich Pushkin, who—

Volkov. They wouldn't give him a visa.

Brodsky. Exactly, they wouldn't give him a visa. So virtually everyone who wanted to was able to go to the West, to live or die. Baratynsky went and died in Italy.

Volkov. Tyutchev lived in the West for decades as well. He came into his own as a poet there.

Brodsky. And no one made a big deal out of it. And Herzen? Well, politics did get mixed in there. A terrific stylist, Herzen, I must say, only he lies a lot. Isaiah Berlin had a student who studied Herzen and dug up some Herzen correspondence. Upon Herzen's arrival in England he wrote back to Russia of the fog. In every letter it's fog, fog, fog. So this English student decides to check it out in the London newspapers—and there was no fog at all! Fyodor Dostoevsky, the Kingdom of Heaven to him, was also an absolutely horrendous liar. I remember strolling through Florence and coming across the house he lived in. He sent desperate letters home saying, Look, I don't have any money. And this house was opposite the Pitti Palace. That is, across the Ponte Vecchio, across from the Pitti Palace. Fancy that.

Volkov. Yanovsky, who was a friend of Dostoevsky, confirms that it was during that very period when Dostoevsky was complaining of terrible want and penury that he was staying in the best hotels, eating in the best restaurants, and going for drives in the best carriages.

Brodsky. That's how an author should behave. I don't blame the author in the slightest. In this he is always right. He's not even lying. Considering the conditions society places on an author, he can allow himself this. I don't even understand why he doesn't steal and murder. For instance, I believe that this idea of Raskolnikov's about killing the old lady moneylender is a purely authorial idea.

Volkov. Dostoevsky wrote *The Idiot* while abroad, and the greater part of *The Devils* was written there as well, and this fact played no important part in how these novels were assessed. Starting at a specific moment, though, this did take on decisive importance—*where* a work was created.

Brodsky. We know starting when. Starting in 1917, when the Soviet revolution occurred. Speaking of Dostoevsky, there is one more curious detail. In many of his novels the main happenings are, ultimately, denouements to events that occurred abroad. Everything starts, everything begins, abroad. Prince Myshkin goes crazy and undergoes treatment . . .

Volkov. The entire action of "The Gambler" . . .

Brodsky. No question about it! The Verkhovensky's pick up these wild ideas abroad and come back . . . And Ivan Karamazov! They all go back to Russia to wind things up. Bakhtin uses the term "carnivalism," which is a completely mistaken term, I think. Scandalism! It's a scandal, not a carnival! That is so much more interesting. Moreover, in his early works, Dostoevsky couldn't describe scandals. In his novel people might gather and start bandying about harsh words and retorts, and afterward Fyodor Mikhailovich would write, "and the fireworks started!" He still didn't understand how to do this. Later he learned how.

Volkov. One of Dostoevsky's constant themes is the acquisition of great wealth. At times it seems to be an obsession.

Brodsky. I've experienced the power of the idea of accumulation myself, actually. I remember, in Ann Arbor once, three and a half thousand dollars suddenly appeared in my account, and I caught myself thinking: "Fuck! I wish it were four!" I felt like—

Volkov. —making it a nice round sum?

Brodsky. Yes, making it a nice round sum! I know people for whom this kind of rounding becomes their chief preoccupation, because you can round in either direction, after all.

Volkov. Here in the West I've taken a fresh look at several issues of Russian literary history, especially those involving money, wealth, and its absence. After all, writers once existed under free market conditions in Russia, and this assumes competition, with all the attendant consequences. Normal capitalism, which they managed to forget about in the Soviet Union. For instance, Dostoevsky complained to his wife that Leo Tolstoy, who had absolutely no need of his literary earnings, was readily paid 500 rubles per 40,000 typographical units by a journal. But he, Dostoevsky, was begrudged 250 rubles. Dostoevsky added, "No, they value me too little because I live by my labor." In the Soviet Union, this motif would have been incomprehensible, but here . . . The other snag is that in the Soviet Union at that time (in the 1960s and 1970s), talking about money, discussing one's earnings, was considered positively indecent. The issue was relegated to parentheses. It was a kind of universal hypocrisy. I was chatting with the great composer Sviridov about Mussorgsky, whose music he had known and loved like no one else and about whom he had some important and interesting things to say. It was a professional conversation, as if among equals, and I commented to Sviridov that it would be good to transcribe and publish it. To which Sviridov made a majestic but wry face, as if to say, let us leave these base, transitory concerns about publication aside. Let us think in eternal categories. All the while, though, he, Sviridov, could easily allow himself to operate exclusively in eternal categories, raking in at least 500 rubles a month from his sinecure as secretary of the Composers Union alone, to say nothing of his royalties and fees for appearances and recordings. I was making what—120 rubles a month—and I cared very much about how I was going to make ends meet. There's your equality among Russian intellectuals.

Brodsky. What you're talking about is very interesting. This problem has two aspects, by the way. Above all, I think the idea of equality is stark raving mad, and I never tire of saying so. Then, there's something else: when you are making money, when you are getting paid—if only 120 rubles— it's still embarrassing. When I was working in a factory in Russia, I felt awkward signing for my pay in the office and getting my money, even though I was working like the proverbial ox. I think it is absolutely not a matter of equality but of the Russian consciousness, although all this is much larger than the Russian consciousness alone. It's the religious traditions. By the way, not just in Russia, but in Europe, too, talking about money is just not done. There are so many political parties, platforms, philosophies, and everything else there, all of which can be discussed with impunity, but no one would ever breathe a word about money. Whereas here, in the States, everyone talks about it. Well, maybe not everyone, but in general, people talk about money quite a lot. Here, it's true, there is another form of hypocrisy. The majority of Americans, in comparison with Europeans, are extremely well off. Nonetheless, a rich American can start making faces because a sandwich seems too expensive to him. Or make a terrible scene about it in a restaurant.

Volkov. I've run into that more than once. Americans are nonchalant about going to a restaurant only when their company is footing the bill.

Brodsky. It's a constant game with the idea of saving, which is also probably of religious—Puritan—origin. In fact, what seems vulgar to a Russian, these American appraisals—"Oh, this person is worth a million dollars, and that person is worth ten million"—has its own logic. The whole political life here, all the political discussions, circle around one thing: how much money is going to be spent on one program or another. Say, how much the Republicans are going to put into defense or education and the Democrats into social needs or the war on drugs. That is, they're constantly talking about money, which makes perfect sense, because the well-being of a given interest group depends to a significant degree on the state's capital investments. That is, money is one of the most important realities. It is much more real than political convictions, platforms, and philosophies. In Europe, they don't hold to that at all. Or in Russia. True, the overall situation there reminds me more of the theater of the absurd, where it's not a matter of money or politics, so that I don't even know what it is a matter of. I remember in Leningrad a woman friend and I went to the Akimov Theater to see a comedy, and we fled from the second act. My friend put it rather nicely: "In Russia, the theater of the absurd and the audience have switched places." That is, what was on stage was total realism, whereas in the audience it was—hell if I know.

Volkov. We have touched on the subject of New York dining. Do you cook for yourself or do you go out?

Brodsky. There's this illusion that it's cheaper to cook for yourself, which is true to a certain extent, but in the final analysis, it's not. There are so many psychological costs involved. First, there's all that chaos. Then endless dilemmas arise: wash the dishes or not? And if so, then now or later? And so on. Therefore, as a rule, I go out in the evening. Sometimes I cook for myself, though, especially when I'm teaching at a college, because the situation there is somewhat different. Ordinarily you don't live at the college itself but in some house or apartment, and in Michigan, for example, you could gallop for three years and not reach any restaurant, so you have your supper where the night finds you.

Volkov. Here, in New York, there are myriad exotic restaurants and exotic cuisines. Which do you prefer?

Brodsky. Chinese—from day one. Chinatown has absolutely terrific restaurants. Not very far away from here there's a stunning Indian joint. And by the way, if you check, all this turns out to be not that terribly expensive. And the difference from our national cooking is fantastic. Above all, there's the variety. In the purely culinary respect, it is simply an absolutely different category of taste, if I can put it that way.

Volkov. What about Armenian and Georgian cooking in the Soviet Union? And all those Asiatic pilafs?

Brodsky. No, that's absolutely wrong. That is ultimately a variation on the same theme. If you were to compare, I would say that Russian cuisine is traditional harmony, whereas Chinese is the twelve-tone technique. Except it tastes good—because I'd rather not have the real twelve-tone scale for dinner. All these Caucasian deals are a refined variation on the traditional harmony—Chopin, say, or some other romantic.

Volkov. A few days ago in the *New York Times,* some local Chinese restaurant announced that it got its food supplies directly from Szechuan, and I thought, that's nonsense. There isn't anything in Szechuan.

Brodsky. I submit that China's Party bosses, and the élite in general—like in the Soviet Union—are chowing down marvelously. Take someone whose opinion I trust implicitly, inasmuch as I was the one who corrupted him on all these Szechuan and Hunan deals—Misha Baryshnikov. Misha went to China to dance, and when he came back I asked him, "Well, how'd you like Chinese cooking in the mainland?" So here's the thing. According to him, the food in China—despite the fact that the overall situation there is catastrophic—the food is still great. For special guests, of course. Still, all these exotic and ethnic cuisines are probably at their peak here, in New York. That is, you can assume they're head and shoulders above what you'd find in their respective countries. With the exception of Italian restaurants probably. French restaurants here are terrific, but the drawback is their incredibly high prices. The conclusion to draw is that its very affordability and diversity make Chinese cooking here the gastronomic equivalent of democracy.

Volkov. What do you show your friends from Russia in New York? What's beautiful and what's ugly?

Brodsky. I don't find ugly what's usually considered ugly in New York. It's simply a different aesthetic category, as I've already said. Therefore I have to show them Harlem, around the 140s and 150s, and on the East Side, not the West. It's a stunning spectacle—the Bronx, with all those awful, devastated blocks. Another mandatory attraction is the New York subway. Moreover, you have to use the subway, ride it and live in it, not just poke your nose down there once. Then the subway becomes one of the most notable attractions in New York. What else? Well, the Circle Line, the ship that circumnavigates the island of Manhattan.

Volkov. What about Coney Island?

Brodsky. No, that's not interesting. But going down to Chinatown is really very diverting. Then there's the southern tip of Manhattan, the Wall Street district, which is a qualitatively different phenomenon, a different principle in the architectural sense. I remember, a friend of mine came to New York for the first time—from England. It's like coming from Russia, the same thing. I took her to the Wall Street district at about seven or eight at night, when it's emptied out, to look at the skyscrapers, and she said a curious thing about those skyscrapers. She said this was all remarkable since these buildings impressed upon you your true scale. Because in Europe the scale is different. There the buildings, even if they're not of normal proportions, they're still more or less within the control of your imagination. In New York, both the proportions and your imagination are absolutely swept aside as totally irrelevant.

Volkov. Have any specifically New York stories happened to you in the time you've lived here?

Brodsky. No, periodically you just find yourself in more or less the same catastrophic situations as you did in the homeland, but nothing special has ever happened. I do remember, though, what seems to me like my first one hundred percent New York dream. I dreamed I had to leave here, leave Greenwich Village, and go somewhere on 120th or 130th Street, which required me taking the subway. When I walked up to the subway, though, I suddenly saw that all of Broadway—that is, from here to Harlem, say, or even beyond—was rising up and becoming vertical! That is, the entire long street was transformed instantaneously into an awe-inspiring skyscraper. The subway ceased to be a subway and became an elevator. So I went up, feeling all the while that Broadway was standing up too! It was a stunning sensation! There was probably some kind of erotica involved. When I reached 120th Street, I walked out the elevator onto the intersection, which was like a staircase landing. This was an absolutely new scale of dream for me.

Volkov. By the way, do you think there's a difference between European and American erotica?

Brodsky. As far as I can tell, being—how can I put this?—a subject as well as an object of this, actually, there is no special difference. People here may be less into reflection, but I think that's a rather universal phenomenon these days.

Volkov. One more point that's rather odd for someone coming from Russia. According to the official data, at least 20 percent of the population of New York is homosexual. Here, in the Village, I think the proportion is the reverse, that is, heterosexuals make up less than 20 percent. As far as I can tell, émigrés from Russia have a hard time getting used to this.

Brodsky. In this sphere, as in all spheres, New York is "the most." Here, right near me, Christopher Street, is the main street for this in the States and, therefore, in the world, but this hasn't made any particular impression on me. There are an enormous number of young women here, plenty for me.

Volkov. Has a man ever propositioned you here, in Greenwich Village?

Brodsky. Never. Only once a very drunk black man started laying the whole thing out for me, but exclusively out of drunken eloquence, I think, and not in any outburst of amorous feelings.

Volkov. A rather significant Russian-speaking community has taken shape in New York. Is the language colony also becoming an artistic colony? Do you think the mutual demand for contact is increasing?

Brodsky. In my case, I'm not making any qualitatively new acquisitions—in the sense of friendships—among my compatriots. The only person I didn't know well in Russia is Misha Baryshnikov. Here he and I see each other fairly often. He is a man of amazing intelligence and intuition. A man who—apart from everything else—knows much more poetry by heart than I do.

Generally, this whole idea of an artistic colony is absolutely fictitious. This idea grew out of the tradition of the nineteenth century. Such a thing is quite simply unthinkable in America, unnatural. That is, it goes against the essence of the country, because the idea of a bohemia, the idea of an artists colony, arises only in a centralized state, as the mirror reflection of that centralization. It's a way of closing ranks, resisting. After all, what is the essence of an artistic colony? The opposition between poet and tyrant, which is possible only when, say, they meet in the evening at the opera. The tyrant sits in his box, the poet in the stalls. The poet sees himself as a Carbonieri, and in his mind's eye he's packing a gun. He mutters something through his teeth and tosses back an angry glance. That's the whole idea of a bohemia.

There is another idea. The idea of uniting people of aesthetic and, in principle, ethical understanding. Like the Irish monks who tried to preserve knowledge, culture, literature, and language. What is happening today—both here and in Russia—actually has nothing at all in common with this, although we all remember that Russia is a country with enormous resources and incredible human potential. No matter what the drain on the culture and the intelligentsia, sooner or later out of its depths it will produce something grandiose and amaze everyone. This is a quantitative effect, if you like. It is simply a vast country and a vast culture and, as far as literature goes, one of the most grandiose of languages. It is absolutely inevitable that in the depths of this language phenomena will arise that are going to drive us all wild. Regardless of where the person speaking or writing this language finds himself—Moscow, Petersburg, Paris, or New York.

Volkov. How did you and Baryshnikov meet here?

Brodsky. It's very odd, but for the life of me I can't remember how he and I met. One thing I can say, though. He made—and makes—a tremendous impression on me. Not with his qualities as a dancer, especially since in that area I am absolutely no kind of specialist, but above all with his incredible natural intellect. Usually I treat people younger than myself with a certain—how can I say this? Well, the way graduates treat freshmen perhaps. I deliberately overlook them, right? And Baryshnikov is almost ten years my junior. But Baryshnikov is an absolutely unique being. He was born on the same day as Wolfgang Amadeus Mozart, and I think they have a lot in common. If we're talking about people whom fate and circumstances have brought me together with outside Russia, then this would be, first of all, Auden. Then Stephen Spender, Susan Sontag, Derek Walcott, Czeslaw Milosz, and Isaiah Berlin. These are the people I've met as a consequence of professional, literary matters. And it is Baryshnikov if we're talking about purely human relations rather than literature or culture. Baryshnikov I don't look at through the prism of his activities.

Volkov. I've met many people here who fled Russia at one time or another, and in my conversations with them I have seen that their defection was a terrible psychological trauma, a wound that won't heal, even if sixty years have passed since that day. Some try to hide the trauma. Others, on the contrary, eagerly psychoanalyze it. You were actually deported from Russia. My wife Marianna and I simply left, although not without considerable difficulty. This, too, was traumatic. The pain has still not eased. Baryshnikov defected. Have you and he talked about this? Have you discussed this problem from the psychological standpoint?

Brodsky. We have. Misha told me the story of how it came about, but it's hard to psychologize, let alone generalize, here, because each instance is a specific, unique occurrence, evidently.

Volkov. Nonetheless it must be rather terrifying to defect, because you burn all your bridges at one fell swoop. Whereas one way or another a "normal" departure is a gradual process.

Brodsky. It seems to me that for a Russian of the modern era there is no more natural thought than defection. It is a natural state of the mind and soul. Moreover, before the October Revolution, no such emotional necessity arose in the Russian, evidently. If it did, then he gave a policeman or the caretaker ten rubles, and a few days later he was brought a foreign passport. This is what Akhmatova used to tell me. That's how she went to France. The very idea of defection is largely impulsive by nature; but in the case of Baryshnikov, he had often thought it beforehand. When I say that for a Russian the idea of defection is fairly natural, I am speaking from experience. I remember that in prison and exile I spent half my time thinking about how to run away. Actually, it was the same at liberty. I had all kinds of plans—for instance, running away in a hot air balloon. Or in a submarine with a chainsaw motor. I can't even remember all the ideas I had, but none of this was very serious. They were just ideas, like inventing the bicycle or a perpetual motion machine. The plan to escape in an airplane went pretty far. I rejected it only at the very last moment. Not out of fear but simply because I began to regret not being able to see certain people, and apart from that, what was I then? A nineteen-year-old kid. Pretty ridiculous. Ever since, the feelings a person has before escaping are more or less understandable to me.

Volkov. Were there also moments in your life when the desire to escape from Russia was sharply exacerbated?

Brodsky. Yes, in 1968, when Soviet troops invaded Czechoslovakia. Then, I remember, I felt like running away, anywhere. Mainly out of shame. Because I belonged to a power that cooked up deals like that. Because for better or worse, part of the responsibility always falls on the citizen of this power. I was in a terrible state at the time.

Volkov. You were drawn into one extraordinary defection here, in New

York, in late August 1979. I'm talking about the defection of Alexander Godunov, a star dancer from the Bolshoi Theater. How did you come to take part in this sensational story?

Brodsky. When was that you say? In August?

Volkov. If I'm not mistaken, Godunov decided to remain here on August 21, a Tuesday.

Brodsky. If it really was August 21, then it's actually funny, because the 1968 invasion of Czechoslovakia took place right around that same date.

Volkov. How did you learn of Godunov's defection?

Brodsky. I was busy with some affairs of my own. I was translating something. It was hot. Moreover, in the city, on the water, the heat is especially trying. My heart, you know. Urgent business. So my reaction was not especially joyful when I received an unplanned call from an acquaintance, who said, "Joseph, do you know of any apartment free outside the city?" I was rather legitimately peeved. "I have no idea." Then I decided some woman had turned up for this guy. The usual. I had to help him. I asked, "How soon do you need it?" "Actually, the sooner the better." All right, I called a few people I knew who had places outside of town. In the summer, people work in the city and go back out to the country in the evening. There isn't any vacant housing. But in one place they told me their small dacha would be free for a few days. I called my friend back. "I've got one. You just have to drive by such-and-such an address for the keys." He, somewhat unexpectedly: "Couldn't you bring the keys to me yourself?" I began to get an inkling that something more out of the ordinary was going on than the usual skulking around of a married man. When I asked, "When do you need the keys?" and he answered, "Right away!" I definitely got the idea that there had been some kind of trouble with the ballet. I could sense a certain tension in the man's voice. The Bolshoi Theater was touring in the city then, and this fellow was closely involved with ballet people. I went by for the keys and set out for his apartment. I arrived, and he tells me this, that, and the other and then, "Allow me to introduce you: Godunov."

Volkov. What was your reaction?

Brodsky. I'd never heard of Godunov. Before me stood an extraordinary figure in the full sense of the word. Imagine this great mass, heavy jaw, blue eyes, long blond hair—the embodiment of 1960s aesthetics. None of it, to be honest, was much to my taste, but gradually you get used to it. Later I thought that in the case of Godunov, there couldn't be any real split between the individual and his art. He simply walked out on stage and this in and of itself was an event. It was the same in life. He didn't simply sit in an apartment, he was *present*. When he stood up, you realized that something had happened. There was one notable aspect to all this: at that moment and thereafter, Godunov displayed amazing dignity. On the one hand, this was part of his image, of course. I'm not talking about the stage now but in life. A man possessing Godunov's mass moves more majestically. That's inevitable. And it's an extremely interesting phenomenon to observe. On the other hand, Godunov had been a star from early on and consequently corrupted to a certain extent by success and admiration. At the moment of his defection he was absolutely alone—no mama, no wife, no friends, no one. He had absolutely no one to turn to, and he could expect nothing but dirty tricks on all sides. Given all this, Godunov's dignity was especially noteworthy.

Volkov. At the time, the Soviet *Literaturnaya Gazeta* tried its damnedest to prove that Godunov had been brainwashed, that he'd been talked into staying in the United States. They wrote that he was "literally besieged everywhere he went by a whole team of troublemakers who promised him mountains of gold and a sea of free booze."

Brodsky. There was definitely nothing like that going on, by the way. As if anyone could have besieged him! Booze was not an issue. This was a leap into the absolute unknown on Godunov's part.

Volkov. I discussed this whole story in detail with Godunov. We planned to write a book together. I got the impression that on Godunov's part the defection was more or less an improvisation.

Brodsky. Events developed in approximately the following manner. Godunov paid my friend a visit, and when they got to talking, Godunov started trying to clarify who he ought to hook up with if and when he did decide to take to his heels. The reply to which was that of course he would get all kinds of recommendations, but there was one attendant circumstance of no little importance. What specifically? "You're saying 'if,' and it's impossible to reply to 'if.'" That is, it's impossible simply to name names and addresses and so forth just like that. Nonetheless, Godunov kept insisting. "But what if I still wanted . . . just to talk . . ." "Well then," my friend told him, "talk to me!" Then he heard Godunov say this: "Here I am. I'm talking." My friend excused himself, went into the next room, and called me.

Volkov. Why you rather than someone from the ballet world?

Brodsky. The American ballet world (in New York especially) is strongly bound up with the Russian colony. It would be a risk to trust ballet people.

And then, there was no guarantee that a ballet person wouldn't turn around and dial up the Soviet consulate. (Crisis situations are always interesting because they show who's the boss and who's the lackey.) One more circumstance dictated caution. Godunov was a ballet star. Instantly people get ideas involving the ballet business and the competition. That is, who, when, and how contracts are going to be signed, and once again, no one could be expected to hold their tongue.

Volkov. How did events unfold?

Brodsky. Well, we got into a car and went to the summer place, since it was clear we had to hide Godunov. My first advice to him was to get in touch with someone from the U.S. State Department. Sasha was a dancer with a name, and I reasoned that he would be invited to go abroad, and he would need papers to leave, and it would be the State Department that would issue those papers. Let them take him under their wing one way or another. It's always better if someone at the top knows you. And that's how things did work out, by the way. The next day we came back to town, where all the necessary manipulations were performed with filling out forms. Sasha sat on the couch, I sat in an armchair, and the immigration official sat on a chair. There were two from the FBI. I interpreted. Afterward they took Sasha to the police department to take his fingerprints (a procedure performed on all émigrés). Well, I thought, all's well. I went home. I took a shower and changed my clothes. I went back to my papers. Suddenly the telephone again: "Joseph, could you take Sasha to Connecticut?" Well, what could I do? The main thing was that he had no tongue, as we say. We spent the next three days in Connecticut.

Volkov. While at the same time in New York a newspaper squall began: "Leading Bolshoi Dancer Asks for Political Asylum in the US!" Everyone brought up Nureyev, Makarova, Baryshnikov. They were from Leningrad, though, and Godunov was the first from the Bolshoi.

Brodsky. We foresaw all this, so after Godunov went through the immigration procedure, our mutual friend called one of the best lawyers in the United States, Orville Schell, one of the most remarkable Americans I have ever had occasion to deal with. A touch naive maybe, like all of them, but not when it came down to business. Schell informed the State Department that he was representing Godunov's interests. Literally fifteen minutes later they called him back. The Soviets were demanding a meeting with Sasha. In fact, according to the consular convention, they had a right to do so. Schell told Godunov, "I have no opinion either for or against such a meeting. That's entirely up to you. If I were in your place, though, I'd meet with the Soviets, if only because you could demand a meeting with your wife as a condition."

Volkov. Yes, there was a fine mess stirred up over Godunov's wife, the ballerina Ludmila Vlasova! They had flown to New York on tour together, but Godunov had remained—alone. I remember, he never did make it completely clear to me what exactly had gone on between them.

Brodsky. We tried to call Mila Vlasova on the very first day of Sasha's defection. First she was in rehearsal, then she was supposed to perform, and then it was too late to call—the KGB established a curfew for artists on tour, after which they couldn't leave the hotel. We kept trying to get a call through to her from Connecticut, but it was quite obvious that Mila was no longer in the hotel. Some Soviet kept answering the phone in her room. We tried to get in touch with Mila by three or four known routes. Nothing worked. Later we found out that she was on the territory of the Soviet consulate in New York. The meeting with Mila was set for Friday at one o'clock. Schell called us and asked us to be ready. Two men from the State Department flew to New York. The moment they landed in New York, they were told that Ludmila Vlasova—escorted by four men from the Soviet consulate—had been put in a car that was heading for Kennedy Airport. That is, the Soviets had violated their agreement with the State Department. That pair from the State Department jumped into their car and set off in pursuit. I think at one point they were less than a mile or a mile and a half behind the Soviet car on the Van Wyck Expressway.

Volkov. Here is where the excitement begins: the confrontation between the two superpowers at Kennedy Airport. The television, radio, and newspapers were screaming about nothing else.

Brodsky. Schell called Godunov. The Soviet plane on which the Soviets planned to fly Mila to Moscow had been detained. It would be good if we went to Kennedy Airport, so we set out, escorted by the FBI, who made a total farce of the situation. They were looking for the way in at Pan Am and they missed it not once but twice. This blunder was the start of three hot days in the airport. We spent the first night in a minivan, the second in town, and on the third they took us to a hotel at the airport. The hotel was crawling with Soviets: consulate workers, KGB, correspondents. Sticking us in there was total idiocy from the FBI's standpoint.

When we drove up to this hotel and I saw what was going on, I said to the FBI guys: "Listen, this is none of my business—explaining things to you—but you really don't get it, do you?"

"What can we do?"

"Well, maybe we could enter the hotel through the kitchen, I don't know."

They made their way over to the kitchen—but there didn't seem to be an entrance there. Then I said, "You see the fire escapes on the left and right? Why not open one of them?" Which is what they ended up doing. Sasha scrambled up the escape like Murzik the cat. It was rather comical. Although the whole story unfolded more tragically.

Volkov. By that time Brezhnev was involved on the Soviet side and Jimmy Carter on the American.

Brodsky. Not yet, because this was still the weekend. When the State Department called Moscow, the Foreign Affairs Ministry, no one was there. At first Moscow proposed that someone from the KGB conduct the talks on their behalf, but the State Department refused to have anything to do with the KGB, inasmuch as those two institutions were unequal in their respective positions in the state hierarchy. The Soviet representatives in New York dug their heels in, though, which was perfectly natural. Any Soviet working there would do everything in his power to avoid being accused of insufficient zeal. Who would ever want to lose such a good posting, their slice of the New York apple? Ultimately, the Americans lost. The fact was that the main goal of the negotiations was a meeting between Sasha and Mila. Not simply for the sake of finding out whether or not Mila wanted to stay there with him but for the sake of letting her decide of her own free will, in a normal situation, outside an airplane, outside the presence of a hundred fellow countrymen. We wanted to get the meeting the Soviets had promised. Blame for the way it ended rests primarily with President Carter and indirectly with McHenry, the American representative to the United Nations, who was put in charge of this extremely delicate affair. McHenry didn't have any real experience in international negotiations, to say nothing of negotiations with the Soviets. In this critical situation, McHenry decided to be extremely cautious.

Volkov. But after all, the Americans were detaining the Soviet airplane with Vlasova on board at the airport. That is, in the beginning they did act fairly decisively.

Brodsky. Yes, and when he got back to his office on Monday, President Carter gave two orders. The first was to the attorney general. Carter gave the police permission to utilize any method that seemed reasonable to him, the attorney general. Carter's other order was to McHenry: show restraint. That is, the left hand took back what the right hand was giving. When it became clear that the Soviets were not going to give their consent to a meeting between Godunov and Mila, Schell suggested, "Why not write Mila a note? She's sitting in the airplane, she doesn't know anything, and the officials are feeding her a line. McHenry can take the note with him to his meeting with Mila and hand it to her. That way Mila can see what set the fur flying. The Soviets aren't about to jump the ambassador and tear up the note."

I said, "What about Mila?"

"They won't jump on Mila because that would be too brazen."

I said, "All right, let's hope."

We composed this note in extremely distinct and so to speak private language. We gave it to Schell, who gave Godunov's note to McHenry. Time passed. Schell walked in. "She said no." We were all crushed. We were gathering up our belongings when I asked, "Well, how did she react to the note?" Schell replied, "The note stayed in McHenry's pocket. He didn't give it to her." I very nearly sobbed. Actually, I think I did. Godunov had to reason with me. I find it painful even to recall. All this cut very close to my heart. After all, I was—how can I put this?—the mouth through which Godunov expressed his thoughts. Not just a mouthpiece. Ultimately, something had happened in my mind, too. I had understood something and tried to explain it to the Americans. The intense nervous tension. The exhaustion. That's why I sobbed.

Volkov. Still, even after dozens of hours talking with Godunov, much about this story puzzles me. I'm thinking about the psychological aspect and that hidden drama that played out between Godunov and his wife—unlike the political confrontation between the superpowers that was visible to all.

Brodsky. For me there is absolutely no doubt that Mila was extremely dear to Sasha. They had been married for seven years, and when seven years of conjugal life goes up in smoke, exclusively due to political considerations, it's unbearable even to contemplate.

Volkov. How do you think events would have unfolded if Mila could have made a choice in a normal situation?

Brodsky. I don't know. I think she would have stayed. Sasha explained to me—literally the day after his defection—that they had discussed such a possibility several times. Nonetheless, in the last few days in New York she had not expressed readiness, although in another instance she evidently had. This seems to me the usual marital story, when today you say no because you know that tomorrow you'll say yes. Or vice versa. I don't think even Sasha's mind was totally clear, because until you actually defect, you don't understand what's involved. Sasha simply could not have thought it all through down to the details, which would have been impossible to imagine anyway! Evidently, he proceeded from the assumption that everything would work out somehow.

Godunov guessed that after New York they were planning to send him back to Moscow. He realized there was no time, that the discussions with Mila would stretch out indefinitely. He might have talked her into it eventually, but the moment would have been lost. It's one thing to make plans to defect in the Soviet Union and another in New York City. That is when Sasha decided to carry out at least the one part of the plan that was paramount for him, because for him the main thing was his self-fulfillment as an artist. After all, Godunov was first and foremost an artist and only then a husband.

For any artist, I think, the main thing is what you're doing and not how you're living apart from this main thing. A woman, when she needs to choose between the known and the unknown, prefers the known. Setting aside the romantic, emotional aspect that might have roused Mila to stay, from the practical standpoint, purely professionally, Mila's course of reasoning could have been this. Godunov was a star. She, due to the quality of her talent, could not expect any special piece of the action. She was seven years older than Godunov. If success came to Sasha in the West, there would be nothing holding him back—assuming we again set aside romantic feelings. Therefore Mila could well assume that her life in the West would not turn out in the happiest possible way. Her ultimate decision would have depended on her degree of attachment to Godunov. In the context that arose at Kennedy Airport, though, her attachment and other romantic emotions retreated into the background and fear came to the fore.

Despite all the tension, all the strangeness and abnormality of the situation, Sasha was still in human surroundings, with people who sympathized with him. His love for his wife did not retreat into the background. On the contrary, everything else did. Evidently the reverse was true for Mila. Even if she had wanted to tell the Soviet official she would stay, she couldn't have. She simply couldn't have! Americans cannot imagine the psychological pressure, the wave that comes crashing down on top of you at such moments.

We came back from the airport in an extremely depressed mood. The next day a press conference was announced. That night we slept all of two or three hours because they kept trying to get us to cancel the press conference. To this day I can't understand why. To me, the Americans' arguments seemed like total drivel, but the pressure was such as I've never felt in all my life, even when I was being interrogated by the KGB. Nonetheless, Sasha stood his ground. At the press conference (about three hundred reporters had gathered) he gave extremely distinct answers. It was an impressive spectacle. Not only the press conference but Godunov's entire conduct during those days. I saw someone who blossomed in crisis situations, and for me this was a memorable experience.

Volkov. In the time you've lived in New York, we have witnessed a curious process of adaptation of émigré Russian culture by the mother country. Chaliapin, Rachmaninoff, and Bunin were partially adapted a long time ago. That is, they joined the ranks of the classics, albeit the waning classics, back when we were still living in the Soviet Union. Later came Stravinsky's and Diaghilev's turn. Gradually, Marc Chagall was transformed from a bogeyman into a good guy. The same thing happened with George Balanchine. Finally, matters went as far as Nabokov and the "Parisian" poets. They even published living émigrés, including you and Solzhenitsyn. Now a repeat process of adaptation is starting up—more complete, more well-meaning and objective—of the same émigré classics: Chaliapin, Rachmaninoff, Bunin, Stravinsky . . .

Brodsky. I'd say they were being coöpted, not adapted. Chaliapin again—Lord! That's really the limit!

Volkov. It seems to me that putting a cultural value into permanent circulation, even if it is scalped and taken out of context, is still more of a plus than a minus.

Brodsky. When I see how they cook up émigré culture, émigré art, in the mother country, when I leaf through their scalped publications or hear about some kind of selective exhibit . . . Maybe when it comes to painting, the fine arts, this kind of approach does bear certain fruits, but for literature it doesn't. On the basis of a scrap of material you can restore or, even better, reimagine a lot of the rest, basically, though, I don't like this kind of attitude. I much prefer an either-or situation.

Volkov. When I arrived in the West in 1976, I was enormously interested to read Lydia Chukovskaya's notes on Akhmatova published here. I remember one note of Chukovskaya's from the 1960s that stunned me. She was writing about Georgy Adamovich, who was living in Paris. She was amazed to find that somewhere something was going on that had nothing to do with the mother country. Someone was still writing and publishing in Russian somewhere there, in Paris, and I remember how, reading this, I was suddenly whisked back to 1960, and I shuddered. For the intellectual milieu of that time, even a concept like a Russian culture abroad really didn't exist. That is, a huge cultural stratum had been completely lopped off, and this had had an extremely negative effect on the cultural balance inside the country.

Brodsky. The fact of this long absence of Russian émigré culture in the mother country can be explained not only by the efficiency with which it was cut or lopped off but also by simple geography. When you think about the West, the Russian émigrés living there now aren't what you think of first. When you think of Paris, what comes to mind first is not that Khodasevich or Adamovich lived there but Valéry and Sartre, right? That is, a normal cultural-geographical principle comes into play which says that you really shouldn't give any special thought to the existence of a Russian cultural island in the West. That's on one hand. On the other . . . I, for instance, knew about Adamovich and that he lived in Paris. Of course, this wasn't 1960, but I remember in about 1967 discovering Adamovich's first collection of poetry, which came out in Petersburg—I don't remember now whether it was in 1914 or 1916. I sent this book to Adamovich in Paris with a female acquaintance of mine. Later this woman turned up in Leningrad with thanks from Adamovich. As for Russian culture abroad as a whole, then naturally, we didn't know the details—who was and wasn't alive, what was happening at any given moment, but what did reach us bore—and this is remarkable, and herein lies the merit of the iron curtain—a timeless quality. That is, in my view it had something of the quality of an absolute.

Volkov. The perception of culture does not gain much when it appears before its audience spasmodically, so to speak, rather than as the result of a natural, ongoing process.

Brodsky. You know, Solomon, that may very well be, but what you are talking about—I will allow myself this sardonic comment—happened after us. I don't know anything about that anymore. In my time, Solzhenitsyn was still at home and so was I, and so was everyone else. And it just doesn't matter anyway. Lord! It just doesn't matter. I simply wanted to say that in my opinion the most valuable thing in Russian culture abroad was always present in our consciousness. To the highest degree. You can't imagine what I read in the 1960s, especially in the latter half! For the most part this was Shestov, then Berdyaev, Lossky, and Frank. And by the way, I had read Eliot's "Notes Toward a Definition of Culture" and Joyce's *Portrait of the Artist as a Young Man* by 1965. This isn't Russian culture, of course, but on the other hand, all this was translated into Russian, although published by the émigré presses in the West.

Volkov. But look at the chronological gap! You were reading what had been created in the West half a century before, in the case of Joyce. What had long since become recognized by the entire world. That isn't normal! In normal cultural circulation, you get what was created today, not fifty years ago!

Brodsky. You know, I don't agree with that either. This is the view not even of our own era but of our own location, so to speak. It is a modern, Western view. If you recall how culture developed over the millennia, it was anything but a temporally unified process. Something was happening in Assyria, something else in Greece, or India, or Byzantium, and centuries passed before one reached the other.

Volkov. Those days are long gone, and for good. Today culture is disseminated instantaneously, and I think the situation is irretrievable. Of course, all this now flows in a powerful current, the bulk of which is dross, but I absolutely do not agree with the complaints about how people are consuming nothing but vileness and banality whereas before they swam in waves of exclusively high culture. In 1830, people in Russia were avidly reading the works of Bulgarin and other such garbage, not Pushkin. Now they're reading Pikul and Nabokov and Pushkin. I'm sure that not only in absolute but even perhaps in relative percentages a much greater number of people are coming into contact with high culture, so to speak, now than they were two or three hundred years ago.

Brodsky. That is, "the cultural output per capita has increased greatly." But this is technology, not a virtue, not a victory for culture as such.

Volkov. Of course it's technology. In that sense even the invention of printing can be looked on as a purely technological innovation.

Brodsky. Well, naturally . . . But no! I am wholeheartedly in favor of finding out about everything instantaneously. On the other hand, though, being a retrograde, I do have certain nostalgic emotions. I know from my own experience that the less information your brain receives, the harder your imagination works.

Volkov. Yes, you used a similar method, as far as I know, in your work on the translations from English and American poets.

Brodsky. And not only in that instance. Take Mandelstam's famous words about acmeism being the longing for world culture. Valéry expressed similar notions. I think that the longing for world culture is an absolutely remarkable phenomenon, because when you long for world culture, you let your imagination off its leash, and it gallops away. Sometimes in the process it overtakes what is happening in Western culture, because naturally world culture is the culture of the West, right? At least, for those times, and for our times, too. It's like archery: sometimes you fall short, sometimes you score a bull's-eye, and frequently, as in Mandelstam's case, there's a flyover. Unlike real archery, those kinds of flyovers are the most valuable thing in culture.

Volkov. I will allow myself to disagree with you, and for this reason. Mandelstam's words are very pretty, but they tend to conceal one thing. When the acmeists proclaimed their longing for world culture, they had ample opportunity to quench that longing—with the stream of cultural information coming in from the West. All those people—Mandelstam and Akhmatova and Tsvetaeva and Pasternak—were fully formed . . .

Brodsky. In the old days.

Volkov. In the prerevolutionary years, Russian translations of new literature appeared almost instantaneously. The same was true of music and painting. And by the way, a countercurrent had begun to take shape—going from Petersburg to Paris. If everything had continued normally, by today modern Russian culture would be a genuinely integrated part of world culture, not some exotic province. Our whole famous Silver Age was made possible by that kind of normal cultural circulation. On the other hand, look what happened when that circulation was destroyed, the tremendous decline that was gradually revealed in the thinking and poetic culture of people who may have possessed great gifts that were, however, never fully realized. I'm thinking of the composer Sviridov again, or Tvardovsky, if you prefer. I think that Tvardovsky had a tremendous poetic gift and an outstanding critical mind and aesthetic instinct. And all this was not realized to its fullest due to the fact that Tvardovsky was artificially cut off from contemporary Western culture.

Brodsky. That may very well be, that may very well be. I can't say anything about Tvardovsky. On the other hand, take Zabolotsky and the Oberiuts. They came into their own while absolutely cut off from everything.

Volkov. What about German expressionism? At the time, German expressionist plays were performed in Petrograd theaters. With dances choreographed by Balanchine, by the way. Ernst Toller used to come. Mikhail Kuzmin and others translated the new German poets. Information came in about the dadaists. When the iron curtain was really lowered, that was when this anemia began, the results of which are felt to this day. Look: generation after generation of talented illiterates.

Brodsky. Well, that's true. Lord! The iron curtain didn't hang for very long altogether. Thirty or forty years. And you can't dump everything on Stalin, because that kind of isolationist policy played right into the hands of all our jingoistic hacks. On the other hand, I remember my feelings, back in Russia, when I started receiving Western postcards. You look at the photograph on a postcard like that and for a second you can't tell where it was sent from. Caracas, Venezuela, or Helsinki, Finland? That is, in a certain sense the iron curtain, for all its obvious defects, helped preserve the purity of the national culture.

Volkov. This would be an argument for the apologists for Sviridov and Tvardovsky. I still think that isolation from the West did them, as well as other Russian talents, more harm than good.

Brodsky. Now when I look at postcards from Moscow, though—especially if the photographs depict new districts, I absolutely can't make heads or tails of where all this is happening. Is it the Bronx or, the reverse, the capital of our homeland?

Volkov. If events had developed in a civilized manner, the Moscow Bronx would have been built much earlier, in parallel with our Bronx, in New York. Now in Moscow they could easily be constructing buildings both good and nationally distinctive. Instead, they are belatedly starting to ape the worst aspects of Western culture, what is most superficial in it.

Brodsky. I agree with you perfectly.

Volkov. When your poems started appearing (or to be more precise, perhaps, to be published once again) in the homeland, not only favorable responses began reaching us, but also some malevolent as well. These basically boiled down to one phrase that I remember, from a long-ago émigré response to your work stating that Brodsky was a man "climbing to the heights of fame over the steps of the Russian language."

Brodsky. I think that's marvelous. Lord! What could be better, right?

Volkov. Simultaneously, many poems that are now being printed in Russian journals, especially by young poets, betray the influence of your poetic manner. Here, in New York, this influence began to have its effect even earlier, paradoxically enough, maybe because you've been teaching here for so long. I remember the literary journal of Columbia University published an interview with you in which one of the questions was, "What would you advise young poets?" Your answer gave me the definite impression that you were actually taken aback.

Brodsky. Yes, because I myself had been in the "young poets" category for such a long time. I think that if I had remained in the Soviet Union, I would still be in it. Up until recently, even Voznesensky and Yevtushenko were still considered young there. It's rather shocking. As for life here, I've had many reasons for thinking, especially in recent years, that everything was basically over. Or about to be. If only for this reason I had not considered myself a young man for quite a long time, but when you're asked these questions you mention and they look at you as if you were a guru, you feel a little strange—at any age, I think, whether you're thirty or sixty. For me, these kinds of things are a constant surprise, although I ought to have grown used to them, since I do teach, and that very fact pretty much implies that you are older, wiser, and so forth than your students. Nonetheless, when they ask you that kind of question, What can you advise young poets? . . . What on earth could I advise them!

Volkov. You were just talking about having the feeling that it would soon be all over. In connection with what?

Brodsky. First of all, the poems. Because you've reached a point in your writing that, at the age you are now, you ought not to have reached yet in principle. If only for this reason you feel older than your years. There are so many other different things, among them the most obvious circumstance—your ill health. I've had several very close calls here. Existence, of course, does not determine consciousness, but it does sometimes determine, say, the tonality of your verse. Not so much the content as the tonality.

Volkov. You've undergone heart surgery here. I hear different things from different people about your health.

Brodsky. Actually, it's all very simple. I had a heart attack, after which I've had a wretched time for a year or two. My condition didn't improve one bit; it actually deteriorated. True, I'm a fine one, too—I was smoking and so forth. Then the doctors decided to cut me open, inasmuch as they had done all kinds of analyses and saw that of my four arteries, three *no pasaran,* right? Completely blocked. They decided to bypass those arteries. They opened me up like an automobile. They shunted it all aside—the blood, the fluid . . . All in all, the operation was pretty massive. So they put in three bypasses, extra paths. Roundabouts, if you like. Subsequently it became clear that of the three paths only two were functioning properly, so they had to repeat the operation. As a result, life can be extremely uncomfortable at times, and at times everything's fine, as if there were nothing wrong. When it hurts, it's truly terrifying. Very unpleasant. And there's nothing you can do. It's not that it's really fear . . . because eventually you do get used to all this, and you get the feeling that when you arrive *there,* it'll say, "Kolya and Masha were here." That is, the feeling that you've already been there, you've already seen and know this. Nonetheless, this illness is rather depressing. It simply puts you out of commission.

Volkov. How did you feel before going in for your first operation?

Brodsky. I was pretty powerfully frightened. It is your heart after all! We're used to identifying ourselves, our notions of ourselves, with our heart. It's an old romantic tradition. In my case this was intensified by something that I believe in general: a person's soul is in his blood, as it's written in Leviticus. Remember? "You shall not eat the blood of any creature, for the life of every creature is its blood . . ." I'd always wondered where a person's soul is, and when I read this, it all became clear to me. Therefore I was somewhat nervous before this blood pumping. For a while it was very scary until a rather simple thought occurred to me. I even remember how it happened. I was almost having a dialogue with myself. I told myself: "Well, yes, certainly, it's the heart. But it isn't the brain after all, is it? It isn't the brain!" As soon as I thought that, I was greatly relieved, and I got through it somehow.

Volkov. I remember in one conversation with you I was cut to the quick by your words, which I still remember, about how we're here not to live but to live out our time. I often repeat these words to myself.

Brodsky. This is really a perfectly plausible point of view, although not the only one. Objectively, this is just how the situation quite often appears. After all, I don't think I'll spend thirty-two years here, as I did in the homeland. It's hard to imagine. After all, both our convictions and our principles were already relatively formed. People of our age are already formed beings, whether we like it or not. The foundation and the initial speedup took place in the fatherland. Our existence in Russia was the cause. Today you have the effect.

Volkov. Didn't you have the sensation when you arrived in New York that this move, on the contrary, would allow you a fresh start?

Brodsky. That I most certainly did not have. I never have that kind of feeling, of a start.

Volkov. What about the feeling of a continuation?

Brodsky. That yes, since a certain point. Since I was about thirty, I think.

Volkov. We were talking about various responses to your poetry in Russia, as well as here, actually, in emigration. People over there have written about other émigrés, too, in approximately the same vein—about very different individuals who quit Russia due to different circumstances, but at the same time there was a common thread: Stravinsky, Nabokov, and Balanchine. Here, in the West, they moved away from anything national toward a greater universality. They became cosmopolitans. And in Russia people took up arms against them for this cosmopolitanism, using expressions very similar to the attacks on you.

Brodsky. You know, I've never thought about that. Honestly. And I never look on what I'm doing in that light or on that level. I'm involved exclusively with my own—I won't even say life, but my own inner history. What worked out, what didn't, when I was wrong, whether due to my own fault or not. In general, purely private matters. The rest doesn't interest me very much.

Volkov. A little while ago I read the first major biography of Nabokov, as well as his correspondence, and I saw how very painful this process, this move from a national culture to a world culture, is. Both outwardly and inwardly.

Brodsky. If you're speaking of attacks, I don't think they merit any phenomenological significance. It's a little unpleasant, that's all. What we see here is just a certain number of wounded vanities. If we're talking on this level, though, we'd do better to recall not even Stravinsky, Nabokov, and Balanchine but Peter the Great. He was in for a really rough ride.

Volkov. Well, Peter also had more administrative opportunities for responding to this criticism.

Brodsky. Psychologically, it's more or less the same thing for me.

Volkov. This problem interests me because the longer I live, the more I am convinced that Stravinsky, Nabokov, and Balanchine, who at a certain moment consciously rejected participation in Russian culture, in the end never did leave it. They rejected certain aspects of it, but as a result, they extended the boundaries of Russian culture incredibly.

Brodsky. This is all terribly interesting, but personally I'm not extending anything. I write my own poems, exclusively. I have no other ideas on this score. Unlike the remarkable gentlemen you mentioned, I didn't even want to leave Russia. They forced me. I wrote Leonid Brezhnev at the time that I would rather he let me participate in the literary process in my own country, if only as a translator.

Volkov. By the way, I saw your poem in the latest *New Yorker.* What, was it written in English?

Brodsky. Oh no, it's a translation. They just didn't put down the translator's name. The translator being me, by the way.

Volkov. I imagined you had begun to write poetry in English, although you assert that you don't want to do this.

Brodsky. And I almost don't. The only thing I write in English with any regularity is essays. Even there, I've observed a certain block lately in this area, simply because my brain won't function in this hellish New York heat.

Volkov. I'd like to see those essays published—in full—in Russia. Not least of all because they're written from the standpoint of world culture, which is what Russia lacks right now.

Brodsky. It's wrong to put it that way—"what Russia lacks." Russia lacks absolutely nothing. Because a longing for world culture exists, but only in certain cultures. English culture, for instance, doesn't have it.

Volkov. Because world culture is present there without any kind of longing.

Brodsky. Yes, one way or another. But then the English have a longing for immediacy, which you find in the East. They are drawn to orientalism, to all those Indian affairs. In general, every culture lacks something, as a rule, and that is what it always strives for. For a total embrace of being, right? That's why it's culture. If you want to get into particulars, though, then the English, for instance, are extremely rational. At least outwardly. That is, they often miss nuances, all those "loose ends," as they say. All that fringe. Say you cut up an apple and peel the skin. Now you know what an apple has inside, but you lose sight of the two bulges, the two cheeks of the apple. Russian culture is interested in the apple itself. It admires its color, the smoothness of its skin, and so forth. It doesn't always know what's inside the apple. These are, roughly speaking, different attitudes toward the world: the rational and the synthetic.

Volkov. When someone connected with one type of culture also masters the working mechanism of another culture, though, that opens up certain new horizons. Stravinsky is a great example of this. Very early on he broke out of his national framework, and having made that leap, he gave a stunning impulse to all of world music. Simultaneously, though, as is now becoming clear, Stravinsky's work had a very powerful influence on twentieth-century Russian music as well. That is, Stravinsky left Russian culture in order to remain inside it.

Brodsky. Possibly. The point is that this belonging to two cultures or, more simply, this bilingualism to which you are either condemned or the reverse, is either a blessing or a punishment, right? It is, if you like, a remarkable situation psychically, because you're sitting on top of a mountain and looking down both slopes. I don't know if that's so or not in my case, but at least when I do something, my vantage is good.

Volkov. An inhabitant of two worlds.

Brodsky. If you like. Well, not so much two worlds. It's always your own spot, right? But still, you see both slopes, and this is an absolutely special sensation. Were a miracle to occur and I were to return to Russia permanently, I would be extremely nervous at not having the option of using more than one language.

Fall 1978–Winter 1990

JOSEPH BRODSKY AT HIS HOME ON MORTON STREET,
GREENWICH VILLAGE, NEW YORK, 1980

9

ITALY AND OTHER TRAVELS

Volkov. Why is there a picture of the St. Mark's lion on the cover of your book *A Part of Speech?*

Brodsky. Because I love that beast so much. First of all, it's the Gospels according to Mark, which interests me more than the other gospels. Second, it appeals to me: a beast of prey—with pretty wings. It's not that I identify with it, but still . . . Third, it's a literate lion, it's reading a book. Fourth, when you get right down to it, this lion is simply a marvelous version of Pegasus. Fifth, take away the wings, and this beast is a sign of the zodiac, the sign of someone extremely dear to my heart, but because he has to fly there, to the top, then he definitely needs those pretty wings. And finally, he's simply painfully good looking! He's simply a beautiful beast! To say nothing of the fact that this Venetian lion is obviously another version of the Petersburg sphinxes. That's why there's a Petersburg sphinx on the cover of my *The End of a Beautiful Era* and a Venetian lion on the cover of *A Part of Speech.* Only the Petersburg sphinx is much more enigmatic. The Venetian lion isn't all that enigmatic, he's just saying: *"Pax tibi, Marce!"*

Volkov. Rome is so welcoming, too.

Brodsky. I spent four months in Rome on a grant from the American Academy. I had a two-story outbuilding a little ways off, with a huge garden. The panorama from there was absolutely stunning: on the right, pre-Christian, pagan Rome, the Coliseum and all of that; on the left, Christian Rome—St. Peter's and all those cupolas. And in the middle, the Pantheon. In Rome, when you're going into the city, you're going home. The city is a continuation of your living room, your bedroom. That is, when you go outside, you find yourself back home.

Volkov. Why do you think that after her trip to Italy in 1964 Akhmatova

189

had the impression of Rome as a satanic city? "Satan built Rome—before it fell," she said.

Brodsky. Akhmatova couldn't have had any other impression. After all, when she went abroad she was surrounded by God knows whom. Also, you have to live in cities like that, not pass through. If you found yourself in Petersburg for just a few days, you wouldn't take away anything less than a satanic impression.

Volkov. But after all, your favorite Italian city is Venice, not Rome.

Brodsky. Unquestionably.

Volkov. Lydia Chukovskaya recalls a conversation about this with Akhmatova. This was in 1955, and Akhmatova said, "We've grown unaccustomed to pigeons, but they were everywhere in Tsarskoye Selo. And in Venice." Chukovskaya adds that she could still picture Tsarskoye Selo with its pigeons, but not Venice, not at all. At the time, Chukovskaya wondered whether this Venice really existed in the world.

Brodsky. That's an old Russian idea.

Volkov. How many times have you been in Venice?

Brodsky. I don't know, I couldn't say. The first time I went there for Christmas of 1972. The fact is that getting to Venice was my *idée fixe*. When I was twenty, maybe a little older, I read a few novels by Henri de Régnier, a splendid writer whom no one knows anything about—even in France. Specialists maybe, but not the reader in any case. I think that in Russian he was even more splendid because he was translated by Mikhail Kuzmin. What attracted me was the name of the translator rather than the writer. As it happened, of the four de Régnier novels I've read, in two the action takes place in Venice in winter. If I learned the construction of a poem from anyone, then it was from de Régnier. Even though he writes fiction. When it comes to construction, my main teachers have been de Régnier and Bach.

Volkov. Perhaps you should number Kuzmin among your teachers as well, because the Russian de Régnier is largely Kuzmin.

Brodsky. I hadn't considered that. That may be. Although de Régnier's constructive ability had absolutely no effect on Kuzmin's own work, strangely enough. Kuzmin's work with de Régnier is, of course, translation. We're dealing with the author, with de Régnier himself. Here is an amazing combination of picaresque novel and detective novel, or psychological novel. The most stunning thing is how it's all done, how these component parts are organized. In a work of art that's the chief element—what follows what. You get a cumulative effect and then *what* is being said becomes important.

Having read about Venice in winter in de Régnier, I developed a fixation on it. A little while passed and someone brought me a *Life* magazine that had a photo story—Venice in winter. Snow and water. When I saw that, it just knocked me out. Later a woman I knew gave me an accordion postcard for my birthday, again with views of Venice, done in sepia. Finally, and last—the fourth by my count—an impression that has weighed somewhat on my mind: *Death in Venice*, Visconti's film with Dirk Bogarde. In Leningrad, this film was shown at some semirestricted viewing at the Institute of Theater, Music, and Film, on St. Isaac's Square. Moreover, they showed a black and white copy. Either there weren't enough color copies, as usual, or else they didn't want to pay royalties.

The film starts out on a very high note, so that everything afterward becomes a plateau. This small ship plowing across the flat water, remember? After that, everything else is much worse. Truth be told, I didn't pay any attention to Mahler's music in this film at the time. So that long before I left the Soviet Union, long before everything, I got this *idée fixe* of going to Venice. Of course, this was pure fantasy. Venice was out of the question, quite naturally. So when I found myself in the States, in Ann Arbor, when I finished teaching my first semester, I took my first free money, hopped on a plane, and flew to Italy.

It turned out much better than I'd imagined. That is, much more interesting. Of course, outwardly, Venice has parallels with familiar places. That is, you could say that Venice is similar to my native city, but in fact there is an absolutely different principle of spatial organization. Above all, there's less of it, less space.

Volkov. And the colors are different. They're much more—not vivid, but fresh, I think. Even the water is more vivid.

Brodsky. In Venice the water plays a special role. But first it's very interesting to compare Venetian architecture with the Roman of the same period. In Rome there must be a kilometer between the figures of the apostles on the pediments. In Venice those same apostles are shoulder to shoulder, crowded, in closed ranks. Like an army. This incredible density creates a special Venetian phenomenon, not baroque but something very different and specifically Venetian.

Yet, what is most stunning about Venice is the water. Water, if you like, is a condensed form of time. If we're going to follow the Book with a capital B, then let us recall what it says there: "And the Spirit of God moved upon the face of the waters." If He did move upon the face of the waters, that means He was reflected in them. He, of course, being Time, right? Or the Genius of time, or its Spirit. And inasmuch as He is reflected in the water, sooner or later H_2O becomes Him. Or rather, it already has. Think about all those wrinkles on the water, the folds, the waves, their repetitiveness. Especially when the water is a gray color, that is, the same color as time ought to be. Hence the idea of Aphrodite rising from the waves. She was born out of time, that is, out of the water.

Volkov. And all this happens in Venice?

Brodsky. Naturally. Because there's a lot of water and everything is reflected in everything. Hence the constant transformations. I don't know how to explain it. Say, a bird is flying over the water. It flies down from high up like a pigeon, but on the other bank—you look—and it appears now in the form of a seagull. The flight over the water is special. It is flight with a tax on the reflection, and apart from everything else, it is incredibly beautiful, because there is this antithesis, this possibility of transformation. When the sun goes down in Venice and the sunset is reflected in the windows, they look like fish with glittering, sparkling scales. Remember all those quasi-Gothic windows, or rather, the Roman mutating into the Gothic? Later, in the evening, when the lights are lit in the windows, they really are fish, illuminated from within, with half-shuttered scales.

Volkov. Has the Russian poetic tradition of describing Venice—Akhmatova, Pasternak—been important for you?

Brodsky. Not in general. In this specific instance Akhmatova's and Pasternak's poems are not all that significant. Akhmatova's "Venice" is an absolutely marvelous poem, "a golden dovecote by the water"—that is very accurate in a way. Pasternak's "Venice" is not as good. Akhmatova is a very capacious poet, and hieroglyphic if you like. She can cram everything into a single line. In Pasternak, Venice sails like a "soaked stone pretzel." That's not quite right. Those two islands and the bridges between them remind me more of two fish on a dark blue plate.

Volkov. When you talk about Venice, you only talk about the water and the architecture. What about the people?

Brodsky. There are no people for me. Naturally, the Italians are enchanting—the black eyes, the mix of tragedy and knavery and all the rest. In fact, though, the people aren't all that interesting. You know more or less what to expect from them. How can I put this? Ultimately, people are incomparably more synonymous than art. That is, people have much more in the denominator than in the numerator, right? Whereas art is a constantly changing denominator. People are connected with the city, of course, but they might not coincide with it at all. On the other hand, Venice has a magnetic effect on visitors. I always find it interesting to observe the neo-phyte arriving in Venice.

Volkov. Celebrating Christmas in Venice—is that your ritual?

Brodsky. I don't have any rituals. It's just that every time I've been in Venice, I've been there for Christmas. Because of the winter break. In the last nine years, I don't think I've missed a single time, except for twice. Both times I was in the hospital. It's not a ritual, of course, I just think that that's the way it ought to be. It's my crazy idea, if you like. The New Year. The changing year, the changing time; time rising up out of the water. I'm re-luctant to talk about it because it's pure metaphysics. These crazy ideas of mine—about time and water—started back in the Crimea. I realized something there for the first time. I remember, I celebrated the New Year in Gurzuf. As midnight approached—at about a quarter to twelve—I went outside to look at the sea and the bay. There was a *cloud* coming in off the bay onto the dry land. Moreover, I was high up on a hillside, so the cloud was moving below me, and I had a good view of it. It was moving like those biblical clouds the Lord or I don't know who is supposed to be inside. I re-member having the feeling that this cloud was a fog risen up from the water, transformed into a giant sphere. Or rather, a disheveled sphere. And it touched the ground at exactly twelve. Of course, you could look on this in various ways. Everything in the world is chemistry, but you can look on this in a somewhat different manner. Think about your native city, which also stands on the water, although in Petersburg it's always winter and cold and there you really don't think about time.

Volkov. You freeze and you think, if only—

Brodsky. —I could have a drink, right?

Volkov. Ezra Pound lived in Venice for many years and died there. He's buried in the Venetian cemetery of San Michele, not far from the graves of Diaghilev and Stravinsky. That section of San Michele is sometimes called the "exiles' graveyard."

Brodsky. Pound and I nearly met. He was participating in the Festival of Two Worlds in Spoleto, where I had been invited. Pound apparently had wanted to see me, or so they told me. I was invited to Spoleto twice alto-gether, the first time when I was still in the Soviet Union. Then the orga-nizers were informed—literally—that I was somewhere on the Baltic Sea, in a submarine. I must have been getting ready to invade Sweden's territo-rial waters. The second time I was already in London and the tickets for Spoleto had been bought. Suddenly, panic, and telephone calls from Gian Carlo Menotti, who ran the festival. Apparently a ballet troupe from

Perm—Diaghilev's homeland, as it were—had been invited to Spoleto, and the Soviet ambassador to Italy had threatened not to let the Perm company out to go to Italy if my Lordship showed up at the festival. As you'd expect, Menotti was terrified and asked me, "What should I do?" I thought about it and said, "Lord! What's there to get so worked up over? I'll be in Spoleto some other time, but for those ballet dancers from Perm, this may be their one chance ever to see Italy." Thus, my rendezvous with Pound never took place. He died that same year, 1972. In 1977, Venice had its Biennale on Dissent, to which Susan Sontag and I, among others, were invited. One day she asked me, "Joseph, what are you doing tonight?" I said, "Tonight? What could I be doing? Nothing." Susan: "Listen, I ran into Olga Rudge on the street here, Pound's mildly famous companion. She invited me over, and I really don't want to go alone. Would you come along to keep me company?"

We showed up at the house where Pound had lived, on a little street behind Santa Maria della Salute. This part of Venice is quite remarkable in many respects. Some great favorites of mine have lived there—Henri de Régnier, for instance. Pound's house is small, two stories: a living room and kitchen downstairs; a staircase; and upstairs apparently two bedrooms, plus above—Pound's study. The living room is small, like a troll's cave. This impression—a mountain king's case—is due to the fact that the first thing you bump into when you walk into the living room is a marble bust of Pound by Gaudier-Brzeska. It's a muscular bust, it stands on the floor, and it involves a certain violation of proportions. By the way, had this Gaudier-Brzeska not died as a young man, he would have been yet another remarkable fascist-monumentalist. The bust is a little smaller than Olga Rudge herself, who was setting out tea and pastries. And suddenly—without any further ado—she starts telling us how Ezra was not a fascist at all, as everyone believes, and how afraid they were that Ezra would be sent to the electric chair, in punishment for collaborating. What an utter terror that was. Olga Rudge explained quite cogently and distinctly, as well as convincingly and energetically, that Ezra had been treated unfairly. She said that during the war Pound was living in Rapallo, and he only went into Rome twice a month, if not less often, to do those propaganda radio broadcasts of his, after which he returned home. Well, perhaps from her and Pound's point of view nothing special really did happen in Rapallo itself. Life went on.

By the way, I went outside today—to mail some letters. A sunny day and all's well. And a helicopter flew overhead—a military helicopter, actually—and I thought, what if *it* had started? What would a day in the new world war look like? It would look like this. The sun would shine, the helicopters would fly, somewhere cannons would be firing. And the world would roll away to its ruin. And this daily apocalypse is going on after all, somewhere in the Middle East . . .

Volkov. Or Afghanistan.

Brodsky. And so, inasmuch as Pound and Olga Rudge didn't go to the movies, this whole horror didn't really affect them, although she is exaggerating, I think. There were German troops there, especially in Tuscany. I think that Pound saw and understood everything, but that's not important. You know, when you have a living person sitting in front of you, and when he says something—even if you don't agree with him at all—but if this person does not evoke in you a definite revulsion of a purely physiological sort, then ultimately you understand—yes, this is a reasonable view of things. Here I was sitting at Olga Rudge's—weakling or not, I don't know, with my Russian upbringing—and I was thinking that ultimately no one is to blame. We're all just great big unfortunate sons of bitches, right? We all need to be forgiven en masse and our souls allowed to repent.

And suddenly Susan said—I have to say that there is this amazing quality about Susan. When the conversation is wrapping up and all's well, everyone's calmed down—suddenly! It all starts in again!

Volkov. Just as in Dostoevsky: "suddenly."

Brodsky. So Susan lays it out to Olga Rudge: "Don't think that Americans were so dismayed by Pound because of his radio broadcasts, Olga. Had it only been a matter of radio broadcasts, he would just have been one more Tokyo Rose."

Volkov. That's the lady who admonished the American soldiers fighting against Japan over the radio during the war?

Brodsky. I nearly fell off my chair! In English, this comes across as lethal. To compare a poet they consider such a major eminence to Tokyo Rose! I'd be hard-pressed to even come up with an equivalent for this.

Volkov. It's like comparing Laurence Olivier to a stripper.

Brodsky. Something like that. But Olga Rudge swallowed all this quite remarkably. She asked, "So then, what did Americans find so repugnant in Ezra?" Susan said, "Well, it's quite simple. It was Ezra's anti-Semitism."

At this, Olga launched into the next hour: Ezra was not an anti-Semite. He had lots of Jews among his friends. Even Mussolini wasn't such an anti-Semite. In fact, he had a Jewish admiral here in Venice. Which in and of itself is rather remarkable. A Jewish admiral! Well, for Venice, it makes sense. As for Pound, we listened to Olga's story about how Ezra went to Eliot's funeral in London, and I don't remember whether Pound did or didn't shake someone's hand. Then we took our leave.

This was an extremely interesting experience. For the first time in my life I had seen a real fascist. Of course, I'd seen German prisoners of war in Russia, but in the first place, how old was I then? And secondly, well, what kind of fascism was that? They were just Germans, former soldiers. Then suddenly in Venice—of all places—I see a fascist by conviction, by ideology, and this fascist is an American lady with a more or less steady income who has spent the greater part of her life in Italy. That is, this house in Venice had belonged to her since I think 1928, and the only thing in the world that interested her was preserving her own status quo. The world through the prism of her own class, through the prism of a petty bourgeois. Well, in and of itself this really isn't so terrible, and it is absolutely no reason to go beat on the petty bourgeoisie, but when for the sake of maintaining the status quo they start exterminating people en masse . . . This didn't seem to penetrate to Olga Rudge, though, which is perfectly understandable, really. It's simply easier like that in many respects, to say nothing of the fact that you're residing in Venice and life is beautiful.

Volkov. How do you explain the support for Pound that came from so many different people, like Auden [who voted to award him the Bollingen Prize] and Robert Frost [who tried to obtain a pardon for him]?

Brodsky. First of all, they treated him like someone who had been buffeted by fate. You need to help whomever is in trouble, regardless. Pound was held in an insane asylum for nearly thirteen years. Holding a poet, no matter what his convictions, in an insane asylum—that really beats all. Auden said that if a great poet has committed a crime, he should first be given a prize and then hanged.

Volkov. Recently, materials have been published showing how unencumbered Pound was in that institution. The entire operation was pushed through by his admirers so that Pound could avoid a trial.

Brodsky. So they wouldn't send him to the electric chair! For better or for worse, Pound was a poet, especially as regards the first third of his work. "Hugh Selwyn Mauberley" is an absolutely marvelous poem, unfailing. Like Zabolotsky, but with an edge.

Volkov. To my own shame, I've never been able to get through the *Cantos.*

Brodsky. You don't have to get through them. You don't even have to touch them, because there's absolutely no point. There are stunningly eloquent bits, but in fact, it is a fictitious reality. Like, by the way, much in twentieth-century European painting. Something that could never be exists, and it's not just that you can live happily without it, but you could live unhappily without it as well.

They were fair to Pound. As a poet he was rewarded, and as a man he got what he deserved. From my point of view, as a poet he got even more than he deserved. They should publish a complete collected works of Pound: all the early poems and the *Cantos* in full. And a volume of his Italian radio talks. Then everything would be set to rights, and no one would get crazy about some injustice being committed against the poet.

Volkov. They say that Olga Rudge played the violin fairly well. Ezra Pound himself was actively interested in music and even wrote an opera to the verse of François Villon. Stravinsky was one of Pound's favorite composers. He liked to say that he learned his craft as a poet from Stravinsky. Moreover, they were both admirers of Mussolini.

Brodsky. I find nothing surprising in that.

Volkov. Stravinsky spoke ecstatically about Mussolini, especially after Il Duce received him at the Palazzo Venezia. We know that in 1936 Stravinsky opened his concert in Naples by playing "Giovinezza," the fascist hymn.

Brodsky. Italian fascism is not such a simple matter. It's simple, of course, but . . . Do you know why they called Mussolini "Benito"? His papa was a man of left-wing convictions. According to one version, he christened his son in honor of Benjamin Franklin. According to another, in honor of Benito Juarez, who in turn is known as the Mexican Lincoln. In fascist Italy, they didn't really persecute Jews. There really isn't any anti-Semitism there. Of course, under Mussolini the Italian Jews came to suffer many trying days. For example, the Roman ghetto—only recently, thirty years later, have Jews started returning to it. Still, it was nothing like what went on, say, in France. There simply were no yellow stars in Italy. I don't say this to defend Stravinsky. On the contrary, this was a tremendous blunder on his part. But you can't expect too much from a musician.

Volkov. Yes you can. Is a chicken not a bird and a musician not a human being?

Brodsky. The fact is that music—like architecture—is an art that depends to a strong degree on finances. If you're a composer, you need an orchestra to perform your symphony. Who provides the orchestra, though? And you can't pull a radio out of your hat. That's probably why the devil knows what goes on sometimes in the minds of these people. The very best architects have worked for the most hideous clients. The poet, the writer—that's another matter. They work on a higher plane of regard.

Volkov. According to the memoirs of the writer Vasily Yanovsky, Merezhkovsky used to talk about meeting Mussolini: "As soon as I saw him in his huge office by his desk, I loudly addressed him in the words of Goethe's Faust: 'Who are you? *Wer bist du denn?* And Mussolini replied: 'Piano, piano, piano.'"

Brodsky. Piano, piano . . . Yes, a fine lot they were!

Volkov. Getting back to Venice, can it be said that this city became one of your worlds?

Brodsky. Yes and no. You know, a person views himself—whether he likes it or not—as a hero out of some novel or movie in which he is always in the frame. My crazy idea is that Venice should be in the background.

Volkov. And the pigeons on San Marco?

Brodsky. The pigeons are not mandatory. Just Venice—better not of earth created. If some idea of order exists, then Venice is the most natural, well thought out approximation of it. And insofar as I have an opportunity to get close to all this, I try—well, I don't know, to hang out there at least for a while because I can't all the time, and I don't need to.

Volkov. My two favorite poems of yours about Venice are "Venetian Stanzas I" and "Venetian Stanzas II." The first is dedicated to Susan Sontag; the second to Gennady Smakov, your friend from back in Leningrad who died in New York in 1988. I wanted to ask you how you come to dedicate a poem to one person or another. Regarding Sontag I can guess, especially given what you've told me, but why is the second poem dedicated to Smakov?

Brodsky. I wanted to dedicate several poems to him. I even have this idea of publishing a volume of Italian poems, that is, poems written about Italy, and dedicating the entire book to him. Simply because his view of Italy and mine were identical. That is, we were two boys looking at this country identically. We saw the same thing, we loved the same thing. For us, Italy was heaven on earth in a sense. Really.

Volkov. Maybe now you can perceive Italy as heaven on earth because for us it is mostly a museum, but all those magnificent pictures and churches, all that marble and so forth—all this was created in the midst of innumerable wars, suffering, and bloody horror.

Brodsky. No, it's not heaven for us. Not even now. Why do I say that Italy is really the only place that could be called heaven on earth? Because living in Italy I see that this is what the world order ought to be. And what it evidently once was. In ancient Rome perhaps. In this sense Smakov and I were, oh, I don't know, Romans, I guess.

Volkov. Which Italian city did Smakov love best? Venice?

Brodsky. Assisi. The first Italian city he ever saw wasn't Rome or Venice but Assisi. Smakov used to tell me that when he first saw Assisi, he started sobbing and couldn't stop. I understood him very well then, because for all his hedonism, Smakov was in fact a Christian mystic. A happy Christian mystic. There have been such people. When Smakov, with all his cultural baggage, saw Assisi, for him everything came into focus. For him, Assisi became the embodiment of the idea of happiness. I remember my own reaction to Assisi, too, which was somewhat different. Smakov and I discussed this at great length. Here was a happy man because he recognized happiness when he saw it embodied. This is why he loved art and why he loved Italy.

Volkov. Did you and he ever travel to Italy together?

Brodsky. No, although we were always planning a trip like that. As it worked out, though, he could go in the autumn but I couldn't because I teach. So we never were in Italy at the same time. For me, purely egotistically, this was a tremendous loss, because I realize that the happiness of discovering or recognizing Italy with Smakov will never happen, and I realize, I know, what could have been. Those few places where we did find ourselves together . . . Well, there's no point bringing that up . . . We were unlucky. And you were asking about the mechanism of dedicating poems. It works in different ways. With Smakov, though, it was all quite simple. He liked a few of my poems very much, and in those instances, I realized I had made no mistake. I felt that. I wanted to dedicate a few poems to him. For instance, "Letters from the Ming Dynasty," because he was the first to really convince me that this was a good poem. I had all kinds of doubts on that score. As for "Venetian Stanzas," I was certain that he would like the poem. Which he did.

Volkov. I see dedications as part of the poem. A dedication gives the whole poem a kind of tuning fork. In this respect I'm a little confused by your dedications in "Venetian Stanzas." They seem intentionally reversed. The second poem talks about the "new Susannah," but it's dedicated to Smakov. Whereas the second, which is dedicated to Susan Sontag, mentions Diaghilev, with whom you'd think it would be more natural, for many reasons, to link Smakov: both are Russians, passionate balletomanes, homosexuals.

Brodsky. It's true the image of the "new Susannah" whom the "new elders"—the Japanese with their movie cameras—are looking at does appear in the second poem, but I simply decided it would be nicer for Sontag if I dedicated the first poem to her. After all, you dedicate a poem to give some-one pleasure. You know once, a long time ago, I heard some absolutely ter-rific music. It was a Bach record, and the work was called "A Musical Offering." You must know this music.

Volkov. I can even guess exactly which recording you mean—a Czech recording put out by Suprafon. That was the only recording of "A Musical Offering" for sale in Leningrad in the 1960s.

Brodsky. Well, at the time I thought I would like to be able to write something like that someday! To make that kind of offering to someone. This emotion I think conceals one of the most powerful inspirational mo-tives for art. You write a poem in order to thank someone. That's where all these poems of mine dedicated to various places and countries come from. Some critic once wrote that with me you get a travelogue. That's idiotic! You write because you were happy somewhere and want to express your gratitude for that. In like coin, so to speak. You pay for art with art. So it's the same coin. You know my poem "Lagoon," written about Venice. I al-ways liked it very much, but that was a long time ago. During that same 1977 Beinnale we were just talking about, I appeared in Venice—I don't remember in which hall, somewhere near the theater La Fenice—but I'll remember the hall all my life. All of it—the walls, the ceiling, everything—was covered with Guardi frescoes, I believe. Imagine this hall, these paint-ings, the dimness. Suddenly, reading my "Lagoon," I felt like I was standing in some kind of energy field and even contributing something to it. It was the end of the world! Once all this has happened in your life, you can absolutely die peacefully. Remember how Baryshnikov used to relate Smakov's words before Smakov's death from AIDS, when he was in the hospital? "What a happy life I've had."

Volkov. You talk about this in the last line of "Roman Elegies."

Brodsky. Yes, exactly.

Volkov. One more thing about dedications, in particular about dedica-tions to women. Let's say you have a romance with a woman. Does this make you want to write a poem and, accordingly, a dedication? What kind of woman makes you want to write a poem, say, and what kind doesn't?

Brodsky. Well, they all make me want to write a poem, I think, but often this happens—how can I put this—post factum.

Volkov. Take those "Roman Elegies" of yours, for instance. Every time I reread them, I come up against the dedication "To Benedetta Craveri." This name has become part of the whole cycle for me, and I try to picture her to myself because I've never seen her and don't know anything about her. Does she have the blue eyes you mention several times in "Roman Elegies"?

Brodsky. Of course not. The blue eye is mine! I don't really know what kind I have—blue? gray? The woman's eye there is brown! It doesn't belong to Benedetta Craveri, though, but to a very different young woman, Michelina. Her name appears there, too. But Benedetta—she's the grand-daughter of Benedetto Croce, by the way—I dedicated this cycle to her because in Rome she was like my Virgil and introduced me to Michelina. In fact, the contrast between the blue eye and the brown in this instance is a north–south opposition. The entire cycle is about a northerner's reactions to the south.

Volkov. Similar to Goethe's *Roman Elegies?*

Brodsky. What's happening here could be described as Goethe-esque, al-though this parallel should not be taken too far. My "Roman Elegies" are dedicated to a specific woman, but the true heroine of the cycle is someone else altogether. That's how it happens sometimes.

Volkov. I understand you have special feelings for Italy, for which, I can guess, there are several reasons. What about other countries? I have the sense that you don't spend much time at home. You're always taking off somewhere. Do you like to travel?

Brodsky. Generally speaking, yes. That is, not so much travel as get somewhere and settle in. Just knocking around from one place to another and looking from side to side—no, I don't much care for that.

Volkov. So you have no purely touristic curiosity? I ask this because I am totally lacking in that kind of curiosity. I'm capable of staying inside for weeks at a stretch. New landscapes frighten me.

Brodsky. I don't have agoraphobia but I don't exactly have an idler's com-plex, either. As for a fear of new landscapes, I think you can experience that somewhere outside the limits of the civilization you're used to—some-where in Africa or, to a certain extent, in the Orient—China or Japan. Maybe in South America. But not in Europe. On the other hand, it is countries with what we see as exotic civilizations that are worth traveling through, to look from side to side, to be photographed on that backdrop. Whereas in Europe—Italy again, for example—when I find myself there, I try to live, to be, and not to file through like a tourist. As a result, in all my travels through Italy I've seen rather little. Fully mastering what I have seen has really taken considerable time and energy. As a result, I don't think I've understood what I've seen. I don't think I know it. Behind any cultural phenomenon, be it a facade or a picture, there is so much information you need to master. You look at every cathedral, at every fresco, for so long and try to understand what's going on there, what brought this miracle to life. These kinds of feelings are especially strong for me in Italy, since it is the cradle of our civilization. Everything else is a variation, and not always successful at that. Your Italian impressions are especially acute, though, because they refer directly to you, to your culture, and you need to study this seriously, not just skim the surface.

Volkov. But you have an extensive "Mexican Divertimento" and poems about England, Holland, Sweden, and throughout you scatter so many expressive local details testifying to a tenacious eye and memory. I've heard from several people that you remember the tiniest details of your travels even from many years past.

Brodsky. Well, that could be, although I give myself no credit for this. I'm simply talking about how no matter how many journeys I make through Italy, it is difficult to become a part of the landscape—precisely because it is the landscape you want to be part of. There is a tremendous temptation here—wholly natural, if you bear in mind how much Russia and many Russians owe Italy.

Volkov. You have fewer poems about Petersburg, I think, than about Italy. Might that be because when you write about Italy or other countries you are in any case comparing them with Petersburg?

Brodsky. It might. More likely, though, I've written less about my native city because for me it is like a given. Why keep writing about Petersburg all the time? I've already worked through that idiom, as they say. The same thing is happening today with New York, which also feels like my city. But Italy or, say, Holland, I still feel like cramming into myself and digesting.

Volkov. Lately you've made frequent trips to Sweden. You obviously like the country. I understand your emotions. For any Petersburger, Scandinavia has to strike a chord: the climate, the architecture, the white nights. Since I've brought up Sweden: in October 1987, they announced you'd been awarded the Nobel Prize. You were in London at the time, weren't you?

Brodsky. Yes, I remember the moment very well. I was having lunch in a Chinese restaurant with John le Carré. That is his pen name, his name is David Cornwell. David's wife was with us. This was in Hampstead, and I was staying with my friend Alfred Brendel, the pianist. Suddenly Alfred's wife runs into this establishment—the restaurant was not far from Brendel's house, literally around the corner—and said, "Come home immediately!" I asked, "What's going on?" She explained briefly. We all went back to the house, where there was already a crowd of reporters with cameras. And the whole circus began. I remember, all this made a rather powerful impression on David. I told him, "I would have given this prize to V. S. Naipaul." To which David replied, "Stop playing the fool! It's all about winning!" Brendel at the time was on tour. Thank God, because he does not take noise well. He's a musician after all, right? Because he didn't need this entire circus, this onslaught, which is exactly what had started.

Volkov. I saw the ceremony where you were given the Nobel Prize in Stockholm on television. What emotions did you experience at the time?

Brodsky. Mixed. On one hand, this is neither the first nor the last time for me sitting on a stage, right? On the other, I'm hoping I don't do anything stupid. I can say, however, that I did not experience any powerful thrill or joy.

Volkov. Why?

Brodsky. For several reasons. In the sense of recognition, the greatest experience for me was not the Nobel Prize but the moment when I was still in Russia and learned that a volume of my poems was being put out by Penguin with a foreword by Auden. That was the most thrilling moment in my life. Everything that happened afterward was an anticlimax in a sense. And of course, it's too bad that my father and mother didn't get to see the Nobel awards ceremony. It's too bad they didn't live that long. That's all I have to say about my feelings in connection with the Nobel. As for the rest . . . There was a certain nervousness about what would come of it subsequently. I realized that my life was going to change, that the quantity of chaos in it would increase, and there would be less time. This presentiment proved accurate.

Volkov. I understand that you would have liked to see your father and mother at the Nobel awards ceremony. Who else?

Brodsky. I also would have liked Yevgeny Rein to show up, and two or three friends from Russia, but at the time that was hard to arrange. Those were still Soviet times after all. On the other hand, everyone I wanted and could see in the flesh at this enterprise did show up.

Volkov. Did you not think of Akhmatova there?

Brodsky. I did, of course. Without her, I might never have been there.

Volkov. I believe you took part in a convocation of Nobel laureates in Stockholm on the occasion of the ninetieth anniversary of the prize.

Brodsky. Yes. It was proposed that all 230 or so laureates still living would gather, but only 180 showed up. This was all rather amusing and pleasant, like an excursion through cherished places. I had several interesting conversations with various people, which I found gratifying, and quite a bit of Swedish vodka was drunk. It's made of wormwood. Instead of being clear it has an infusion of certain herbs, something like a liqueur, although the locals for some reason don't drink it.

Volkov. What do they drink?

Brodsky. Beer, like all Scandinavians. Nothing really interests the Scandinavians but beer. Women don't interest them, drugs don't interest them, and cars don't interest them either. I even think that Sweden's high suicide rate is due to the fact that they drink beer there instead of vodka.

Volkov. Lately you've traveled widely throughout Europe. Do you agree with those European intellectuals who complain that modern mass culture is erasing national distinctions?

Brodsky. Oh no! Look at Italy, at that sharply expressed ethnic milieu, which has fiercely resisted any leveling. In fact, when you land, say, in France, you find that the French are actually too French. In Germany the Germans are too German. I won't even start in about the English or the Swedes. The only place where I don't think about the country as such but about the continent as a whole is Holland. I recently spent a few days in Leiden and suddenly I had the feeling that this was a completely different space, a completely different world. It was a very intimate feeling, I would say. Basically, to understand what one country or another or one place or another is in any real way, you have to go there in the winter. In winter, life is more real, more dictated by necessity. In winter, the contours of a foreign life are more distinct. For the traveler, this is a bonus.

Winter 1979–Winter 1992

BRODSKY, NEW YORK, 1980

10

REMEMBERING
ANNA AKHMATOVA

Volkov. It is a rather fragile thing—the human memory. You talk with people and you see how events of the relatively recent past dissolve, their outlines becoming more and more fluid. I would like in this conversation with you to attempt to rescue certain details connected with Anna Akhmatova from oblivion.

Brodsky. With pleasure, if they haven't drowned in it irretrievably. I just know that I am incapable of answering all the questions. Everything that has to do with Akhmatova is a part of my life, and talking about life is like a cat trying to catch its own tail. It's unbearably difficult. I'll say one thing: every meeting with Akhmatova was an exceptional experience for me. When you physically sense that you are dealing with someone better than you. Much better. With someone who by her intonation alone transforms you. And Akhmatova transformed you into *Homo sapiens* with just the tone of her voice or the turn of her head. Nothing like it ever happened to me before or, I think, after. Perhaps because I was young then. Stages of development do not repeat themselves.

In conversation with her, or simply drinking tea or vodka with her, you became a Christian, a human being in the Christian sense of that word, faster than by reading the appropriate texts or attending church. The poet's role in society largely comes down to just this.

Volkov. We started out speaking about memory. Looking back, do you divide your life into periods?

Brodsky. I don't think so.

Volkov. Haven't you ever said to yourself: that happens to me once every three or maybe five years, or such and such a season is propitious for me?

Brodsky. You know, I don't remember that ever happening to me. I've lost track. I can't say precisely whether something happened, say, in 1979 or in 1969. All that is so long ago, right? Life changes into a kind of Nevsky Prospect. Everything recedes so quickly in its perspective and is lost—forever.

Volkov. My point is that in her lifetime, Akhmatova lent tremendous significance to cyclicity, to the recurrence of specific dates. In particular, I remember, she considered August a sinister month.

Brodsky. Akhmatova was in much better shape than I when it came to memory. The quality of her memory was stunning. No matter what you asked her about, she could always cite the year, month, and date without any special effort. She remembered who had died or been born when, and indeed, specific dates were very important to her. Personally, I've never lent any particular significance to such matters. I remember a few times substantial troubles began for me in late January, but that was pure coincidence. The difference in this attitude toward details and dates evidently comes down to one's education—or self-education. As far as I remember myself, I was always trying to shake off a given reality as quickly as possible rather than trying to hold onto anything. As a result, this tendency became an instinct, whose victim are the circumstances not only of your own life but also of others'—even a life dear to you. Naturally, this was dictated by my instinct for self-preservation, but everything has its price, self-preservation included. I never did learn to remember from Akhmatova—if indeed you can learn that.

Volkov. When and under what circumstances did you meet Akhmatova?

Brodsky. If I'm not mistaken, it was in 1961. That is, I had turned twenty-one. Yevgeny Rein took me to see her at her *dacha.* What is most interesting is that I don't remember those first few meetings very clearly. Somehow I just didn't realize whom I was dealing with, especially since Akhmatova had praised a few of my poems, and praise did not interest me particularly. So I had been at her *dacha* three or four times with Rein and Nayman, and then one fine day, coming back from Akhmatova's in a jam-packed commuter train, I suddenly realized—you know, suddenly, it's like a curtain falling—whom, or rather what, I was dealing with. I remembered a phrase of hers, or a turn of her head, and suddenly all the pieces fell into place.

After that it wasn't so much that I went to see Akhmatova often but that we saw each other fairly regularly. I even rented a *dacha* in Komarovo one winter. Then she and I saw each other literally every day. It was scarcely a matter of literature but of a purely human and—I dare say—mutual attachment.

By the way, there was once this remarkable scene. We were sitting on her verandah, where all our conversations took place, as well as breakfast, supper, and everything else, just as it should, and suddenly Akhmatova said, "Really, Joseph, I don't understand what's going on. You couldn't possibly like my poems." Naturally, I rose up and began protesting vociferously to the contrary, but to a certain extent, as I look back on it, she was right. That is, those first few times I went to see her, I really wasn't very interested in her poetry. I hadn't even read much of it. In the final analysis, I was an ordinary young Soviet man. "The Gray-Eyed King" was definitely not my cup of tea, like the "glove off her left hand." None of those things seemed like such great poetic achievements to me. That's what I thought until I came across her other, later poems.

Volkov. Which Russian poets did you revere at the time?

Brodsky. Tsvetaeva and Mandelstam.

Volkov. You say that you were an "ordinary young Soviet man" at that time, but Tsvetaeva and Mandelstam were anything but the standard fare during those years. When did you read Mandelstam for the first time?

Brodsky. In 1960 or 1961, one of the happiest periods of my life. I was knocking around without work, after a season in the field on a geological expedition. They'd given me a job in the Crystallography Department at Leningrad University. The Institute of the Earth's Crust. Actually, I did fairly decent work there building vacuum chambers for them and other things, all just like I was supposed to. With my own hands. It was interesting work. Overall, though, it bore a somewhat comic nature. The working day at the university began at nine. I would arrive by ten, because the library opened at ten. I registered at the library the day after I started the job, and since I was registered as staff and not a student, I had more privileged access to books. I checked out tons of them. In particular, I took out Mandelstam's *Stone* (because I'd heard a rumor about a book by that title) and *Tristia.* Well, naturally, this just knocked me out. "The Lutheran" and "Petersburg Stanzas" made an especially strong impression on me at that time, and several poems lodged firmly in my mind.

There is something absolutely stunning about your first reading of a great poet. You find not only simply interesting content but above all linguistic inevitability, which is probably what it means to be a great poet. After that, you're speaking a different language.

After *Stone* and *Tristia,* nothing of Mandelstam's came into my hands for two or three years. Even after meeting Akhmatova. The KGB bosses suspected her of corrupting youth, giving them poems by forbidden classics, but there was absolutely nothing like that going on. It never even occurred to me, for example, to ask her for Mandelstam's poetry. When I subsequently read poems by Mandelstam that were new to me, that happened via circuitous routes. Shady figures, total strangers—young women or ladies as a rule—would suddenly pull out of their purses God knows what. It was pleasant and interesting to give these poems to someone else to read if I knew he was unfamiliar with them. I would retype the poems, duplicating them.

Volkov. Shouldn't all those "young women and ladies" have been admirers of Akhmatova principally?

Brodsky. It's entirely possible that they were, but they evidently assumed that I was already well acquainted with Akhmatova's works, which absolutely wasn't the case, because I knew only a rather narrow selection of her poems—twenty, or about that many.

Volkov. I'm interested in talking a little about the Leningrad subculture of the late 1950s and early 1960s. Did you get together and read poems—Mandelstam's—to each other?

Brodsky. No, there was absolutely none of that. I remember, we used to ask each other, "Have you read this? And this?" From time to time we would get together at someone's place, but then we only read our own poems. That began when I was twenty-two or twenty-three.

Volkov. Whose place did you gather at?

Brodsky. All kinds of people's. At first we didn't even really gather. You would simply show your poems to someone whose opinion you respected or else whose support or approval you cared about. Then a rather harsh discussion would begin. Not that he would start taking your poems apart. Not at all. He would simply set your poem aside and make a face, and if you had it in you, you would ask him what was wrong. Then he would say, "Well now look, this really won't do." My main teacher was Rein, a man whose opinion I value to this day. To my mind, he possesses absolute pitch. There were four of us: Rein, Nayman, Bobyshev, and me. Akhmatova used to call us the "magic choir."

Volkov. "Magic choir." Is that an allusion to something?

Brodsky. No, I think it's of her own devising. You see, Akhmatova felt that Russian poetry was undergoing a renaissance. Actually, she was not far from the truth. I may be overreaching myself, but I think that it was we, this "magic choir," who gave the impetus for what is happening in Russian poetry today.

When you read new poems regularly, as I do, you see to a significant extent (I don't know, perhaps I'm overreaching again) this imitation of our group. It's not that I've harbored any patriotic or nostalgic ideas about our group, but these devices, this diction, first appeared among us, in our circle.

Akhmatova believed that a kind of second Silver Age was under way. I always regarded this pronouncement of hers with a certain suspicion, but you know, it may well be that I was wrong, and for one simple reason: Akhmatova dealt with a much broader circle of poets, or people, with an interest in poetry. We weren't the only ones visiting her in Leningrad. And young people brought her their poems in Moscow as well as Leningrad. This was an extremely diverse (not to say ill-assorted) public.

Volkov. Now, looking back, could you say that the four of you formed a certain literary group, a school?

Brodsky. Looking back, certainly. That's what occurred to me not long ago after reading Lev Loseff's poetry. Indeed, at one time in Leningrad a group arose that in many respects was similar to Pushkin's Pleiad. That is, there were approximately the same number of figures: an acknowledged leader, an acknowledged idler, and an acknowledged wit. Each of us repeated a certain role. Rein was Pushkin. Delvig, I think, that was probably Bobyshev. Nayman, with his caustic wit, was Vyazemsky. I, with my melancholy, evidently took the part of Baratynsky. Like any parallel, this one shouldn't be made too much of, though.

Volkov. Indeed, here we do have a curious similarity of temperaments. With the exception of Rein, perhaps. We don't have to talk about comparing their talents, but even simply the stamp of character and temperament.

Brodsky. Nonsense. You just don't know Rein!

Volkov. I'm not talking about Rein's poetry, of course, but take his articles and reportages.

Brodsky. The man is making a living! I can imagine what Pushkin would have done under Soviet power! It's dreadful even to contemplate!

Volkov. One thing I can say for certain: they wouldn't have let him into the archives so he couldn't have written his *History of the Pugachev Rebellion* or *History of Peter the Great.*

Brodsky. Something odd is going on with Petersburg in general. It's not pure mysticism but it's getting very close. In the early part of the century the situation was similar; a kind of group arose. Of course, it was somewhat more spread out over time, but still: Blok, Mandelstam . . . Really, you don't know which of them has more rights to the Pushkin role. Mandelstam was not really a leader. That role belonged more to Gumilyov, with his Poets' Guild. They actually used to call themselves the Poets' Guild! To our credit, we did not rise to such heights.

Volkov. What did Akhmatova tell you about the first Silver Age?

Brodsky. You know, as someone with a deficient education and upbringing, I wasn't very interested in all that, all those authors and circumstances. With the exception of Mandelstam and subsequently Akhmatova. Blok, for example, I don't like, now passively, but before, actively.

Volkov. Why?

Brodsky. For his bad taste. In my opinion, this is an extremely banal man and poet in many of his manifestations. A man capable of writing: "Under the embankment, in a ravine filled with grass,/ She lies and watches, so life-like,/ A colored scarf thrown over her braids,/ Beautiful and young." Well, really! "Beautiful and young!"

Volkov. Behind this stands Nekrasov and an entire stratum of Russian poetic culture. Then, too, there was the cinema, which Blok loved.

Brodsky. Well, yes, Nekrasov, the cinema. Still, the twentieth century had already begun, and to say that a woman, especially a dead woman, was "beautiful and young" . . . I understand that this is an era, that this is a poetic device, nonetheless, it makes me flinch every time. After all, Pushkin doesn't say "beautiful and young." Mandelstam doesn't have anything like it either. Take note, by the way, that the "Baratynsky" current runs strong in Mandelstam. Like Baratynsky, he's an extremely functional poet. Pushkin had his own Pushkinian clichés. For example, "on the wild shore." You know where the "wild shore" came from? This, by the way, is Akhmatova's observation, and a very interesting one. The "wild shore" came from French poetry: this is *rivage* and *sauvage,* a standard rhyme. Or say, Pushkin's passing rhyme, *radost'* (joy) and *mladost'* (youth). You find it in Baratynsky, too, but in Baratynsky, when he's talking about joy, then it's a very concrete emotional experience. For him, youth is a very specific age, whereas in Pushkin this rhyme simply plays the same part as a stroke in a painting. Baratynsky is the more economical poet. He wrote less, too, and because he wrote less, he paid more attention to what he put down on paper. Like Mandelstam.

Volkov. Baratynsky wasn't a professional man of letters in Pushkin's understanding of the term. He could afford to live on his estate and not publish for years at a stretch.

Brodsky. Well, had circumstances been different . . . But the larger reading public, which, in those days, wasn't all that large . . .

Volkov. That's how it seems to us now. Proportionately, the public was fairly large. In 1823, fifteen hundred people bought the literary miscellany

Pole Star in the space of three weeks, and it cost twelve rubles a copy, a huge sum in those days.

Brodsky. The poet's audience is always at best one percent of the entire population. No more than that.

Volkov. The early Baratynsky was just as popular with the contemporary Russian reader as the most famous names in our day.

Brodsky. Not for long. I would like to quote a remarkable letter from Baratynsky to Pushkin: "I think that here in Russia a poet can hope for great success only with his first immature attempts. All the young people are on his side, finding in him nearly their own feelings, nearly their own thoughts, cloaked in brilliant colors. The poet goes on to write with greater circumspection and more profound thought, and then he bores the officers, and the brigadiers can't reconcile themselves to him because, after all, his poems aren't prose."

Volkov. Baratynsky was disenchanted and wounded by his loss of popularity. His *Twilight* is a very bitter, bilious book.

Brodsky. That's not bile and bitterness. It's sobriety.

Volkov. Sobriety, which came after bitter disappointment.

Brodsky. Oh well, for a poet, disappointment is a pretty valuable thing. If disappointment doesn't kill him, it makes him a truly outstanding poet. In fact, the fewer illusions you have, the more seriously you treat words.

Volkov. To my taste, Baratynsky's *Twilight* is the finest book in Russian poetry. I especially love "Autumn."

Brodsky. "The Goblet" is really much better in *Twilight*. And if we're talking about Baratynsky now, I would say that the best poem in Russian poetry is "Desolation." Everything about "Desolation" is brilliant: the poetics, the syntax, the perception of the world. The diction is utterly incredible. In the end, where Baratynsky says about his father: "Long ago the rumor of him fell still around me,/ His distant grave received his ashes./ My memory has not preserved his face . . ." It's all so precise, isn't it? "But here yet lives." And suddenly this stunning adjective: "his accessible spirit." And Baratynsky goes on: "Here, friend of dreaming and of nature, I will sense him full well." This is Baratynsky about his father. "*He* roils inside me with inspiration, *He* commands me praise the forests, valleys, waters." And you listen further, such stunning diction: "*He* firmly prophesies the country/ Where I shall inherit a spring without end,/ Where there's no decay,/ Where in the sweet shadow of unfading oaks, Among creeks running ever full." What stunning sobriety about the other world! "I meet a shade most dear to me." In my opinion, this is a great line. Better than Pushkin. This is my old idea. That world, the meeting with one's father—well, who has ever spoken of this like that? The religious consciousness doesn't allow for a meeting with your papa.

Volkov. What about *Hamlet?*

Brodsky. Okay, Shakespeare. Okay, the Greek classics. Okay, Virgil. But not the Russian tradition. For the Russian tradition this way of thinking is utterly unique, as Pushkin noted about Baratynsky, remember? "He among us is unique, for he thinks. He would be unique anywhere, for he thinks in his own way, correctly and independently, all the while feeling strongly and deeply."

Volkov. Did Akhmatova ever discuss Baratynsky?

Brodsky. No, we never got around to him. And the blame for this falls not so much on Akhmatova as on everyone around her, because during the Soviet period literary life passed to a great degree under the banner of Pushkin studies. Pushkin studies were the only flourishing branch of literary scholarship. True, this situation is gradually starting to change now.

Volkov. The absence in Akhmatova's conversations of another poet— Tyutchev—also seems odd to me.

Brodsky. I recall a conversation about Tyutchev in connection with the publication of a small volume of his poems with a foreword by Berkovsky. Oh well, for all my positive feelings toward him, Tyutchev is not all that remarkable a poet. You and I have touched on this topic already, I think. We keep saying, Tyutchev, Tyutchev, but in fact you can only come up with ten or twelve really good poems by him (which is, of course, a lot). For the rest, no sovereign ever had a more loyal author. I've already spoken about this. Remember, Vyazemsky talked about the "overcoat poets"? Tyutchev was very much an "overcoat."

Volkov. What did Akhmatova have to say about the acmeists and symbolism?

Brodsky. Akhmatova liked to repeat, "No matter what you say, symbolism was the last great movement in Russian literature." And not only Russian, I think. This was truly the case. It had a certain integrity and scale, a certain breadth to its contribution to culture. In my opinion, it was truly a movement.

Volkov. Didn't Akhmatova distinguish acmeism as a special trend in Russian poetry? In their day the acmeists set themselves in quite distinct contrast to symbolism.

Brodsky. Quite true. But you know, by the 1960s, none of that was left. Not in conversations or behavior, to say nothing of stances. By then it was impossible to resurrect the pathos of that contrast, that polemic. All that had already ceased to exist long before. In addition, Akhmatova was fairly reserved and modest.

Volkov. Why did Akhmatova speak about Mikhail Kuzmin as a bad person? What about him was so distasteful to her?

Brodsky. Nothing of the kind! That's a lie, a myth. She looked favorably on Kuzmin and his poetry. I know this because I was of a much worse opinion of Kuzmin's poetry than Akhmatova was—because I didn't know him very well—and I spoke out in that spirit. Of course, Kuzmin has poetic dregs aplenty. Akhmatova greeted these attacks of mine quite coldly. If Akhmatova did have any problems with Kuzmin's poetry, they had to do with her *Poem Without a Hero,* a work she greatly treasured. Naturally, there were those who pointed out the similarity between Akhmatova's rhythm in *Poem Without a Hero* and the rhythm that Kuzmin used for the first time in his little book *The Trout Breaks the Ice,* and those people said that Kuzmin's rhythm was much more avant-garde.

Volkov. But didn't the Akhmatova rhythm in fact take its origins from Kuzmin's *Trout?*

Brodsky. You know, it's hard to say that with complete certainty. In any case, the music of the Akhmatova rhythm is absolutely independent. It possesses a unique centrifugal energy. That music is utterly enchanting, whereas Kuzmin's rhythm in *Trout* is pretty well rationalized.

Volkov. Memoirs that began to come in from the Russian émigrés—by Georgy Ivanov and Sergei Makovsky—could have affected Akhmatova's attitude toward Kuzmin. They inflated Kuzmin's role as Akhmatova's teacher, which annoyed her tremendously.

Brodsky. Georgy Ivanov's memoirs absolutely enraged her because so very much of it was fabricated. That really infuriated Akhmatova.

Volkov. I also remember her indignation at Makovsky's *Parnassus of the Silver Age.* She said approximately the following: Makovsky was a rich gentleman who wouldn't let Mandelstam and Gumilyov across his threshold, as they say. He considered them callow youths, tramps, and himself a great poet and connoisseur.

Brodsky. Right, a patron. That I remember.

Volkov. Akhmatova used to say that they attempted to depict her as a lady dilettante whom Kuzmin and Gumilyov, through their joint efforts, made over into a poet.

Brodsky. That, of course, is stark raving mad. What Akhmatova could not stand was this attempt to lock her up in the 1910s and 1920s. All those conversations about how she had stopped writing, how in the 1930s Akhmatova was silent—all that enraged her no end. It's understandable. I, for example, when I later read and reread Akhmatova, I was much more interested in those later poems of hers. In my opinion, they are more important than her early lyrics.

Volkov. Did Akhmatova ever discuss Kuzmin's homosexuality?

Brodsky. Not specifically. In Russia even the intellectual milieu was still quite puritanical. I don't remember any conversations with her on the level of gossip.

Volkov. It seems to me that at times Akhmatova was far from averse to gossip. She indulged in it with great relish.

Brodsky. Of course, of course. You know, this is the fault of my memory. I remember that in conversations with Akhmatova—no matter whom they were about—there was always a large measure of irony present. An earned irony on her part, a snobbish irony on ours.

Volkov. Wasn't there some irony in Akhmatova's attitude toward Pasternak?

Brodsky. There was, yes. Irony and, in many instances, moral condemnation, if you like. Akhmatova greatly disapproved of Pasternak's ambitions. She disapproved of his desire, his thirst for the Nobel. Akhmatova condemned Pasternak rather harshly. As a poet of that scale deserves, actually.

Volkov. Akhmatova loved reading her own poems out loud—not from the stage but to the people close to her. Did she ever ask you your impression?

Brodsky. Yes, she did read them, and she did show me what she had written. And she was always extremely interested in our opinion. We would sit there and suggest corrections: Nayman, Rein, Bobyshev, and me. We would say what specifically, in our opinion, didn't work. Not often, but it did happen.

Volkov. Would Akhmatova agree?

Brodsky. Certainly. She was quite attentive to our ideas.

Volkov. Could you point out some concrete instance?

Brodsky. I remember a correction Rein made in Akhmatova's "Ode to Tsarskoye Selo," where she had a line about drinking "tsarist vodka" [*aqua regia*]. Rein told her: "Anna Andreyevna, you're wrong. Tsarist vodka is an oxide." I don't remember anymore of what. Basically it's a chemical formula, and for Rein, who was an engineer by education, this was perfectly obvious. Akhmatova had something else in mind with her tsarist vodka, so she corrected it to say, "drinking vodka 'til late in the night." And I remember even more important corrections.

Volkov. Poem Without a Hero—she must have read that to you as well.

Brodsky. Yes, numerous times. Especially new bits. She was always asking whether something fit or not. She was constantly writing and rewriting it. I remember reading *Poem Without a Hero* in its initial version and being powerfully impressed. Subsequently, when it grew so much larger, it began to seem unwieldy to me.

Volkov. I got the impression that Akhmatova worried a great deal about *Poem Without a Hero,* about how others would see this work.

Brodsky. Perhaps, but in fact you write primarily and specifically for yourself. Akhmatova was interested in how people would react to it, how well they would understand it, but this whole process of writing and rewriting had more to do with her than with outside reactions. First of all, in this instance Akhmatova was in the thrall of the rhythm itself. I remember her teaching me. She would say, "Joseph, if you want to write a long poem, first of all you have to come up with your rhythm. That's how the English do it." The English really do this up in grand style. Almost every poet invents his own rhythm. Byron, Spenser, and so on.

Akhmatova used to say, "What killed Blok in his *Retribution?* The long poem itself may well be marvelous, but the rhythm isn't his, and this borrowed rhythm engenders an echo that shouldn't be there. It overshadows everything." This principle makes extremely good sense. On the other hand, of course, Akhmatova ended up in the thrall of her own invention. The fact is that a poet doesn't write poetry every day, and when he can't write poetry, living, as Akhmatova herself said, becomes "extremely uncomfortable." It's perfectly natural that Akhmatova kept going back to her own rhythm. Or rather, that this rhythm kept coming back to her. Like a dream—or like breathing. And then all this adding and inserting and so on began.

Secondly, correcting, constructing, and compiling can gradually turn into a goal in itself. It's an occupation that can bewitch you. Gradually a situation arose in which we—the closest of the *Poem*'s readers—and Akhmatova herself ended up more or less on a par. That is, we were no longer in any position to judge whether some new bit was in its right place in *Poem* or not. You find yourself so dependent on this music that you lose track of the proportion of the whole. You forfeit your ability to relate to the whole critically. Were Akhmatova alive today, I think she would still be writing *Poem Without a Hero.*

Volkov. Don't you think that something paradoxical happened with *Poem Without a Hero?* Might it not actually have been intended for herself? To the outside reader, her theme and allusions are fairly enigmatic.

Brodsky. Well, it's all easily enough deciphered!

Volkov. Still, *Poem* requires a certain preparation for the reader, more so than any other Russian verse epic.

Brodsky. There is a tendency in Russian poetry—dictated by the country's dimensions, the size of its population, and so on—to believe that the poet is working for a broad audience. To one degree or another, we have all been gripped at one time by the thought, "I have a huge audience." On the other hand, though, in his heart of hearts, any more or less serious poet knows that he is not working for his audience, that he is writing because language is dictating to him. He is doing this—for the sake of the music of the language, for the sake of these words and suffixes.

So that in the case of *Poem Without a Hero,* I don't see any contradiction. Naturally, Akhmatova was interested in learning her listeners' reaction, but if what had most interested her in the world had really been the accessibility of *Poem Without a Hero,* she wouldn't have added all these little bits.

Volkov. The real paradox is that *Poem Without a Hero* turned into a symbol of the Silver Age and the era before the First World War. Strangely enough, we now look on this era through the prism of the decoded *Poem Without a Hero.*

Brodsky. By the way, do you know Pasternak's comment on *Poem Without a Hero?* He used to say that it was like a Russian folk dance, when the circle moves in, closes up, and steps back, opening. Akhmatova was very fond of this statement of Pasternak's.

Volkov. For years, Akhmatova thought about doing a ballet libretto based on the *Poem Without a Hero.* Unfortunately, she only left fragments.

Brodsky. Akhmatova wrote a play as well, by all accounts a terrific piece, which she evidently burned. Once in my presence she reminisced about the beginning of the first scene: the stage is empty except for a conference table covered with a red cloth. A servant comes in, or I don't know now who, and hangs a portrait of Stalin.

Volkov. This is an almost surrealistic image.

Brodsky. There's plenty of that in her poetry, especially the late poetry, and this sense of the surreal often came through even in daily life. I remember at the *dacha* in Komarovo, she had a china cabinet. There was a lull in our conversation, and since I had nothing else to praise in the place, I said, "What a marvelous cupboard," and Akhmatova replied, "What cupboard! It's a coffin upended on its ass." Her sense of humor was characterized by just such flights of the absurd.

Volkov. Tsvetaeva used to call Akhmatova a "lady." It seems to me that you, with your experience—the factory, the morgue job, the geological expeditions—were more the exception in her milieu. Your life in the homeland was not quite the norm for a Russian poet: both prison and the farm work.

Brodsky. Not at all, I lived like everyone else. For all its defects, in the class sense, Russian society is still the most democratic.

Volkov. A Russian poet ordinarily proves more democratic in his poems than in real life. In one of her early poems, Akhmatova says of herself: "On my knees in the garden/ I am weeding goosefoot." Lydia Ginzburg recalled how much later she realized that Akhmatova didn't even know what goosefoot looked like.

Brodsky. That's very far from the truth. The Russian writer never really detaches himself from the people. There's really all kinds of riffraff in a literary milieu, but if we're talking about Akhmatova, what do you do with her experience of the 1930s and much later: "Like the three hundredth in the queue with a parcel will you stand at the Crosses?" And what about all those people who used to visit her? These were by no means poets necessarily, and it was by no means engineers who collected her poems, or scientists. Or dentists. And anyway, who are the people? Typists, nurses, all those old ladies—what other kinds of people do you need? No, this is a fictitious category. The writer is himself the people. Take Tsvetaeva: her poverty, her trips lugging her own bags during the Civil War . . . No. No matter where you point, no poet in our beloved homeland has ever been able to break away from the common people.

Volkov. In the final years of her life, Akhmatova became more accessible.

Brodsky. Yes, people came to see her almost daily, both in Leningrad and in Komarovo. That isn't even including what all went on in Moscow, where they had a name for this great babel—an *akhmatovka.*

Volkov. Describe this *akhmatovka* in more detail.

Brodsky. It would happen mostly when Akhmatova stayed in Moscow, with the Ardov family. First of all, it involved a constant stream of people, and in the evening, the table where the tsar and tsarevich, the king and prince, sat. Ardov himself, for all his defects, was an extremely witty man. His entire family was like that, both his wife Nina and his boys Boris and Mikhail. And their friends, all Moscow boys from good families. As a rule, they were journalists working for remarkable enterprises like the Novosti press agency. These were well-dressed, hardened, cynical people. And very cheerful. Amazingly witty, in my estimation. I've never met wittier people in my life. I don't remember laughing more than I did then, at the Ardov table. That is again one of my fondest memories. Often it seemed that witty repartee comprised the sole content of these people's lives. I don't think they were ever overwhelmed by sadness, but perhaps I'm being unfair. In any event, they adored Akhmatova. Other people came to see her, too: Koma Ivanov, and the brilliant Simon Markish, editors, theater critics, engineers, translators, critics, widows—you could never name them all. At seven or eight in the evening, the bottles appeared on the table.

Volkov. Akhmatova liked to drink.

Brodsky. Yes, about two hundred grams of vodka a night. She didn't drink wine for the same simple reason I don't especially: grape resins narrow the blood vessels, whereas vodka expands them and improves the blood's circulation. Akhmatova had a bad heart. By then she'd already suffered two heart attacks. Later she had a third.

She was a terrific drinker. If anyone knew how to drink, it was Akhmatova and Auden. I remember a winter I spent in Komarovo. Every evening she would tell either me or someone else off over a bottle of vodka. Of course, there were people around her who couldn't bear this. Lydia Chukovskaya, for example. At the first signs of her appearance, the vodka was tucked away, and a particular expression reigned on our faces. The evening passed in extremely proper and intellectual fashion. After the nondrinker's departure, we would pull the vodka out again from under the table. As a rule, the bottle was kept on the floor beside the radiator, and Akhmatova would utter a more or less unvarying sentence: "It was getting warm."

I remember our endless discussions on the subject of the bottles, which seemed bottomless. At times in our conversations there would be these tortuous lulls: there you were sitting in front of a great person and you didn't know what to say. You realized you were wasting her time, so you asked a question just to fill in that lull. I remember very distinctly asking her something about Sologub, what year did such and such an event occur. Akhmatova had already brought a shot of vodka to her lips. Hearing my question, she swallowed and replied: "August 17, 1922." Or something like that. And then she drank down the rest.

Volkov. When people poured for Akhmatova, they asked her how much, and Akhmatova would put out her hand, as if to say, enough, and inasmuch as this gesture, like everything she did, was slow and majestic, the glass managed to get filled to the brim. Many of the variety of people who came to see Akhmatova, following Russian custom, probably came not so much for poetic counsel as for more mundane advice.

Brodsky. I remember one such episode, very typical. It happened one winter when I was sitting with Akhmatova at Komarovo. We were drinking and talking when a certain poet showed up with this marvelous lady-like locution: "Oh, my hair is not done yet!" Akhmatova whisked her away to this storeroom she had there, and I could hear this sobbing. This poet had obviously not come to read her poetry. Half an hour passed, and Akhmatova and the lady reappeared from behind the screen. When the lady was a good ways away, I asked, "Anna Andreyevna, what's the matter?" Akhmatova said, "The usual situation, Joseph. Me administering first aid."

Ladies especially brought Akhmatova their woes. She would console them, calm them down. She would give them practical advice. I don't know what. The simple fact that these people were prepared to lay out all their problems to her was sufficient therapy for them.

Volkov. I wanted to ask you about one thing in particular. I've never seen a photograph of you and Akhmatova together.

Brodsky. That's right, there is no such photo. It's funny. Only yesterday I was talking about this with a friend of mine, the wife of a rather remarkable poet. I said to her, "Give me your photograph," and she replied, "I don't have one. In this marriage, I'm the one taking the pictures."

Volkov. In the book about Akhmatova by Amanda Haight there is a picture reproduced of you and Nayman deep in thought. You have a short-wave radio in your lap.

Brodsky. We're probably listening to the BBC. I don't remember who took that. It was either Rein (because both of them came to see me in Norenskaya), or else I put the camera on a timer. On the same page is a portrait of Akhmatova that's my work. I shot her several times. The photograph there of Akhmatova's desk at Komarovo—that's mine, too.

Volkov. When did you live in Komarovo?

Brodsky. I think it was the fall and winter of 1962 to 1963. I rented the *dacha* of the deceased academician Berg, whom my father had once studied with.

Volkov. Is there a Komarovo mystique? Or is the place in and of itself not that remarkable and only became famous thanks to Akhmatova?

Brodsky. There was very simply a writers' house in Komarovo. Viktor Zhirmunsky, whom we saw rather often, lived there. Next to Akhmatova settled a rather sweet man who was, in my opinion, a fine translator, primarily from oriental languages, the poet Alexander Gitovich. Lots of people came to visit, and great dinners were organized in the summer of Akhmatova's *dacha*, in her "booth." Khanna Gorenko, a marvelous woman who lived with Akhmatova as a rule during the summer periods, helped with the household. For many years she was considered the straw widow, if you like, of Akhmatova's brother, who lived and died here, in the United States. Once, Akhmatova showed me the man's photograph: broad shoulders, a bow tie—a senator, right?—and she said, "A good-looking"—then a pause—"American." He bore an incredible resemblance to Akhmatova. The same gray hair, the same nose and brow. By the way, Lev Gumilyov, her son, also looks more like his mother than his father.

Volkov. How did Akhmatova's brother ever wind up in America?

Brodsky. He was a sailor, a midshipman from the last prerevolutionary batch. At the end of the Civil War, he and Khanna, to whom he was married then, found themselves in the Far East. His surname, like Akhmatova's maiden name, was Gorenko. He was a kind of Joseph Conrad, but without literary ambitions. When he left Khanna, he spent quite a long time traveling through China and Japan—which he later called "undesirable places." He sailed there in the merchant marine, and when he got to the States after the war, he became a security guard. Akhmatova's first news of him came through none other than Shostakovich, because it so happened that Gorenko was hired to guard Shostakovich during his visit to the States. That was how Akhmatova learned that her brother was alive. Before that I don't think there had been any contact between them at all. You can imagine what might come of such contacts.

Only toward the end of her life, when times again became more or less vegetarian, could Akhmatova think again about correspondence, if only extremely irregularly. Gorenko sent Khanna and Akhmatova a few things—shawls and dresses, which Khanna took great pride in. When Akhmatova was unwell and she had her third heart attack, they sent him a telegram. But what could he do? Go to her? He was married to an American and living in Brooklyn.

When Khanna returned to Russia from the Far East, she did, it seems to me, time—hard time. But maybe not. You know, it's a sin not to remember that. We were very fond of and well disposed toward each other. I dedicated some poems to her. But that's what happens to the memory. Or maybe it's not so much the memory as the piling up of events.

Volkov. What did Akhmatova tell you about her father?

Brodsky. Andrei Antonovich Gorenko was a naval officer and taught mathematics at the Naval College. By the way, he knew Dostoevsky. No one knew that, but in 1964, two volumes of memoirs about Dostoevsky came out, and in them were printed the memoirs of the daughter of Anna Filosofova about how Gorenko and Dostoevsky helped her solve the math problem about the hare and the tortoise. I was living in the village then. I read these memoirs and putting two and two together figured out that this was Akhmatova's father, so I wrote to her about it. She was extremely grateful. Later, when we saw each other, after my release, she said something like, "See, Joseph, before there was just the family legend about Dostoevsky, that my mother's sister, who studied at the Smolny Institute, read *Diary of a Writer* and then turned up at Dostoevsky's door! She went right up the stairs and rang the bell. The cook opened the door. Our Smolny girl says, 'I would like to see the gentleman of the house.' The cook replied, 'I'll go call him,' and went away. My aunt stood in the dark vestibule and saw a light gradually coming toward her. A gentleman holding a candle appeared wearing a dressing gown and an extremely sullen expression. Either he had been woken up from a nap or else interrupted in his righteous labors. In a rather curt voice he said, 'What do you want?' Whereupon she turned on her heels and rushed out headlong."

And, as I remember, Akhmatova would add, "To this day this was our sole family legend about our acquaintance with Dostoevsky. Now I tell everyone that my mother was jealous because of my father's attachment to the same lady Dostoevsky wooed."

Volkov. There's a shade of self-parody in this commentary of hers because creating legends was well within her nature. Or am I wrong?

Brodsky. To the contrary, she liked to strip things bare, although there are legends and legends. Not all of them displeased her. Still, Akhmatova did not like making things more obscure than they already were.

Volkov. One legend—which I now think she had a hand in creating—Akhmatova protested against her whole life.

Brodsky. Yes, the legend of her romance with Blok. Akhmatova used to say that this reflected "popular hopes." According to her it never was, and Akhmatova is someone whose every word I believe unquestioningly.

Volkov. This was probably a "literary" romance, as they say. On her part, in any case. Just reread the poems she addressed to Blok. Late in life, Akhmatova had ambivalent feelings toward Blok. In *Poem Without a Hero* she describes him as someone "with a dead heart and a dead gaze." In one of her poems from the 1960s she calls Blok "the era's tragic tenor." If you think about it, this is by no means a compliment.

Brodsky. But in Bach's *St. Matthew Passion,* the Evangelist is the tenor. The role of the Evangelist is the tenor's role.

Volkov. That never occurred to me.

Brodsky. This poem was written right during the period when I was bringing her Bach records.

Volkov. In Akhmatova's poetry, especially the later poetry, music is often mentioned: Bach, Vivaldi, Chopin. It always seemed to me that Akhmatova had a fine feeling for music, but I've heard from people who knew her well, although probably not terribly well disposed toward her, that Akhmatova herself didn't understand a thing about music but only listened closely to the opinions of people around her. They used to say more or less that Akhmatova's statements on Tchaikovsky or Shostakovich were the words of Punin, and on Bach and Vivaldi of Brodsky.

Brodsky. Well, that's ridiculous. That is untrammeled and unfounded stupidity. It's just that when Akhmatova and I met, she had neither a record player nor records at her *dacha,* and only because no one had done anything about it. They never got around to it.

Volkov. Akhmatova made an insightful comment about the music of Shostakovich's Eleventh Symphony. You hear sometimes disparaging comments about the Eleventh Symphony, but Akhmatova said that in it "the songs fly across a terrible black sky like angels, like birds, like white clouds." At the same time, she did not perceive the charms of the "Jewish" vocal cycle by Shostakovich. There she heard only the words, which are awkward from a poetic standpoint.

Brodsky. Well, she was a poet. Above all, she noticed the verse.

Volkov. Shostakovich presented a lofty musical "portrait" of Akhmatova in his vocal cycle, *Six Poems by Marina Tsvetaeva.* Did she ever discuss Shostakovich with you?

Brodsky. She may have mentioned him a few times. She and I often spoke about Stravinsky and listened to the Soviet pirate record of his *Symphony of Psalms.* I remember one of Akhmatova's comments about Stravinsky. This was in 1962, during Stravinsky's visit to the Soviet Union. At that moment I was in Moscow, and from my taxi, en route to seeing Akhmatova, I saw Stravinsky, his wife Vera, and Robert Craft. They were coming out of the Metropole Hotel and getting into a car. I knew that the night before the Stravinskys had been planning a visit to Akhmatova. When I arrived, I said, "Anna Andreyevna, guess who I just saw on the street—Stravinsky!" And I started describing him: short, hunched, a big hat. Basically, I said, all that's left of Stravinsky was his nose. "Yes," added Akhmatova, "and his genius."

Volkov. I had the opportunity to be convinced that Akhmatova's opinions about music were weighty and specific: about Vivaldi, and Bach, and Purcell.

Brodsky. I was constantly bringing her Purcell. She and I also spoke a lot about Mozart.

Volkov. Despite her Pushkin bias, she even held to the progressive view that Salieri had nothing to do with Mozart's death.

Brodsky. Well, of course, what doubt could there be? By the way, did you know she adored Koussevitzky? I heard that conductor's name for the first time from her.

Volkov. The *Symphony of Psalms* was commissioned by Koussevitzky. Did you discuss this Stravinsky composition with Akhmatova?

Brodsky. During that period we were discussing the idea of setting the Psalms—the whole Bible really—in verse. We got the idea that it would be good to put all those Biblical stories into verse accessible to the broad reader. We used to discuss whether or not it was worth doing and, if so, then just how to go about it. And who could do it best, so that it came out as well as with Pasternak.

Volkov. Akhmatova considered Pasternak's a success?

Brodsky. We liked it, both of us did.

Volkov. By the way, in connection with the idea of transposing the Bible, what do you think of the engravings Favorsky did for the Book of Ruth?

Brodsky. They're very fine. Favorsky is really a great artist. I've admired him for a long time. The last time I looked at Favorsky's engravings, though, was many years ago. Favorsky belongs more to the sphere of reminiscence than to my visual reality.

Volkov. Don't you think that Favorsky and Akhmatova are similar artists? And that there is some kind of link between his engravings and, say, Akhmatova's Biblical poems?

Brodsky. Yes, there is a certain similarity in the devices, but only insofar as you can liken the fine arts and *belles lettres* at all—which really ought not be done. There's a definite point of similarity—not so much with Akhmatova as with literature in general. I would say that Favorsky is basically a literary artist, in the sense that the conventions he resorted to are fairly literary.

Volkov. And Akhmatova's Biblical poems are graphic.

Brodsky. Everything Akhmatova writes is graphic. Just as everything Favorsky depicts is didactic.

Volkov. For me, the "Biblical" Akhmatova is more didactic than the "Biblical" Pasternak.

Brodsky. I'm very fond of Pasternak's poems from *Doctor Zhivago.* They're remarkable poems, especially "Christmas Star." I think of them often. At one time I considered writing a poem every Christmas, and as a rule, when Christmas draws near, all this comes to mind once again.

Volkov. Akhmatova's poems are being set to music more and more often. One of the most outstanding compositions of this sort is *Requiem* by the English composer John Tavener. It was performed in London and later at a festival in Edinburgh.

Brodsky. Yes, I heard about that. You see, a poet is the last person to rejoice at his poems being set to music, since he himself is primarily concerned with linguistic meaning, and as a rule the reader does not master that all at once. Even when the poem is printed, there is no guarantee. When music is added on to the verse, then from the poetic standpoint, there is an additional obscuring. So that, on the one hand, if you're a trendy guy, it's flattering that a composer has written music to your poems, but if you are truly concerned with the public's reaction to your text—and this is where your art begins and what it comes down to in the end—then there's absolutely no cause for celebration here. Even if you're dealing with the best composer in the world. Generally speaking, music removes poetry to a completely different dimension.

Volkov. Of course, contact with music diminishes poetry in a certain sense, but that new dimension you're talking about is what lends this interaction special interest. Take *Requiem* again. This is a notable text, but fairly straightforward. The music can deepen this straightforwardness and maybe even unexpectedly illuminate some new stratum in the verse.

Brodsky. No, the text of *Requiem* is anything but straightforward.

Volkov. Sure, there are two levels here: real biography—Akhmatova and the fate of her arrested son; and the symbolic—Mary and her son Jesus.

Brodsky. For me the main thing in *Requiem* is the theme of splitting, the theme of the author's inability to have an adequate reaction. Akhmatova describes in *Requiem* all the horrors of Stalin's "great terror," but at the same time she is constantly talking about how close she is to madness. Do you remember?

Already madness dips its wing
And casts a shade across my heart,
And pours for me a fiery wine
Luring me to the valley dark.

I realize that to this madness
The victory I must yield,
Listening closely to my own
Delirium, however strange.

This second stanza may be the best in all of *Requiem*. Those last two lines pronounce the greatest truth. Akhmatova is describing the state of the poet who is looking at everything that is happening to her as if she were standing off to one side. For the poet, the writing of this is no less an event than the event she is describing. Hence her reproaches to herself, especially when it's a matter of the imprisonment of a son, or whatever the misfortune might be. You start cursing yourself horribly: what kind of monster are you if you can be seeing this whole horror and nightmare as if it had nothing to do with you?

Arrest, death (in *Requiem* people are constantly on the brink of death)—these kinds of situations really exclude any possibility of an adequate reaction. When someone is weeping, that is the weeper's private affair. When someone writing weeps, when he is suffering, he actually gains something from the fact that he's suffering. The writer can suffer his grief in a genuine way, but the description of this grief is not genuine tears or gray hair. It is only an approximation of a genuine reaction, and the awareness of this detachment creates a truly insane situation. *Requiem* is constantly balancing on the brink of insanity, which is introduced not by the catastrophe itself, not by the loss of a son, but by this moral schizophrenia, this splitting—not of consciousness but of conscience. The splitting into sufferer and writer.

Akhmatova's *Requiem* unfolds like a true drama, like a true chorus of voices. We're constantly hearing different voices—first a simple woman, then suddenly a poet, then before us is Mary. This is all done as it should be, in accordance with the laws of the requiem genre, but in fact Akhmatova was not trying to create a folk tragedy. *Requiem* is after all the poet's autobiography. The rationality of the creative process assumes a certain rationality of emotion, a hardened heart. That is what drives the author mad.

Volkov. In this sense, though, isn't *Requiem* really mirroring a real situation? As I understand it, Akhmatova did feel a certain indifference toward her son's fate, didn't she?

Brodsky. No, there was never any real indifference on her part. Indifference—if the word is applicable here at all—came with her art. Akhmatova was tormented and suffered incredibly over her son's fate, but when the poet Anna Akhmatova started writing . . . When you write and try to do it as well as you can . . . That is when you submit to the demands of the muse, the language, the demands of literature. It is a greater truth than the truth of experience. You are striving to create a tragic effect in one fashion or another, with one line or another, and inadvertently you sin against the ordinary truth, against your own pain.

Volkov. Lev Gumilyov, Akhmatova's son, reproached her several times for not doing enough for him—either in childhood or in his prison camp years. I was talking with an old Latvian painter who was in a camp with Lev Gumilyov. When I mentioned Akhmatova, his face turned to stone, and he said, "She sent the very smallest packages." It was like hearing the reproachful voice of Lev Gumilyov himself.

Brodsky. Lev did blame her, and he said something to her that tormented Akhmatova greatly. I think it may have been the cause of her heart attack, one of the causes in any event. This isn't an exact quotation, but the sense of Gumilyov's words was this: "For you it would have been even better if I'd died in the camp." He meant "for you as a poet."

Even if an old friend had said it, my first thought would have been, "What a pig you are really." But this was her son saying it! Lev Gumilyov spent eighteen years locked up, and those years apparently maimed him. He decided that because he had endured so much, he could do anything, that from then on everything would be forgiven.

In the case of Lev Gumilyov, all kinds of psychological elements are layered in here as well. Above all, in the absence of his father, he was the man of the family, and although she was both a mother and a poet and Akhmatova, nonetheless, she was a woman. Therefore he thought he could tell her anything he felt like. All of this is the poor man's Freud, of course, but that's apparently how he manifested his masculinity. I gave this quite a lot of thought at one time—and Akhmatova would be the first to condemn me for getting mixed up in this—but her son did not end up occupying the high ground here. With this sentence about its being "better for her," he showed that he had let the camps cripple him, that ultimately the system had got what it was after.

Volkov. I think that attempts to set *Requiem* to music are going to continue.

Brodsky. Music, I fear, can lend this text only the aspect of melodrama. *Requiem*'s drama is not in the horrible events it describes but in what these events transform your individual consciousness into, your notion of yourself. The tragedy of *Requiem* is not the perishing of millions but the impossibility of the survivor coming to terms with this perishing. We're used to the idea that art somehow reacts to events in real life, but reaction is out of the question—not just to Hiroshima but to more minor occurrences as well. Occasionally you can create some kind of an artistic formulation that expresses your state of shock in the face of the horrors of reality, but this is a fortunate coincidence—in particular for the author's reputation. Take *Guernica.*

Volkov. In 1910, in Paris, the young Anna Akhmatova met Amedeo Modigliani. She was just starting out as a poet, and he was already a mature artist. From Akhmatova's memoirs about their romance, however, it's obvious that she understood the significance of what Modigliani was doing only with hindsight.

Brodsky. That's how it should be in love. It's much better, much more natural than the reverse. Akhmatova's memoirs of Modigliani don't mention art. These are simply the personal relations of two people.

Volkov. There is a drawing of Akhmatova by Modigliani (from 1911, probably). According to her, there were sixteen of these drawings. Akhmatova's memoirs are not entirely clear about the fate of the drawings: "They were destroyed in the Tsarskoye Selo house in the first years of the revolution." Did Akhmatova speak of this in more detail?

Brodsky. She did. Red Guards were quartered in the house, and they smoked up Modigliani's drawings. They made hand-rolled cigarettes out of them.

Volkov. In Akhmatova's description of this episode, you sense a certain evasiveness. Did she understand the value of these drawings? Might she herself have thrown them to the winds?

Brodsky. What would be the point? I'm sure she always had enough paper at home. She was writing poetry after all. Evidently this happened in her absence, though.*

Volkov. Do you think Akhmatova's relationship with Modigliani was important for her?

Brodsky. As a happy memory, no question. After she gave me her notes about Modigliani to read, Akhmatova asked, "Joseph, what do you think of all this?" I said, "Well, it's *Romeo and Juliet* performed by the royalty." Which amused her no end.

Modigliani, by the way, was not the only one courting Akhmatova during her sojourn in Paris. None other than the famous pilot Blériot . . . Do you know that story? I don't remember anymore where the three of them were eating there in Paris: Nikolai Gumilyov, Akhmatova, and Blériot. Akhmatova used to tell the story. "That day I'd bought myself new shoes, and they were a little tight. So I slipped them off under the table. After dinner,

---

*A number of previously unknown drawings by Modigliani, depicting Akhmatova, some of them in the nude, turned up at the 1993 exhibition in Venice, entitled "The Unknown Modigliani: Drawings from the Collection of Paul Alexandre"—S.V.

Gumilyov and I went home. I took off my shoes—and found a note with Blériot's address in one shoe."

Volkov. Which means he kept his head!

Brodsky. A Frenchman, a pilot!

Volkov. Don't you think foreign men occupied a rather large place in Akhmatova's life: Modigliani, Jozef Czapski, Isaiah Berlin? For a Russian poet, that is rather unusual.

Brodsky. What foreigners! Sir Isaiah Berlin was born in Riga (which, by the way, has given the world many remarkable people). Czapski was a Pole, a Slav. What kind of foreigner was he to a Russian poet! Anyway, her relationship with Czapski could only be surreptitious. After all, as far as I know, he was engaged in counterespionage for General Anders. What could they talk about at all, especially in those sultry times! In Tashkent, I think, they had a horde dogging their every step. Most of Akhmatova's conversations with Sir Isaiah, as I understand it, came down to who, what, where, and how. She was attempting—twenty years after the fact—to find out about Boris Anrep, Arthur Lourié, Sudeikina, and other friends of her youth. All those who had wound up in the West. He was the first person to come from there in nearly twenty years—and six of those twenty had been taken up by the Second World War.

Volkov. Sir Isaiah published his reminiscences of his meetings with Akhmatova between 1943 and 1946, and these encounters turn up in many of Akhmatova's poems. If you compare the two versions, you get the impression that they are talking about two different events. In Akhmatova's treatment, their meeting was one of the causes of the Cold War. And on a purely emotional plane, judge for yourself: "He shall not be a husband dear to me,/ But the two of us will make the Twentieth Century blush." You won't find anything like that in Sir Isaiah.

Brodsky. I don't think Akhmatova was that far off the mark in her assessment of the consequences of her meeting with Sir Isaiah in 1945. In any case, she came closer than many think. As for Berlin's memoirs, they are extremely eloquent, but you can't write in English splashing your emotions out all over the table. Although, of course, you're right that he did not lend such global significance to his meeting with Akhmatova.

Volkov. In his memoirs, Berlin insists that he was never a spy, as Stalin accused him, but his reports from the British Embassy in Moscow—and previously from the British Embassy in Washington—correspond full well to Soviet notions of espionage activity.

Brodsky. Soviet, but not Akhmatova's. As a diplomat in the service of the British empire, Berlin was dealing with people whose official activities were not subject to caprice, whereas the conduct of Stalin was sometimes dictated by totally extraneous considerations.

Volkov. That outburst of rage with which Stalin greeted the news of Akhmatova's meeting with Berlin now seems totally irrational. According to Akhmatova, he cursed her in the foulest language possible. The impression you get is that she had struck a very personal chord in him. It makes it seem like Stalin was jealous over Akhmatova!

Brodsky. Why not? But not so much of Berlin as Randolph Churchill, I think, Winston's son and a journalist who accompanied Berlin on that trip. It's very possible that Stalin felt that Randolph ought to meet with him and only him, that he, Stalin, was Russia's main show.

Volkov. This whole story reminds me very much of the novels of Dumas *père* in which empires crack over an incautious glance cast by a queen. Or a dropped glove.

Brodsky. Quite true, and that's just as it should be. After all, what was Russia in 1945? A classical empire; and really, the "poet and tsar" situation is an imperial situation.

Volkov. Akhmatova described the chain of events as follows. She had a meeting with Berlin, which lasted until morning, much to Stalin's fury. Stalin took his revenge against her with a special resolution of the Communist Party Central Committee, which, Akhmatova firmly believed, was written by Stalin himself (as Lydia Chukovskaya comments, "There's a most august mustache poking out from behind every paragraph"). This resolution, when it was published in 1946, shocked Western intellectuals, who prior to this had gazed quite equably upon the Soviet Union. The atmosphere was spoiled—and for a long time to come. The Cold War had begun. Do you agree with this interpretation of events?

Brodsky. It's very close. Of course, I don't think the Cold War broke out only over Akhmatova's meeting with Berlin, but that the persecution of Akhmatova and Zoshchenko poisoned the atmosphere, of that I have no doubts whatsoever.

Volkov. Do you like Akhmatova's cycle, "Sweetbriar in Blossom," dedicated to Berlin?

Brodsky. Those are great poems. They have that in them, too, *Romeo and Juliet* as played by royalty. Although, of course, it's much more *Dido and Aeneas* than it is *Romeo and Juliet*. This cycle has no equal in Russian poetry for its tragic quality. Maybe Tyutchev's "Denisieva" cycle. But in "Sweet Briar" you're hearing something new in all its monstrosity: the voice of history.

Volkov. There is a curious story about how Akhmatova learned of the 1946 resolution against her and Zoshchenko. That day she hadn't read the papers, but she met Zoshchenko on the street and he asked her, "What are we going to do now, Anna Andreyevna?" Akhmatova, not understanding what Zoshchenko meant specifically but assuming he was posing a metaphysical question, replied, "Endure." At which they parted. It's a small town, Petersburg.

Brodsky. She was very fond of Zoshchenko. She told quite a few stories about him. In his final years he couldn't eat; he was afraid they were going to poison him. Akhmatova felt Zoshchenko was losing his mind. She explained Zoshchenko's death as the result of his own heedlessness. A meeting had been arranged for them both with a group of English students who had come to Leningrad. One of the students asked an extremely awkward question about how Akhmatova and Zoshchenko felt about the 1946 resolution. Akhmatova rose and replied curtly that she agreed with the resolution, but Zoshchenko started explaining: "At first I didn't understand the resolution, then I agreed with it in some parts and in some not." As a result, Akhmatova was given the chance to exist by her literary labors—through translations and so forth, whereas Zoshchenko had everything taken away from him, once and for all.

Volkov. Akhmatova liked to repeat that she was prepared for the 1946 resolution if only because it was not the first Party resolution to affect her: the first was in 1935. She also used to say that Stalin had taken offense at her poem "Slander" without noticing the date—1921. He took it as a personal affront.

Brodsky. I think that Mandelstam also disappointed him seriously with his ode. Say what you like, but I repeat and insist that his poem about Stalin is brilliant. This ode to Stalin may be the most stunning poem Mandelstam ever wrote. I think that Stalin suddenly understood what it was all about. Stalin realized that Mandelstam wasn't his namesake but he, Stalin, was Mandelstam's [in Russian, Osip=Iosif=Joseph].

Volkov. He realized who was whose contemporary.

Brodsky. Yes, I think it was this that suddenly hit Stalin—and served as the reason for Mandelstam's death. Evidently Stalin felt that someone had come too close to him.

Volkov. Is Akhmatova's quatrain "No more shall I cry for my own" dedicated to you?

Brodsky. I don't know. People say it is, but I never asked.

Volkov. The epigraph to Akhmatova's poem "The Last Rose" is your line addressed to Akhmatova: "You will write about us on a slant." Do you remember the story of the appearance of "The Last Rose"?

Brodsky. Akhmatova was very fond of roses. Every time I came to see her, I would buy flowers—almost always roses.

Volkov. How did you find out that Akhmatova had chosen your line for an epigraph?

Brodsky. I don't remember.

Volkov. You don't remember?!

Brodsky. Good Lord, I don't remember! In that sense I really am to a serious extent not a professional. Well, of course, when you find out about something like that it's very nice. But that's all. That line—"You will write about us on a slant"—is taken from a poem I wrote for Akhmatova on her birthday. (There were two poems, both really rather hopeless, in my opinion. At least today.) The only thing I remember about this poem is that I wrapped it up rather hastily. Nayman and I, we were on our way from Leningrad to see Akhmatova in Komarovo, and we had to race to the station to make our train. I remember the rush. I don't understand why things like that get remembered.

Volkov. What did Akhmatova say when she read your poem?

Brodsky. I don't remember. I think she liked that phrase. The beginning of the poem is feeble—well, maybe not feeble but there's too much unnecessary expressionism there. But the ending is good. More or less genuine metaphysics.

Volkov. Akhmatova told me that for the first journal publication of "The Last Rose" she was asked whether Ivan Bunin was the author of the epigraph, inasmuch as it was signed with the initials "I.B." [I.B. were Brodsky's Russian initials as well: Iosif Brodsky]. Akhmatova wouldn't say, but by 1965, when this poem appeared in her collection *The Flight of Time*, the conjectures about Bunin's authorship were moot. The epigraph was gone.

Brodsky. Oh well, no hard feelings, as they say.

Volkov. Did you and Akhmatova discuss Nikolai Gumilyov's execution?

Brodsky. No, we never talked about it especially.

Volkov. What about Gumilyov in general?

Brodsky. We talked about him as a poet. I remember our last conversation about Gumilyov had to do with the fact that someone had brought Akhmatova poems supposedly written by him in his cell. We tried to guess whether the poems were genuine or not.

Volkov. Akhmatova said that the material against Gumilyov was fabricated, that he had never participated in any anti-Bolshevik plot. She counted Gumilyov one of the greatest Russian poets of the twentieth century. Do you agree with her?

Brodsky. I don't like Gumilyov and never did. When Akhmatova and I discussed him, I wouldn't express my honest opinion—exclusively so as not to disappoint her. Her sentiment with regard to Gumilyov could be defined by one word: love. I didn't try to hide the fact that from my point of view Gumilyov's poetry was no big deal, though I remember a rather long conversation with Akhmatova about Gumilyov's microcosm, which at the moment of his arrest and execution was beginning to stabilize and become his own mythology. It's perfectly obvious that if anyone was killed at the wrong time it was Gumilyov. I said something to that effect to Akhmatova.

After Akhmatova's death, I read the four volumes Gumilyov put out in the United States, but my opinion did not change. I remember, during that period I stopped in to see Zhirmunsky. I told him, "Here, Viktor Maximovich, I was given some books you might find interesting: the author's complete collected works." I didn't name the author and went on. "I don't find him very interesting, but they may be of some use to you in some academic research. So I would be perfectly happy to give you these books." Zhirmunsky said, "Who is it?" I replied, "You know, I feel awkward, but it's four volumes of Gumilyov." To which Zhirmunsky replied, "Hello! I said back in 1914 that Gumilyov was a mediocre poet!"

Volkov. When people talk about Gumilyov, they sometimes forget that he was among the very few Russian poets whose destiny was decided directly by Lenin.

Brodsky. You know, regardless of how a usurper deals with a poet—nobly or ignobly—it doesn't change my attitude toward him in the least. A person who ruined so many lives . . . What can you say? Even if he had saved Gumilyov from execution . . .

Volkov. . . . or let the ailing Blok go to Finland, as Gorky asked him to.

Brodsky. That still wouldn't have changed anything. There is no saving grace for that gentleman, unfortunately.

Volkov. Gumilyov had been involved in the so-called Petrograd Military Organization affair. The investigation was handled by Yakov Agranov, later a close friend of Mayakovsky and the Briks. Lili Brik recalled that after Mayakovsky's death, Akhmatova would come to the Briks for dinner. I remember how surprised I was to hear that, because Akhmatova always spoke rather brusquely about the Briks. She used to say that in the late 1920s, when art in Russia was "abolished," as she put it, the authorities left only the Briks' salon, "where they had billiards, cards, and secret policemen."

Brodsky. That sounds right. Akhmatova was profoundly negative about the Briks. There was definite unanimity between us on that score. But Akhmatova was always saying that it often makes sense to deal with obvious scoundrels, professional informers in particular, especially if you need to convey something "on high," to the authorities, because a professional informer will repeat everything he's been told precisely. He won't distort anything. You can't count on that in the case of someone who is simply fearful or neurasthenic.

Volkov. Did you and Akhmatova discuss Boris Pilnyak, to whom her poem "All this you alone divine" is dedicated?

Brodsky. We had a rather brief conversation in connection with my meeting someone in Moscow who turned out to be Pilnyak's son: a handsome, oriental-looking man. I remember I was somewhat peeved by the fact that Akhmatova harbored such great sympathy for Pilnyak. In those days I was a spiteful boy, you know. We were all asserting our tastes then at the expense of our predecessors. In the West I reread Pilnyak and found no grounds for altering my opinion of him. The only author about whom my opinion changed for the better here is Zamyatin. His shorter pieces, not *We.*

Volkov. Zamyatin was also a brilliant essayist.

Brodsky. Yes, I came to appreciate that here, too.

Volkov. Why did Akhmatova respond so devastatingly to Zabolotsky's later poetry?

Brodsky. That's not true. Akhmatova used to say, "Zabolotsky doesn't like me, nonetheless . . ." And so on.

Volkov. Akhmatova suspected that Zabolotsky was an inveterate misogynist, and as became clear, she was right. According to memoirs, Zabolotsky expressed himself in this vein: "Art has no room for broads."

Brodsky. All those quotes aren't worth squat. When someone hasn't been allowed to express himself fully during his lifetime, we, his descendants, inevitably seize upon snatches that don't amount to anything. Zabolotsky might say one thing today and tomorrow, another. Fate stuck Zabolotsky into a certain image, a certain frame, but he was bigger than that frame.

Volkov. What was the relationship between Akhmatova and Pasternak?

Brodsky. Extremely close, extremely friendly. By the way, Pasternak twice proposed marriage to Akhmatova.

Volkov. And what did Akhmatova have to say about that?

Brodsky. Well, first of all, that this was an offer made while his wife was still living. Moreover . . . Pasternak was shorter than Akhmatova. And younger. So that nothing ever came of that song and dance. I don't think Akhmatova ever took the emotional aspect of her relationship with Pasternak seriously. She knew, of course, that Pasternak's wife, Zinaida, hated her with a vengeance. Akhmatova was very fond of Pasternak, although, as I've already said, she was extremely prejudiced against his desire to nab the Nobel. Nor did she approve of his relationship with Olga Ivinskaya. I dare say you've read Ivinskaya's memoirs.

Volkov. In her notes, Chukovskaya tells a noteworthy story. Akhmatova met with Pasternak in 1956. He had just written fifteen new poems for a collection that was being prepared for publication at Goslit. He explained to Akhmatova regarding the collection: "I told Goslit that I needed parallel money." To which Akhmatova replied, "What happiness for Russian culture, Boris Leonidovich, that you need parallel money!" As you understand, he was speaking about money for Ivinskaya.

Brodsky. I must say that they were all fatally unlucky in their personal lives. Akhmatova was unlucky with husbands—fatally. Tsvetaeva was unlucky—fatally. Pasternak with his wives and lovers—incredibly so. The only person who was lucky with his wife was Mandelstam, but with the other women in his life he was once again fatally unlucky.

Volkov. In her memoirs, Nadezhda Mandelstam writes about the "fantastic inheritance" left by Akhmatova and about the strife around that inheritance. Her son Lev Gumilyov laid claims to it and so did the Punin family, with whom she had lived.

Brodsky. Well, I don't know what in Nadezhda Mandelstam's lights was a "fantastic inheritance." A few things remained, pictures. There simply were no possessions as such. Akhmatova was not one of those people who has possessions. The main thing that remained was her literary archive, which the Punins sold, earning huge sums in the process.

Volkov. Do you believe that the truth was on Lev Gumilyov's side in the fight over the Akhmatova archive?

Brodsky. Of course. The Punins are one of the foulest phenomena I've ever had occasion to observe.

Volkov. Why did Akhmatova wind up so closely linked with them?

Brodsky. She lived with them when Punin himself was still alive. Later, when Punin was arrested and perished, Akhmatova felt that if it wasn't her fault, then she had at least brought this disaster down on him: "This disaster I brought down on dear ones,/ And they have perished, one by one." Akhmatova felt obligated to look after Punin's daughter Irina, and, as a consequence, Punin's granddaughter, Anya, who, strangely enough, looked a little like Akhmatova in profile—the old Akhmatova, not the young one.

All those years, Lev Gumilyov was in camps. When he was released, they expected him to be rehabilitated quickly and then he and Akhmatova could be together. In the meantime, though, she was still living with the Punins. Irina Punina had an interest in this, inasmuch as she existed to a significant extent off Akhmatova's earnings.

I understand why Akhmatova did this. She was basing herself on ordinary practical considerations. After rehabilitation, they might give Gumilyov a big apartment, but in absence of rehabilitation—what could the two of them together count on? And Irina Punina egged her on: "Stop it, Akuma, wait until they rehabilitate Lev." (She called her Akuma. It seems Punin brought this word back from Japan; it means "witch.") In general, Akhmatova listened to Irina. She told her son that for now it was better they not move in together. Better they should wait until they were given separate housing. At this, Lev Gumilyov was beside himself and he flew into a rage. In my opinion, he's a remarkable person, but with this major fault, which I've already mentioned. He feels that after prison camp he can do almost anything. In the last years before Akhmatova's death, they didn't see each other. The Punins, who trembled for their prosperity, made systematic attempts to sow strife between them. They were extremely successful.

Akhmatova took the fallout between herself and her son very hard. When she was lying in the hospital after her third heart attack, Gumilyov went to see her in Moscow. But the Punins sent Anya to see him, and she conveyed what were purportedly Akhmatova's words (which in fact had never been uttered), words to the effect that "now that I'm in the hospital with my third heart attack, he comes crawling to me on his belly." After which Lev never went to see Akhmatova in the hospital.

When Akhmatova got out of the hospital, she moved in with the Ardovs, lived there two weeks or so, I think, went to Domodedovo, and died there. Nayman, who was with her at the time, conveyed to me her final words: "Really, I feel very bad." She said this when they had started injecting her with camphor. It's a sin to say it, but I have a bad heart and I recognize those words. Those are the words that come out when your heart is failing.

Volkov. What was the fate of the Akhmatova archive?

Brodsky. The entire archive fell into the Punins' clutches. Moreover, I'm partially to blame for that, I and Nadezhda Mandelstam. After Akhmatova's funeral, we returned to Leningrad. I remember a conversation in

Akhmatova's apartment on Lenin Street. I said to Nadezhda Yakovlevna, "Do you remember what happened to Pasternak's archive when he died? And with Sologub's archive?"

Volkov. What did happen with those archives?

Brodsky. They were immediately seized by the authorities, and no one ever saw them again. Nadezhda Yakovlevna replied, "I understand you, Joseph. I'll get it." After which she went into the room where the council of war was being held, at which, besides her, were the Punins, Koma Ivanov, and Arseny Tarkovsky. I don't remember who else. And right then and there the Punins realized that Akhmatova's archive had to be taken in hand immediately, before it was too late. The Punins sold this archive in three places: in Moscow to the Central State Literary Archives and in Leningrad to the Pushkin House and the Public Library, getting fancy prices for them. Naturally, the archive should not have been broken up into three parts, but they did this.

As you know, he sued the Punins but eventually lost, although the sale of the archive by the Punins was, in my opinion, illegal. They could not have done this without the support of the state, given a living heir. Legally, they could not have circumvented Lev Gumilyov. Those who acquired the archive ought to have asked certain questions. Evidently this sale was sanctioned from on high. The Punins did not have any peculiar motivations in this instance. The only thing that interested them was the money. That's what had always interested them. The Punins were paid not so much for the archive itself, I think, as for the temporary restrictions on its use. Now the archive is sealed for seventy-five years, I believe. The authorities knew that Lev Gumilyov would not impose a prohibition on the use of the archive. He himself would have been interested in sorting through it. The Punins couldn't have cared less, though, and for this they were rewarded in commensurate fashion.

Volkov. As had happened with Pasternak, Akhmatova's funeral too turned into a political event.

Brodsky. The Punins took no interest in Akhmatova's funeral. They handed me her death certificate and said, "Joseph, find a cemetery." In the end, I did find a plot—in Komarovo. I must say I had my fill in connection with this. The Leningrad authorities protested, offering a plot in one of the municipal cemeteries, and the authorities in the resort district, under whose jurisdiction Komarovo falls, were also decisively opposed. No one wanted to give their permission, and everyone dug in their heels. Endless negotiations began. Zoya Tomashevskaya helped me enormously. She knew people who could be helpful in this matter—architects and so forth.

Akhmatova's body was already in the Cathedral of St. Nicholas. They had already started the funeral while I was waiting at the Komarovo cemetery, not knowing whether they would bury her there or not. I find it hard even to think about this.

As soon as we heard that permission had been granted and the gravediggers had been given their bottle apiece, we jumped into the car and raced to Leningrad. We caught the tail end of the service. There were police cordons all around, and in the cathedral Lev Gumilyov rushed about pulling the film out of the cameras of people taking pictures. Later Akhmatova was taken to the Writers Union for a civil funeral, and from there to Komarovo. I have heard talk about how Komarovo is Finnish land, not Russian, but in the first place, I don't think Russia is ever going to give Komarovo back to Finland, and secondly, Akhmatova *walked* on this very ground. The funeral—and all the events that followed—were in every respect a gloomy story. It's a sin to dispute God's will, but I don't think that's what led to Akhmatova's death; it was simply an oversight.

Volkov. On whose part?

Brodsky. On the part of the people who knew and loved her. In Moscow, after the hospital, she was moved into a cramped room. It was stuffy and right next to the kitchen. Then, the sudden transfer to Domodedovo. And imagine, after her third heart attack, spring collapses on you.

To put it bluntly, Akhmatova was homeless and—I'll use her own expression—shepherdless. Her close friends called her the "hobo queen" and truly, especially when she rose to meet you in the middle of someone's apartment, there was something of the vagabond, a sovereign without shelter, in her face. She changed her place of residence about four times a year: Moscow, Leningrad, Komarovo, back to Leningrad, back to Moscow, and so on. The vacuum created by her nonexistent family was filled by friends and acquaintances, who worried about her and took care of her as best they could. She was extremely undemanding, and more than once when I visited her, especially at the Punins', I found her hungry, although she was constantly paying them back for everything.

This existence was not comfortable. Nonetheless, it was happy in the sense that everyone loved her so much and she loved so many people. In some spontaneous way a field always rose up around her to which crud had no access. Belonging to this field, to this circle, determined for many years afterward the character, conduct, and attitude toward life of many—almost everyone—who inhabited it. Each one of us bears, as a light tanning of the soul, the extraordinary generosity that came from her, this heart, mind, and moral force.

We did not go to her for praise, or literary recognition, or any kind of approval for our work. Not all of us, anyway. We went to see her because she set our souls in motion, because in her presence you seemed to move on from the emotional and spiritual—oh, I don't know what you call it—level you were on. You rejected the language you spoke every day for the language she used. Of course, we discussed literature, and we gossiped, and we ran out for vodka, listened to Mozart, and mocked the government. Looking back, though, what I hear and see is not this; in my consciousness surfaces one line from that same "Sweetbriar in Blossom": "You do not know you've been forgiven." This line tears itself away from rather than bursting out of the context because it is uttered by the voice of the soul, for the forgiver is always greater than the offense and whoever inflicts it. This line, seemingly addressed to one person, is in fact addressed to the entire world. It is the soul's response to existence.

It is this, and not the ways of verse-making, that we learned from her. "Joseph, you and I know all the rhymes in the Russian language," she used to say. On the other hand, verse-making is also a breaking away from context. Those of us who knew her, I think, were tremendously lucky—more so, I think, than if we had known Pasternak, say. No matter what, she taught us how to forgive. Actually, I probably ought to be careful with my pronoun, "we." Although I remember that when Arseny Tarkovsky began his graveside speech with the words "With Akhmatova's departure, an end has come . . ." everything inside me resisted: nothing was over, nothing could or can be over as long as we exist. Whether we're the "magic choir" or not. Not because we remember her poems or write our own but because she became a part of us, a part of our souls, if you like. I would also add that, without believing overmuch in the existence of the other world and eternal life, nonetheless, I often find myself gripped by the feeling that she is observing us from somewhere outside, watching over us from somewhere, just as she did in life. Not so much watching as safeguarding.

Fall 1981–Winter 1986

BRODSKY AT HIS DESK, NEW YORK, 1978

11

REREADING
AKHMATOVA'S LETTERS

Volkov. I wanted to talk with you about the three letters that Akhmatova sent to you in exile and that were published not long ago.

Brodsky. I haven't reread them.

Volkov. The first of them is dated October 24, 1964.

Brodsky. Good God!

Volkov. In it Akhmatova says that she is having nonstop conversations with you, day and night, which are supposed to tell you everything that has and hasn't happened. What is this? A reference to her famous ability to conduct conversations "over the barriers," so to speak?

Brodsky. To some extent. This isn't even a reference but a statement of a fact we all knew.

Volkov. Akhmatova spoke of this in her memoirs of Modigliani: "What amazed him most of all in me was my ability to guess people's thoughts, to see other people's dreams and other trifles to which those who knew me had long since grown accustomed." In her letter to you she almost makes you her medium. You "are supposed to know" what she is thinking about you. Is this correct?

Brodsky. Yes, more or less.

Volkov. Akhmatova believed that for poets, reading other people's thoughts and other psychological "tricks" are a commonplace, right?

Brodsky. Yes. After all, we poets know everything about everything.

Volkov. In her letter to you, Akhmatova quotes from her so-called little epic, "By Way of All the Earth," two short lines: "And here fame's/ lofty threshold . . ." And she adds that this has already "happened." Is she talking about your trial, your celebrity in the West?

Brodsky. Yes, that was one topic in our conversations. At the time, Akhmatova was planning a trip to Italy, where she was supposed to be awarded a literary prize. Then there was supposed to be a trip to England, to Oxford. Akhmatova took these trips very seriously. Or else this quotation may be connected with the fact that we—how can I put it?—we had become famous, right? That is, it had already "happened." It had come about, taken on reality. It's basically these two different things that Akhmatova probably had in mind.

Volkov. When Akhmatova discussed the trial against you with the people close to her, she liked to repeat that the authorities were "creating our redhead's biography" single-handedly. She took the view that persecutions create fame for a poet.

Brodsky. Yes, yes! She also liked to quote two lines: "Going to sleep, pray that you/ Do not awaken suddenly famous." I don't know whether those are her lines or someone else's.

Volkov. In the same letter, Akhmatova cited her line to you: "It's dawning—it is the Last Judgment." She goes on to write about your inherent "divine fusion with nature." What is this, consolation over your exile? Or something more philosophical? I remember in the late 1950s she wrote in her diary that nature had long reminded her of nothing but death.

Brodsky. No, in this case I don't think the allusions go that far. Nor do I think Akhmatova here is shutting herself up inside her own verse. It seems to me her words about the Last Judgment are a commentary on reality. That, unfortunately, is reality.

Volkov. In the next message to you, dated February 15, 1965, Akhmatova reports that she has sent you candles from Syracuse.

Brodsky. Yes, I remember! These were two candles, which either arrived all by themselves by mail or else someone brought them—I don't remember anymore. From Syracuse. Remarkably beautiful—you know, the way they make them in the West: translucent candles. Archimedean.

Volkov. In it she writes that she recalls "our last autumn with music, the well, and your cycle of poems."

Brodsky. Dear God, I don't remember which poem cycle she's talking about. The well is probably the well at Komarovo, where I drew water for her, and the music, that's the records I brought to her in Komarovo. There were lots of them—Haydn, Handel, Vivaldi, Bach, Mozart, Pergolesi's *Stabat Mater,* and especially her two favorite operas, Monteverdi's *The Coronation of Poppea* and Purcell's *Dido and Aeneas.* By the way, I wasn't exactly bothered but I was somewhat embarrassed at the part in Nayman's memoirs about Akhmatova where he describes her musical enthusiasms in the 1960s. It turns out that he, Nayman, did have something to do with this, but he obviously got confused because as far as I remember I was the one who brought Akhmatova all those records.

Volkov. In two of the three letters to you, Akhmatova quotes your aphorism, "The main thing is the grandeur of the design." This statement became quite popular, by the way, in Russian artistic circles. People cite it apropos and not, and sometimes in an ironic sense. Do you remember in what connection this came up?

Brodsky. This I do remember quite well. Akhmatova and I were sitting together once and she said, "Joseph, what's a person to do (she meant, of course, a poet, but we almost never used the word *poet* because Akhmatova did not approve of that. She would say, "I don't understand these big words, *poet, billiards*)—so, what's someone to do if he knows himself by heart, all his favorite devices and so forth? What's the solution to this situation? And off the cuff, I replied, "Anna Andreyevna, the main thing is the grandeur of the design!" At the time, I recall, I thought that if you faced a great task, it spurred you on to new technical devices. Akhmatova liked this notion a lot because she was probably thinking about herself when she asked this question about creative inertia. She was thinking about her work on *Poem Without a Hero.* My answer was very much to the point for her. Well, and later in conversations with her I developed this thought. I told her that even if the great design fails as a result, the game was still worth the candle. And there I think I'm right.

Volkov. In one of her letters to you, Akhmatova praises your poems on the death of T. S. Eliot. She says the thought that these poems exist make her happy. The letter was written in February 1965, and you composed this poem in January. I see that your poems reached Leningrad rather quickly from exile.

Brodsky. Yes, my friends saw to that.

Volkov. In another letter Akhmatova informs you that she and Nayman are finishing up her translation of poems by Giacomo Leopardi. Nayman once gave me this volume of translations, which came out in 1967. In it, some of the poems are marked as having been translated by Akhmatova and some appear over Nayman's signature. In his book about Akhmatova, however, Nayman insists that the distribution of these translations under one name or the other was quite arbitrary, inasmuch as they were done jointly. Moreover, Nayman writes that as far as Akhmatova's translations went, you couldn't be certain of her authorship at all in any given instance because Akhmatova often got help from various literary colleagues. He says that it would be better all around not to include her translations in her collected works. What do you think?

Brodsky. I think this is a complicated question. Starting with the fact that when there is collaboration and you are doing this four-handed, then you really can't remember who did what anymore. As for the translations from Leopardi, I think that Nayman probably was much more enthusiastic about this project than Akhmatova. Just think, outside, God help us, it was 1965! Apart from everything else, this was a way for Nayman to participate directly in culture. That is, it must have been more interesting for him than for Akhmatova to translate Leopardi, so he may well have done more in this collection. However, he may also be exaggerating a little. Ultimately, though, it doesn't matter exactly who translated this poem or that. The main thing is that Akhmatova took this work seriously, and that seriousness must be respected.

Volkov. You did quite a lot of translating yourself as a young man: poems by Poles—Gałczyński, Norwid, Miłosz—and Italians—Umberto Saba, Salvatore Quasimodo. You translated John Donne. You even translated Tom Stoppard's play *Rosencrantz and Guildenstern Are Dead.*

Brodsky. A fine play! And the translation's not so bad either, I don't think.

Volkov. In a letter to you, Akhmatova praises your drawings, even compares them with Picasso's famous illustrations for Ovid's *Metamorphoses.* Has it ever occurred to you to collect your drawings and publish them?

Brodsky. Except that the drawings aren't in my possession. If we're talking about portraits, for example, I don't even remember whom I drew or when. The only person who I know tried to collect my drawings was Era Korobova, Nayman's ex-wife. She even published an article about the drawings in *Russkaya Mysl.* By the way, I recently saw reproduced somewhere my portrait of Sergei Dovlatov. I really like that drawing! I think it's a terrific likeness!

Volkov. You probably saw it on the cover of Dovlatov's book that was published in Moscow. By the way, Dovlatov liked to tell a story about that portrait. He showed it to an American acquaintance, who pointed out that the nose wasn't drawn quite right. To which Dovlatov replied, "That means I'll have to have plastic surgery on my nose." I've also seen your portrait of Loseff, which is also a wonderful likeness. It's reproduced in his book of poetry.

Brodsky. A new career!

Volkov. Let's get back to our conversation about Akhmatova's letters to you. In one of them, she quotes the following quatrain:

Your maddened eyes
And speech ice cold
And confession of love
Before our first hello.

Why did this quatrain appear in the letter to you?

Brodsky. Nothing comes to mind. Maybe it has to do with her relationship with Isaiah Berlin, but he certainly does not have maddened eyes. Which of her friends had maddened eyes? Maybe Nedobrovo? I think the maddened eyes belonged in part to Gumilyov and in part to Punin. And also probably to Shileiko.

Volkov. But it was Vladimir Garshin who really had thoroughly maddened eyes, isn't that right? That man was off his rocker!

Brodsky. There, you see? Even better. More significant here, though, is something else. I don't know anymore why Akhmatova cited this quatrain specifically in a letter to me, but what I personally see in all these encounters that did and didn't take place are her passing rhymes, rather like in Pushkin. So I don't really distinguish one from the other.

Volkov. Well, Akhmatova seems to have squeezed everything out of her encounters. Even her non-encounters by some miracle became important episodes in her biography. Her abortive romance with Blok was discussed by the entire Russian reading public. What about speculation that reached me in Leningrad about a romantic relationship between Akhmatova and Nayman?

Brodsky. I've heard this many many times. Despite all the scabrousness, shall we say, of my imagination, nonetheless I believe that this is absolute bullshit.

Volkov. Nayman writes that Akhmatova "always seemed to be finding" poems. He cites as an example the same quatrain that Akhmatova quoted in her letter to you. In your letter, Akhmatova explains that she had forgotten and lost this bit of poetry and now it has suddenly "surfaced" among her papers.

Brodsky. This was a matter of the chaos in her papers. She was always tucking things away. In Komarovo, I remember, she would sit at her desk—she had a kind of tall desk that was chest height or maybe a little lower. This desk had a shelf below where she kept all kinds of folders and papers and so forth. Akhmatova was in the habit of rifling blindly through this shelf, and from time to time she'd pull out a piece of paper on which there might well turn out to be some forgotten poem. She also had notebooks in which she wrote down all kinds of bits and pieces: poems, prose, drafts of letters, various excerpts, addresses . . . It's quite possible that in leafing through such a notebook she might come across some verse from a relatively distant period. Then she would say the poem had "surfaced."

Volkov. Akhmatova also played more complicated games with these surfaced poems of hers. In the 1950s and 1960s, she wrote down poems in her notebooks and put the dates 1909 and 1910 under them—and that's how she published them, as her early poems. By the way, in the twentieth century, when firsts in the realm of artistic devices became important in art, many people pulled such tricks. Malevich, for example, when he arrived in Berlin in the late 1920s, drew an entire cycle of pictures and gave them pre-revolutionary dates.

Brodsky. That could very well be! First of all, there could be ordinary coquetry behind that or some rivalry with someone, with some idiom or certain thoughts that his or her contemporaries had stated at one time. When Akhmatova did anything like that, I think she actually felt justified in doing so. Maybe she told herself, I thought about all that before X or Y. I discovered it before them. To say nothing of the fact that one poem or another might simply have been finished later. Say, two or three lines existed back then, and these two others were added only now. Why should I use the later date when I could date it much earlier? That's even better, right? There's another circumstance, too. There was a period when Akhmatova wrote rather few poems. Almost nothing. She didn't want people to think that of her. At least, she herself didn't want that to be the case. In general, Akhmatova's dating of her poems is chronological insanity. The young Akhmatova began on an amazingly mature note. Purely stylistically, it is extraordinarily difficult to establish the chronology of her poetry. What you can trace is the sentimental chronology, that is, the dialectic and development of her sentiments. In that respect she did achieve increasing depth, but in many instances things occurred to her from the very outset that in their spirit belong to a much later era. Take anything, say:

What makes our century the worse?
Has it, dazed with grief and fear,
Touched the blackest sore of all,
Yet not had strength enough to heal?

Beneath this poem, of course, is a date—1919. In fact, though, it's impossible to say when it was written. This is a language and style that in general does not undergo significant development. It's for all time.

Volkov. Akhmatova always said that the chronology of her poems was very important, though. I remember her getting angry at foreign editions of her poems in which the dates were omitted under her poems: "They want to pass all this off as recently written."

Brodsky. Of course she was angry! As you rightly noted, though, she was also playing all kinds of additional games. When a young woman researcher would come to see her, for instance, they would start arguing because Akhmatova ascribed a certain poem to an earlier period. In compiling the future academic edition of Akhmatova's poems, a researcher will stumble into additional problems. He or she will have to verify the dates set by the author critically.

Volkov. What about you? Don't you plan to sort out your own early poems someday? And make firm decisions as to which should and shouldn't be published?

Brodsky. You know, I probably ought to do that, but my hands never get around to it. Or rather, my head. Anyway, all those early poems, they're in Paris. I simply don't have them here, in New York.

Volkov. Akhmatova used to say that prose always seemed to her both "a mystery and a temptation." She used to repeat: "From the very beginning I knew all there was to know about poetry, but I've never known anything at all about prose." What do you think of Akhmatova's prose? I would point out, by the way, that in one of her letters to you she gives a magnificent description of her trip to France in 1965, how she saw it out her compartment window.

Brodsky. I adore Akhmatova's prose! She heard it from me, but I've continued to say so all my life: in the twentieth century, the best Russian prose has been written by poets. Well, with the exception of Platonov maybe, but that's an entirely different matter. Despite the fact that Akhmatova wrote very little prose, what there is of it is absolutely terrific: Pushkin studies, memoirs of Modigliani and Mandelstam, memoir notes. Apart from the content, their interest lies in their absolutely remarkable stylistics. For clarity, this is model Russian prose, true clarism. She simply has no extraneous words.

Volkov. But Akhmatova also tortured herself working on her prose. She wrote, "There seemed blasphemy in approaching it, or else it meant a rare emotional balance for me." Akhmatova used to add that she "either feared or hated" prose. I remember, in conversations with her, she was constantly letting slip a strong ambivalence toward her own prose experiments.

Brodsky. Ambivalence in connection with what?

Volkov. I think that Akhmatova was afraid of her own idea: writing a major autobiographical book. She just couldn't grope out the necessary form for this contemplated book. Something similar happened with Yuri Olesha, who long sought a form for his last volume of autobiographical prose. He went through incredible contortions, approaching it first from one angle and then another. After his death they found a great number of fragments. Other people attempted to gather these into a single whole. I also remember, in the mid-1960s, Olesha's book coming out, posthumously, under the title "No Day Without a Line." In his preface to it, Viktor Shklovsky made a stab at declaring this book Olesha's great creative success, but there was no book; it was nothing but a heap of fragments, albeit brilliant, but producing a rather sad impression overall. Don't you think that something similar happened with Akhmatova?

Brodsky. To a certain degree, yes. If you assess the situation post factum. Really, though, fragmentariness is a perfectly natural principle present in the consciousness of any poet. It is the principle of collage, or montage, if you like. An extended form is what a poet, simply by virtue of his temperament, cannot bear. The extended form is the hardest of all for a poet to master. Not because we're short-winded but because the principle of condensation is so crucial in the poetry business. If you start writing this kind of condensed phrase, then no matter what, no matter how you twist and turn, it comes out short.

Volkov. What about Pasternak's *Doctor Zhivago?*

Brodsky. We can only marvel at Pasternak! What an idea for a poet—to write a novel: an introduction, a first part, a second, all those descriptions and tremendous paragraphs. Akhmatova, on the contrary, had absolutely no desire to become a novelist. She was still a poet, and of the old school, moreover. A true poet writes prose out of duty or necessity. The only thing Akhmatova wrote out of her own desire were the Pushkin studies.

Volkov. But after all, all these excerpts and fragments were supposed to make up her memoir book.

Brodsky. You have to bear in mind how dangerous doing this was. Writing memoirs of any sort in the Soviet Union was a perilous activity, and for Akhmatova doubly so. The authorities were very much afraid of what she might remember. And Akhmatova remembered absolutely everything. She not only remembered who, when, and with whom, say, she met, she also remembered days of the week and times of day. I can't tell you how many times I stumbled across this, and it always took me aback. This is not even just a different upbringing but a different biology, which to others might seem like a pathology.

Volkov. Yes, in conversation Akhmatova was always drawing parallels—this happened fifty years ago, twenty years ago, ten. When you talked with her, you yourself got drawn into this game, too—the echoing of events, the endless round dates . . .

Brodsky. This is what no researcher of her work can penetrate because we are people of a different culture. We no longer have this ability to correlate events in time and space. This kind of disposition is possible only given a specific degree—not of tranquillity exactly, but of a different biorhythm. It's not the same glut of events, phenomena, and so forth that has collapsed on us. I think that in prerevolutionary Russia, and even after that whole remarkable revolution, this other rhythm still—at least partly—defined a person's existence. That kind of rhythm is a marker of a different era—the turn of the century.

Volkov. When Akhmatova used to talk about her future memoir, she used to call it the cousin of Pasternak's *Safe Conduct* and Mandelstam's *Noise of Time.* That is, to a certain extent she was thinking in terms of these two books, which were by then classics—if not officially then among the intelligentsia. How would you compare Akhmatova's memoir prose with *Safe Conduct* or *The Noise of Time?*

Brodsky. Both these books—Pasternak's and Mandelstam's—are marvelous. *The Noise of Time* is dearer to me. If you look at them both from a distance, though, then these two books even have something in common in the texture, in how detail is used, how a sentence is constructed. I think that if Akhmatova called her planned book the cousin of those two, then she was in fact pointing to the true state of affairs, to what was going on in her consciousness as an author, because I think she was incapable of writing prose this way. Her prose was nothing like Mandelstam's or Pasternak's, and she recognized that fact. She recognized the advantage of their prose and to a certain extent this perspective must have hypnotized her—that she wouldn't write *like that.*

Volkov. Yes, Akhmatova did write that about her book: "I'm afraid that in comparison with its luxurious cousins, it's going to seem a sloven, a hick, a Cinderella."

Brodsky. This fear of hers was what held her back to a certain degree. It slowed her work. Akhmatova was phenomenal with details, but once again, she was primarily a poet, and in that sense she could have given every detail in one sentence. Whereas Pasternak or Mandelstam, when they came across a detail or a metaphor, they worked it, as a rule. Like a rose. You're always feeling the centrifugal force in their work. Which is present in a poem when it seems to spin itself apart.

Volkov. On the contrary, though, Akhmatova complained that when she wrote she saw much more behind her words than was poured out on the page. She was afraid that the reader wouldn't catch all the smells and sounds she pictured when she recorded her memories.

Brodsky. Quite true. Because Akhmatova's main lingo is aphorism. She is a supremely aphoristic poet. The very length of her poems attests to this. Akhmatova never spills over onto the third page. Her attitude toward history is aphoristic as well. When she addresses modernity, what interests her is not herself so much as the expressiveness of the modern language. People who didn't know her well were used to thinking of Akhmatova as a regal lady who spoke the language of the Smolny Institute for Well-Bred Young Ladies, whereas Akhmatova adored all kinds of vulgar expressions.

Volkov. If you wanted to explain what Akhmatova is in terms of English-language poetic culture, whom would you compare her with?

Brodsky. She has a parallel in American literature—Louise Bogan. The similarity is unusually strong. I thought about the similarity between them for the first time when I saw Bogan's photograph—an incredible resemblance to Akhmatova. But Americans treat their remarkable people with somewhat greater restraint than we do ours.

Volkov. Sometimes it seems to me that we are even more enthusiastic about their poems. I always think of Henry Wadsworth Longfellow's *Song of Hiawatha,* which is very popular in Russia, for which we have to thank its translator, Ivan Bunin. Here people rarely recall Longfellow.

Brodsky. Akhmatova, as we know, liked to say that in Russia, English and American authors were famous whom no one had ever heard of in England or America.

Volkov. Where is the similarity between Akhmatova and Bogan—in their themes or their technique?

Brodsky. Both, and it's unusually strong, too. First of all, both begin their poem from the very beginning. There's no "machinery." Notice, the greatest impression in a poem is usually produced by the last stanza because it's been led up to by the momentum of the entire meter. When you start reading a poem, quite often you don't hear the music, you only hear the preparation for it. It's like in an opera: the singers warm up, the violins saw away, and only then does the curtain go up. In Akhmatova and Bogan the curtain goes up immediately. With regard to their poetic themes, both—if we're talking about this with a certain male bluntness—took their first romantic enthusiasms too seriously. For Akhmatova, this was Gumilyov. For Bogan, over many years there was her romance with the remarkable American poet Theodore Roethke. Bogan's life also turned out quite unhappily—dreadfully, I would say, but at least this was a private drama and not a matter of external circumstances, as in the case of Akhmatova. Neither wrote that much.

Volkov. Is there a parallel in Bogan to Akhmatova's prose, her memoirs, her Pushkin studies?

Brodsky. Bogan doesn't have any literary scholarship, but she did leave a stunning diary. This is terrific prose. In English-language prose of the last few decades, with the exception of Faulkner, it is generally the women who are the most interesting to me. When I read prose, I'm not interested in the plot or the crafting of the story but simply in the literature, the writing. You always have to delineate whom you're dealing with—the author of a novel or a writer. In happy instances they coincide. Too often, though, the novel becomes the writer's goal, whereas the writer's goal should be something else: the expression of a world view by means of language. Not by means of plot. And from this standpoint I'm wild about the fiction of Jean Stafford, Janet Flanner, and Jean Rhys. These are all great authors and as yet completely unknown in Russian.

Volkov. Don't you think that the writing about Akhmatova by her contemporaries is disappointing for the most part? I have in mind the linguistic analysis. The works by Eikhenbaum and Vinogradov, for all their brilliance, are devoted to particular issues. Zhirmunsky's book, published in 1973, which encompasses Akhmatova's entire career, is rather superficial.

Brodsky. That's not quite right as far as Zhirmunsky goes. I value his 1916 article, "Overcoming Symbolism," very highly. Akhmatova liked that article too, by the way. It contains one extremely important idea. Zhirmunsky talks about Gumilyov, Mandelstam, and Akhmatova, and he comes to the conclusion that Gumilyov and Mandelstam really did remain symbolists. In the final analysis, Mandelstam is a hypersymbolist. From Zhirmunsky's point of view, it was Akhmatova who was the only genuine acmeist, and I think that is a fair thesis.

Volkov. Akhmatova insisted on including herself in the acmeist school—moreover, to her final days. She quite grieved when people who read her *Poem Without a Hero* didn't understand something in it. She said, "I'm an acmeist. Everything of mine should be understandable." On the other hand, she got angry when they tried to "brick her up" in the 1910s, as she put it. Akhmatova felt there was some special conspiracy on this score. She especially suspected foreigners and Russian émigrés of this. That was why she so attacked a few émigrés in particular.

Brodsky. I know what you mean, but Akhmatova treated the most outstanding Russian émigrés with extreme respect. Stravinsky, for example, she adored. I remember several conversations with Akhmatova about Nabokov, whom she valued very highly as a prose writer.

Volkov. I don't think I've missed anything of what you have published here in the West about Russian poets, and I'll say frankly that at first it seemed to me you were almost consciously distancing yourself from Akhmatova.

Brodsky. Nothing of the kind! It's simply that Akhmatova was very widely known here, whereas Tsvetaeva was almost completely unknown. I was trying to draw attention to her. Mandelstam is also less known here than Akhmatova. Now the situation with Mandelstam is changing.

Volkov. Thanks mainly to Nadezhda Mandelstam's two volumes of memoirs. As far as I can tell, here, in the West, the popularity of his widow's prose far exceeds anything Mandelstam wrote.

Brodsky. No, this is going on completely independently of Nadezhda Mandelstam's memoirs. Mandelstam has been translated into English quite uselessly, right? Nevertheless, his use of images grips poets here very powerfully.

Volkov. Akhmatova loses much more in translation than Mandelstam. Her love poems rendered into English look quite sentimental. Which there's not a hint of in the original. Now that the authorities in Russia no longer regulate contact between the reader and literature, Akhmatova is emerging in third place for popularity—behind Pushkin and Blok.

Brodsky. When you cite Pushkin and Blok, I must say I'm not so sure when it comes to Blok. I really don't have all that clear a picture of contemporary Russian reality on this level. It does seem to me, though, that the reader had this kind of free access to literature in Russia a long, long time ago, before 1917.

Volkov. Akhmatova miraculously combines the uncombinable, which defines her continuing popularity. On the one hand, her love lyrics have retained all their freshness, and young men today can declaim these poems to their girlfriends when they want to seduce them. On the other hand, it's not at all embarrassing to recite these poems out loud, to declaim them to even the strictest connoisseurs of poetry. Whereas Blok or, say, Esenin, who traditionally has been extremely popular in Russia, contains a strong element of kitsch. Sometimes you start reading their poems aloud and you think, "Oh, Lord!"

Brodsky. What's interesting with respect to Akhmatova is just how vital her work has proved to be, or rather, how enduring and applicable to the times specifically because she is a poet of minor forms. You could say that the essence of *belles lettres* is the short poem. Modern man has an extremely short attention span, as they say. And to a certain degree poetry counts on precisely this. That is, not that it's counting on it, but poetry knows precisely that this is so.

Volkov. On the other hand, epic poetry does exist, and even if we talk only about contemporary figures, say, you and Derek Walcott, aren't you trying quite consciously to stretch the reader's attention span?

Brodsky. Well, maybe in the final analysis we're making a major mistake. Although I don't think so, naturally. What survives is the art of minor forms, the art of condensation. I say all this also because in the last few days I've looked through twenty or thirty issues of a newspaper called *The Humanitarian Fund*, which is published in Moscow. The authors are these quasipunks, young people from twenty-five to thirty-five years old. This is today's Russian avant-garde. When you read this newspaper, you see what has young people excited right now in literature, painting, and music. Well, as far as music goes, it's true, it makes no sense talking about it here, because it's rock. As for poetry, though, the picture here is quite remarkable because there's not one word in it about Akhmatova or Pasternak or Blok. Moreover, the poems come in from all over the country, so that it's a representative cross-section.

Volkov. Whose poems are an example for them—Boris Grebenshchikov's?

Brodsky. Yes, Grebenshchikov's, but even Grebenshchikov is fading from the scene, from their point of view. This newspaper is interested exclusively in what they care about or, at worst, what is modern, and they print a lot of nonsense, but sometimes you read some absolutely remarkable poems. All this is fairly interesting with respect to the question of what survives in culture and what dies out.

Volkov. Did you and Akhmatova ever discuss Freud?

Brodsky. Yes, several times. I even remember a quotation: "Freud is the number one enemy of creativity." Akhmatova used to say, "Of course, creation is sublimation. But I hope you understand, Joseph, that it is not only sublimation. For there is as well the influence and intervention of powers that are if not seraphic then at least purely linguistic." Akhmatova and I agreed on that point. I don't even know which is really the sublimation of which. Is creation the sublimation of the sexual principle or vice versa? Is sexual activity the sublimation of the creative, constructive element in man?

Volkov. Being an enemy of Freudianism, Akhmatova nonetheless subscribed to modernist culture. She read Joyce, Kafka, Valéry, Proust, and Eliot closely. These figures were dear to her.

Brodsky. Unquestionably! From my point of view, Akhmatova was a true modernist. By modernism I mean a unique sensation that had not registered in Russian literature before that time. Hers was the tragic world view, but much more restrained and focused than among the majority of Russian modernists. That is, when you're completely torn up and you still obey specific aesthetic requirements, which impose certain bonds on you. When the poet cannot allow himself to rant and rave, regardless of what is happening to him. But this is restraint, not deficiency, as people sometimes think. Akhmatova is much more restrained, in my view, than Mandelstam. She has the same thing that is present in Cavafy: a mask.

Volkov. Here's something else interesting about Akhmatova. In her early years, she created love poems that young Russian lovers will be reading to each other a hundred years from now. That alone would be sufficient to go down in the history of Russian culture, but Akhmatova made an unbelievable leap. In connection with the First World War and the revolution, she composed a series of stunning civic poems, compositions that you might say predicted and described all the horrors of the twentieth century. She was the first Russian poet to be frightened by the twentieth century, if you don't count Blok's "Voice from the Chorus," which seems to me the strongest of his prophetic compositions. The poems Akhmatova wrote in

1914 are amazing for their absolutely unexpected breakthrough to affairs of state. When a poet becomes the voice for an entire nation.

Brodsky. That's absolutely correct! Remember we were talking about this poem of hers, "What makes our century the worse?" This is one of her most stunning compositions. It says everything about the twentieth century.

Volkov. Akhmatova was one of the first to understand what a nightmare totalitarianism could turn into, what horrors a totalitarian state could doom the individual to. In this sense, she became the first Soviet poet in a way, even before Soviet power.

Brodsky. I understand what you mean, but this terminology—"Soviet/non-Soviet"—if I were you, I wouldn't use it.

Volkov. This isn't a qualitative definition after all. I'm using Soviet to designate a certain historical period of the Russian state.

Brodsky. Oh ho! I know what I'm about to hear! A few years will pass and this so-called Soviet period is going to be looked on in academic circles in precisely this way—as high classicism, right? Isn't that what I hear you saying?

Volkov. Fine. Let's formulate the question in a different way. Does there or does there not exist a Leningrad period in Petersburg literature? And is Akhmatova a participant and part of this period?

Brodsky. Well, I probably have to answer this question in the affirmative.

Volkov. In the history of twentieth-century Russian poetry, there is an unofficial Big Four: Mandelstam, Tsvetaeva, Pasternak, and Akhmatova. Take Tsvetaeva. Of this foursome, she seems the most powerful to me in her poetic gift.

Brodsky. Unquestionably!

Volkov. Pasternak, at least the young Pasternak, has the most highly strung and unique voice, unlike anything else. Mandelstam is the strongest technician of the foursome, right?

Brodsky. Yes.

Volkov. Akhmatova doesn't have as strong a gift as Tsvetaeva, or as unique a voice as Pasternak, and her poems are not always as powerfully sculpted as Mandelstam's, but in the long run, I think her work has proven to be the most vibrant and the freshest of the entire foursome.

Brodsky. You know, Solomon, I have a different theory about this. It's a bizarre and perhaps fantastic idea, and if it seems stark raving to you, then just toss it out. The fact of the matter is that everything that happens in culture ultimately comes down to this, to the four famous temperaments: melancholic, sanguine, phlegmatic, and choleric. That's what I think. It seems to me that our Big Four can also be divided up according to these temperaments, inasmuch as all of them are actually very distinctly represented in the group: Tsvetaeva is unquestionably the choleric author. Pasternak is sanguine. Mandelstam is melancholic. And Akhmatova is phlegmatic. Together they cover the whole poetic universe.

Fall 1991

BRODSKY, NEW YORK, 1990

12

ST. PETERSBURG:
MEMORIES OF THE FUTURE

Volkov. Let's talk about Gennady Smakov. You and he were friendly for so many years, both in Peter in your youth and here, in New York. Smakov's fate resembles yours in some ways: living in Leningrad got too dicey for him as well, and he made his way to New York, with a lag of just a few years behind you. You got to America in 1972 and Smakov in 1975. He was a member of the intellectual élite in Leningrad, but when he moved to the West he didn't get lost in the shuffle. He put out several books on ballet, including a biography of his friend Mikhail Baryshnikov, wrote reviews, and translated. And suddenly, a tragic end. In 1988, Smakov died of AIDS. He was forty-eight years old. To begin, I'd like to ask you when and how you met Smakov. And how did this acquaintance develop?

Brodsky. I think Smakov and I met when I was about eighteen. I had come to the School of Philology of Leningrad University, where there were some girls I knew, to read my poems. I might never have remembered this event, but Smakov subsequently recounted it to me several times. He said that my reading made a very strong impression on him. Evidently he was more receptive then and I was more energetic. That is, both of us were sufficiently young. After all, Smakov and I are practically the same age; he was all of three months older than I. So there was a mutual biological understanding between us. I had and have lots of all kinds of acquaintances, but they are either older than I or—alas!—younger, and that's not quite right. But Smakov is someone who truly was—well, I don't want to say my alter ego, but in a certain sense I had more reason to trust him than anyone else, and not only because he was one of the most highly educated people of his day. Which in and of itself created a tremendous—if not respect, then at least, tremendous grounds for trust. This was not only because he had read and knew everything but because he and I really were cast in the same mold.

Volkov. Did you and Smakov see each other often in Leningrad?

Brodsky. Often, more often than here. We had lots of friends in common, including foreigners, because Smakov hung around with them a lot. We had simultaneously read many books. This is so important, that the books we read came into our life more or less simultaneously. When I found I needed some book that I'd heard of vaguely, that something interesting had come out in the West but I couldn't find it in the Leningrad bookstore, then I always knew where to go.

Volkov. To Smakov?

Brodsky. Well, of course! Moreover, we more or less simultaneously became involved in translation. Very often we were translating the same authors or found ourselves competing for the same translation. With the one difference that Smakov really knew the languages he was translating from and I didn't.

Volkov. Did you consult with Smakov on your translation work?

Brodsky. Yes, if there was something I didn't understand in a text, I called him and asked; him more than anyone else. I knew him about as well as my own subconscious. And vice versa, right? That's how he and I got along.

Volkov. Did you and he talk about theoretical problems of translation?

Brodsky. No, there was no discussion on the theoretical level, but we were constantly discussing the effectiveness of what we were doing: what worked, what didn't, and why. You have to understand, though, that translating was far from our most important point of contact, although we earned our livings that way—both he and I. Actually, Smakov also had other sources of income, but he and I talked about everything under the sun, including movies, theater, and so forth. He and I chased girls together—at that time, at any rate. Very often the objects of our pursuit even coincided.

Volkov. You worked with Smakov on the translations of the poetry of Constantine Cavafy. How did that come about?

Brodsky. The fact is that we started translating Cavafy back in Russia. Moreover, we began more or less simultaneously, but each of us spontaneously, independently of each other. Although I do remember in this previous—Peter—incarnation of mine I showed Smakov two or three of my translations of Cavafy. Now, in hindsight, I realize that these translations were beyond the pale. Subsequently, here in the United States, I wrote an essay on Cavafy, and Smakov continued to translate him all those years, but three or four years before his death he sat down to it in earnest. Indeed, he translated all of Cavafy—everything that was in the two-volume Greek edition of Cavafy, with the exception of two or three poems, and during those last few years he would show me these translations, and I would correct them immediately, on the spot. During these meetings, by the way, Smakov would sit right there where you're sitting now.

We kept putting off a true collaboration on these translations for the future. But the future is by definition something that is constantly receding. You have to earn your living, you have to survive. In this regard Smakov had lots of other urgent plans. He spent a great deal of time in close contact with the Libermans—Alex and especially his wife Tatiana, quite a remarkable woman, as you know. He became like a member of the family. So we abandoned our joint work on Cavafy somehow, but when he got sick, I said, "Give me these Cavafy translations of yours. Let's see what we can do with them." I decided to do this not so much to entertain Smakov as to distract him a little. As a result, twenty poems were edited. What Smakov undertook to do with Cavafy is a huge job. It's incredible that one person did all that, and did it in a situation when he had no prospect whatsoever of seeing it in print. It's a crazy story.

Volkov. What do you think of the volume of Cavafy translations by Russian poets that came out in Moscow?

Brodsky. An extremely mediocre edition, even though I'd prefer not to say anything bad about the people who took part in the enterprise. The Cavafy volume was edited by a very professional woman, Sofia Ilyinskaya, who was the first to present this poet to the Russian-speaking public. Both the editing and the introductory essay are quite good, and in it there are several excellent translations, but there are also many horrendous careless errors. Many poets evidently feel that translations permit what they would never allow in their own verse.

Volkov. So you still feel that Cavafy should be presented to the Russian audience in Smakov's translations?

Brodsky. Without a doubt. Above all, because Smakov knew modern Greek, and in the edition you mentioned, only the editor knew the language. But I don't think even her translations in this volume are completely satisfactory. That is, she knows what she's dealing with but she can't reproduce it. This does require poetic intuition, or at least a certain technical knack, and even though highly professional people were brought in to do the translations in this volume of Cavafy, it was the technical aspect of the matter that came out so dismally with them, and that is inadmissible.

Volkov. This is what interests me in connection with Smakov. He used to go around Leningrad like some kind of peacock, his tail spread, this was his own expression. His knowledge of foreign languages, his emphatically sophisticated manners, all this made an exotic figure of him. In addition, he was a well-known homosexual and balletomane. He was perceived as a pure Petersburger, in the tradition of Mikhail Kuzmin. Americans call someone like that a quintessential Petersburger. But in New York, the sculptor Ernst Neizvestny told me that Smakov came from the Urals, that all his stories about the governesses who supposedly taught him foreign languages when he was a child were pure fantasy . . . and so forth. How can someone make himself over into that kind of "quintessential Petersburger"?

Brodsky. You see, basically I believe that a person can become a genuine snob only if he does come from the provinces. When I talk about snobbery, I don't mean it in the negative sense. On the contrary. Snobbery is a form of despair. I don't remember anymore who said that, it might even have been me. Someone from the provinces simply by definition has a stronger appetite for culture than someone who grew up inside this culture, this milieu. If you look at Smakov not as a specific person but as a kind of symbol, he went through all the stages of cultural development. He was born in the provinces and at first looked on culture from a great distance. Gradually he approached it by taking enormous leaps, until he landed in Italy. When you take the next step, the next jump, that is, when you transpose yourself to the United States, a paradoxical situation arises. In a way you have dug a tunnel through culture—you know, like a mole—and come out at the other end. Then you're looking at culture from the other side, that is, from the other province. I don't know whether I can explain all this to you coherently. Let's take a similar example. One of the most, I would even say perversely, refined beings in English literature was D. H. Lawrence, who came from a miner's family, from somewhere in the north of England. And look what he made of himself.

Volkov. You know, I used to discuss this topic with Andrei Bitov, and he thinks that in Petersburg everything educates the person—the boulevards, the buildings, even the stone. And the water, too. That is, you get a literary education just walking around the city. When you're in contact with the Petersburg stones you immediately find yourself in a certain literary context, and in this way you become a Petersburger, even if you came from somewhere else.

Brodsky. We all projected ourselves onto the old Petersburg. Every period, every culture, has its own version of the past. There is an eighteenth-century German ancient Greece. There's an English ancient Greece. There's a French ancient Greece. Worst of all, there's a Greek ancient Greece, and so forth. Inside each of these major strata, though, there is also a breakdown by generation, and for every successive generation the view of the past culture changes and, naturally, becomes more and more diffuse. What is interesting for me in all this is what specifically each generation chooses to place under the magnifying or diminishing glass. That is, what it picks out in the culture of the past and what it ignores. And it is just this mechanism of cultural survival through a given generation that interests me: what specifically endures, and what perishes.

Volkov. You believe that it is we who animate the stones, and not vice versa.

Brodsky. Whether it's the stones or not, explain it however you like, but in Petersburg there is this enigma, and it truly does influence your soul, shapes it. A person who grew up there or at least spent his youth there, it's hard to mix him up with other people, or so it seems to me. That is, for starters, it's hard to confuse us, say, with Muscovites, if only because we speak Russian differently.

Volkov. If I'm not mistaken, Blok was the first great Russian poet to be born in Petersburg. For us, Pushkin is so closely linked to Petersburg that we forget he was born in Moscow. Dostoevsky was born in Moscow, too. They went to Petersburg to study. Or take another example, from the Soviet era. For me, the poets of the Oberiu group were true Petersburgers, and indeed, Kharms and Vvedensky were born in Petersburg, but Zabolotsky, for example, was born outside Kazan and grew up in Vyatka and Urzhum. Oleinikov is really a Cossack from somewhere in the Kuban. But the poems they both wrote were thoroughly Petersburgian.

Brodsky. I don't get that feeling from that group. Even Zabolotsky, of whom I'm very fond, even though he did write some great poetry about the Obvodny Canal and about that famous beer pub, the Red Bavaria. This is a completely different route, not Petersburgian. Let's not talk now about all of Petersburg culture because it's limitless, although one could sit down, of course, and list who does and doesn't belong to it. If we're talking only about *belles lettres* in Petersburg, then there is a precise tone characteristic of it. I think it was Mandelstam who talked about Pushkin's "Hellenistic paleness," right? There is this concept, the genius or spirit of a place, the *genius loci*. The reason we talk about the genius of a place is that the place itself is different, it's changed. Nonetheless, if we talk about the *genius loci* of Petersburg, then it does indeed inform the city's literature with a certain "paleness of face."

Volkov. I understand "paleness" not in the sense of the color of its face but as understatement. Mandelstam, as I recall, used to talk about the "pale young shoots of our life."

Brodsky. The Petersburg face, on the metaphorical level, seems untanned and, if I can put it this way, starved for culture and light.

Volkov. As in Slutsky's poem: "They fed him. But they fed him badly." Also written about a poet.

Brodsky. The point is that Petersburg *belles lettres* bear the patina of an awareness that all this is written from the edge of the world. From somewhere on the water. And I'm not talking about some fusion with the environment, with the elements. This is not something biological. But if we can talk about a certain pathos, or tonality, or tuning fork of Petersburg *belles lettres,* then it is the tuning fork of being pushed to the side. Even if you are a Blok and are planning or starting to talk about the fate of the entire country and the future of the nation. Even Blok, even he had a sense of this restraint, which is taken in a certain sense from the dampness, what we could call the "Petersburg rot." This may be the only air worthy of landing in human lungs.

Volkov. It's odd when a novel that is typically Muscovite in its setting and devices, Andrei Bely's *Petersburg,* comes to be considered the model Petersburg composition, whereas the texts of the Oberiu group are pushed outside the Petersburg tradition. Akhmatova used to say that there was nothing Petersburgian about Bely's novel. Whereas she held the prose of Kharms and the compositions of Zoshchenko in extremely high regard.

Brodsky. Just a second! Zoshchenko is a terrific writer, no doubt about it. As for Kharms, I remember Akhmatova's words about how he could describe a man walking outside, walking, walking, and then suddenly flying off, and she added: "Only with Kharms could that ever work. Never with anyone else." If you consider that the task of prose is to describe just such extraordinary situations, then Kharms, too, can be considered a great author. At the same time, though, this is not Petersburg prose, and the poetry of the Oberiu group is not Petersburg poetry. At least, I cannot connect their compositions to the idea of Petersburg, even though all these people were writing in that city in the 1920s and 1930s. But I'll say one terrible thing about Bely right off the bat: he's a bad writer.

Volkov. Most importantly, he's a typical Muscovite! As for the Oberiuts, how do you explain the coincidence of the heyday of this group of surrealists and dadaists in Leningrad, which at that time may have been the most surreal city on earth?

Brodsky. Forgive me, but in this same city at this same time there was also Konstantin Vaginov, an utterly phenomenal author and a true Petersburger, in my opinion. Or, to a somewhat lesser extent, Leonid Dobychin.

Volkov. I share your enthusiasm for Vaginov, but he leaned toward the Oberiuts, and some scholars even include him in it. Whereas Dobychin always stood apart. In Leningrad, people compared him to Joyce and Proust, although he wrote microscopic stories. You can find common features in all of Leningrad prose of the 1920s and 1930s: in Kharms, Vaginov, Dobychin, Alexander Grin, and Zoshchenko, whom all of us adore, thank God.

Brodsky. Well, Zoshchenko is notable above all as a kind of *vox populi* in literature. Something of that sort.

Volkov. But his later prose, those whetted novellas, isn't that typically Petersburgian literature? Don't they have that paleness you were talking about?

Brodsky. Wait a minute, do you mean *Before Sunrise?* I never noticed any whettedness in that book of Zoshchenko's. I think a homebred Freudianism overshadows everything there.

Volkov. But what naked, simple words!

Brodsky. Unfortunately, they are overshadowed.

Volkov. So what about Vaginov's homebred Bakhtinianism? After all, Vaginov belonged to Bakhtin's circle in Petersburg. Don't Vaginov's philosophical digressions annoy you?

Brodsky. I adore that gentleman.

Volkov. I sense the fabric of Vaginov's novels and poems as typically Petersburgian.

Brodsky. It's the fabric that we need to be talking about here, because the fabric of Vaginov's works is this kind of disintegrating curtain, right? What attracts me especially in Vaginov's texts is the sensation of a sort of untensed muscle—not a flabby muscle even, but a relaxed one. You feel this constantly in his structures and intonation both.

Volkov. Where would you include Vladislav Khodasevich—in Moscow's literary school or Petersburg's?

Brodsky. Personally, I include Khodasevich with Petersburg, although his works contain many other tendencies as well. His intonation, though, especially his blank verse—for me this is definitely Petersburg. I recall very distinctly the first time I encountered Khodasevich's verse. I read his collection *By Way of a Grain of Corn* when I was probably twenty-one or twenty-two—in that same Leningrad University library where I also sought out Mandelstam's *Stone*. Mandelstam goes without saying, but strangely I also remember many of Khodasevich's poems by heart.

Volkov. What about Nabokov?

Brodsky. I read his *Laughter in the Dark* when I was twenty-two or twenty-three, I think. It was the first Nabokov work I'd ever come across. Within a few years I had read everything by Nabokov you could get a hold of in the Soviet Union at that time. All the same, Nabokov was an émigré, like Khodasevich. Matters were always a little more complicated with émigré literature in the Soviet Union.

Volkov. Did you read Nabokov's *Other Shores* in Leningrad as well?

Brodsky. *Other Shores*, oddly, I read only in the West in its English-language version, *Speak, Memory*, and this book didn't produce the same impression on me as it did on most readers.

Volkov. Didn't reading Nabokov make you at all nostalgic?

Brodsky. Definitely not. To me, Nabokov, strangely enough, is mainly a writer not from Petersburg but from somewhere else. I see him more as a kind of Moscow–Berlin writer. I think Nabokov's appetite for reality scares me off to a certain extent. The gentleman is very firmly tied to the material world, and it is in this sense that he is too "modern" for me.

Volkov. Remember, you were once telling me that you perceive all of Nabokov's life and work as a kind of gigantic rhyme. That is, his two "Lolitas," the Russian and the English, rhyme, the two versions of his book of memoirs, and even more broadly, his Russian and English-language novels, and even the fact that Nabokov wrote both prose and poetry. You explained this by saying that all his life Nabokov really wanted to be a poet, although his poems, as we know, do not stack up well against his prose. So here he was rhyming his whole existence. Hence, the literary figure of the double that Nabokov loved so well.

Brodsky. Yes, the principle of rhyme permeates Nabokov's entire work. Here, contradicting myself, I might say that in this it's not hard to catch the

Petersburg influence, since it is in his native city that the idea of reflection was always extremely strong, and naturally enough.

Volkov. Remember Dostoevsky! No wonder there was the concept of a "Petersburg Hoffmaniada." A "Moscow Hoffmaniada" would be unimaginable. For me the following picture is emerging. Stravinsky, Nabokov, and Balanchine—and not only they, but mainly these three—carried on the legend of Petersburg in the West at a time when this legend was being driven underground in the Soviet Union. This image of Petersburg, preserved in the West through Western radio, books smuggled into the Soviet Union, as well as the tours of Stravinsky and Balanchine's dance troupe, was transferred to Russia and helped the Petersburg legend survive in Russia before it was ultimately restored.

Brodsky. Something of this kind did occur, although it seems to me the restoration you're talking about began somewhat before the Stravinsky and Balanchine tours. True, here I can speak only of myself. Between the ages of twenty and thirty I read quite a few works by future émigrés—Khodasevich again, and Georgy Adamovich, and Georgy Ivanov—published either before the revolution or during the first postrevolutionary years. You must remember the remarkable secondhand bookstores we had in Leningrad.

Volkov. What do you mean! For three rubles you could buy Khodasevich and Kuzmin and—

Brodsky. Yes, whatever you wanted! And of course, Russian-language Western radio played a huge role—all of a sudden you hear, I don't know, Vladimir Weidle or someone, in all his eloquence, informing you about the "Silver Age." I wonder when you talk about Balanchine or Stravinsky, because for me Balanchine is a purely visual phenomenon, first of all (maybe because for me ballet was never a very great reality), and secondly, to a certain extent foreign, not of Petersburg. The same goes for Stravinsky. I don't associate his music in my consciousness with my native city. True, I don't associate Shostakovich with my native city either. "Petersburg" means a clarity of thought and a feeling of responsibility for the content and a nobility of form. There you go. No, let me try this again. . . . Since "nobility of form" doesn't sound very convincing, somehow. If I try more precisely, then it's a sobriety of form. A sobriety of consciousness and a sobriety of form, if you like. Not a desire for freedom for the sake of freedom but an idea evoked by the spirit and architecture of the place, an idea of order, no matter how compromised. It is a desire for genre order, in contrast to the erasing of genre boundaries, the erasing of form. It is what the Greeks used to call the *kosmos,* that is, order. After all, when the Greeks spoke of the *kosmos,* they had in mind not so much the cosmos of heavenly bodies as the cosmos of military formations and the cosmos of thought. Here Petersburgian culture closes ranks with Hellenism, according to Mandelstam. This is the idea that order is more important than chaos, no matter how congenial the latter is to our sense of the world. The aesthetic equivalent of stoicism—that's what Petersburg and its culture is.

Volkov. What would you say about the imperial idea in Petersburg culture?

Brodsky. What imperial idea?

Volkov. After all, Petersburg was conceived of from the very beginning as the imperial capital. Hence the legends about how Peter the Great himself dug the first ditch on the site of the city's foundation and how an eagle soared above him while he was doing it.

Brodsky. What? Eagles there, in that locale? It was probably ravens soaring over Peter's head.

Volkov. Remember that old Russian idea of Moscow being the Third Rome? Constantinople was considered the Second Rome, and Peter the Great projected this idea of the Third Rome on the Petersburg he founded.

Brodsky. Peter? The idea of the Third Rome? On Petersburg? What's wrong with you? Whatever Peter had in mind, it wasn't that!

Volkov. There was a reason why Peter transformed himself from a Russian tsar into a Russian emperor—in which, by the way, the Old Believers saw yet another proof that Peter was the Antichrist, since they understood Rome as the reign of the Antichrist. The seal of Petersburg, specialists believe, contains transformed motifs from the seal of the city of Rome. You can tick off a number of these symbolic details and cues.

Brodsky. What do I personally find appealing in Peter the Great? What makes him great, or, if you wish, horrible? The fact that he actually did move the empire's capital to the edge of the world. What rational grounds he had for doing that, I don't know, but he utterly rejected that biological Muscovite notion. That is, this was someone who rightfully felt himself a sovereign! There were two directions in Peter the Great's mind, north and west. No others. The east didn't interest him. Even the south didn't interest him particularly. This was a man who spent a good half of his life in contact—either traveling or warring—with the west and north. It was in these directions that he moved, and he was moving toward an absolute. He was first and foremost a sovereign, that is, a political being. Not some heir to the Roman idea, no matter what the form. The idea of a Third Rome in Russia is an Orthodox idea primarily, and I think that Orthodoxy held little interest for Peter the Great. I think his mind was utterly free of it. At least, that's how I see Peter the Great.

Volkov. In the light of all that's just been said, how do you feel about the restoration to the city of its historical name of St. Petersburg? What were your emotions when you learned of this?

Brodsky. I was extremely happy. Extremely! I say this in all earnest and without a single hesitation or reservation, even though the situation today is paradoxical: there is a city of St. Petersburg in the Leningrad Region. Or I get a letter from there with the return address of Kosygin Street, St. Petersburg. This can all drive you slightly nuts, but in this case we need to think not so much about ourselves as about those who are going to be living in this city, who have yet to be born in it. Better they live in a city that bears the name of a saint than a devil.

Volkov. The mystique of a name wields an influence over reality?

Brodsky. Certainly, that's true. For me it's always been important that the people—even during those years when the city was called Leningrad—persisted in calling it Peter.

Volkov. When you and your friends during those youthful years called the city Peter or Petersburg, didn't this help you maintain a certain independent position vis-à-vis the Soviet state?

Brodsky. That was the least of our concerns. We simply liked the word Petersburg more, and I can say that our use of this word was dictated not so much by the struggle against the Soviet state as by the definite charm this name holds. Moreover, the charm is really extrasemantic, purely euphonic. Have you noticed that to the Russian ear, the *g* at the end of Petersburg has a solidity akin to that of a stone? There may even be more solidity to the city's name than to the name and image of Peter himself, don't you think? I can say one thing more. When during the Soviet years we insisted on calling the city Petersburg, we were mainly thinking of a certain cultural succession, if you like. This was a means, if not of establishing it, then at least of hinting at that succession. That was how we felt privately.

Volkov. I have to admit I was amazed at Solzhenitsyn's suggestion that Leningrad be renamed Saint Petrograd. I understand that he wanted to Russify the city's name, but it's strange that he, a writer who ordinarily is so attentive to the sounds of words, didn't sense how cumbersome and awkward his proposed variant was.

Brodsky. Yes, well, I have no wish to speak of this gentleman.

Volkov. The mission for which Petersburg was created (if you agree that there was such a mission)—has it already been accomplished, completed? That is, can this city lay claim to a future comparable to its brilliant past?

Brodsky. I wouldn't be in any hurry to bury the place. I don't even know why. There is the opinion, of course, that a city that has a beginning must have an end as well. And that unlike, say, Rome or Paris, Petersburg, as they say at the racetrack, is a "done" city. That is, those capitals developed naturally and gradually, whereas the building of Petersburg was decided on in advance. This definition of Petersburg as a done city is, I feel, a modern paraphrase of Dostoevsky's words about Petersburg as the most "abstract and premeditated" place in the world. However, I would be warier about taking these kinds of historical leaps, especially when it comes to this city. For the most varied reasons. Naturally, at a certain point it really did skid into provincial status.

Volkov. Well, formally it became a provincial city the moment Lenin moved Russia's capital back to Moscow, in March 1918.

Brodsky. You know, yes and no. I think that even after the capital was moved to Moscow it took the death of a few more generations for this feeling of being the center to really evaporate from Petersburg. Today's Petersburg is not Alexandria naturally, but I think it would take an invasion of new, truly uprooted generations, that is, generations bereft of historical memory, for Petersburg to become wholly provincial, although it's not even a "hero city" anymore, as Leningrad was called after the Second World War.

Volkov. On the other hand, I think it has acquired a new status, as a "martyr city." As a result of the horrible misfortunes that befell Petersburg in the twentieth century, as a result of Russian history.

Brodsky. You know, twentieth-century Russian history seems terribly vague to me at this moment. With regard to Petersburg I can say one thing: we are all becoming victims of demography. The Petersburg population's physiognomy is tending very strongly toward broader cheekbones and shorter height. But inasmuch as the squares, and the boulevards, and the water, and the bridges over it, and the horizon, and the sky remain . . .

Volkov. That is, the stage sets that dictate the actors' behavior and lines . . .

Brodsky. You may be right. It may truly be that the sets determine an actor's repertoire in a way. For us, what is most important is the kind of actor a person is and how he's prepared to appear before this backdrop.

Utter horror sets in because the present era, with its population explosion and tectonic dislocations of nations, is preparing our consciousness for a populist perception of the world: that everyone is alike, everyone is equal. That everything more or less moves at a certain middle level, that there are no heights and therefore those heights don't need to be scaled. For us, for our generation, both the city and its setting were very important, but even more important was what we as actors in this spectacle were reared on. Because we were reared not simply on this set but on what was created on this set when it was still a real perspective in which we saw Akhmatova and Mandelstam, then Blok and Annensky. Even these latter may have been less essential for the consciousness that arose in Petersburg than everything that happened in this city in the first quarter of the nineteenth century, when Pushkin, Krylov, Vyazemsky, and Delvig lived there. When Baratynsky used to visit. And I'm not citing nearly all the important names. It is the contemplation of this Petersburg perspective that gives us definite grounds for some kind of hope. Because you can observe that some kind of creative splash occurs in this city approximately every twenty or thirty years, so there's no guarantee there won't be another splash in the future, too—in altered fashion, naturally. Even if we live to see this splash, though—and I think it's almost certain we won't—then it's altogether likely we won't recognize it. It does have to recur, I think, though, if only because the Petersburg landscape hasn't changed. The ecology hasn't changed either. I would say this, too, that every splash like this has and will have something in common, inasmuch as Petersburg is a city by the sea, so the notion of freedom—perhaps phantasmagorical, but very powerful—inevitably arises in the consciousness of anyone living there. In this city, the individual is always going to strive to reach beyond because the space in front of him is not limited or delimited by land. Hence the dream of unlimited freedom. This is why I think that in this city it is more natural to reject the whole existing world order.

Volkov. You feel that the Petersburg stage set makes you an outsider. This applies to Smakov, a stranger in both Leningrad and New York, whom you deem the quintessential Petersburger. In Leningrad he was a stranger, first of all, as a translator from Western languages, that is, as someone attempting to bring contraband Western values onto Soviet territory. Then he was suspect as a homosexual. And finally, as a balletomane, since the ballet in Russia has always existed more as a commodity for export, whereas inside the country only a very few were enthusiastic about the ballet. Smakov belonged to an isolated and eccentric little group. Did you ever go to the ballet in Leningrad?

Brodsky. You know, I didn't. Odd, isn't it? I know a tremendous number of ballet dancers—ballerinas, male soloists—nonetheless, ballet never particularly interested me. It still doesn't. Although, I must say, when I see Baryshnikov on stage, it's a stunning sensation. I even think that it's not really even ballet, what he is doing.

Volkov. And what is that exactly if not ballet?

Brodsky. In my opinion, it's pure body metaphysics. Something that has burst from the framework of ballet.

Volkov. During your youth in Leningrad, did young poets discuss ballet as something worthy of respect?

Brodsky. In my circle—never. All of us—now how many of us were there? You could count us on your fingers—so, we all had the typical officer's attitude toward the ballet, if I can put it that way. The ballerinas, the flowers . . .

Volkov. What, were you trying to resist the official aura around ballet?

Brodsky. If we're talking about official auras, then that had more to do with what we felt somewhat closer to—cinema. Because the chief source of more or less significant earnings for us was cinema—writing all kinds of texts for documentaries and even features. That's why movie people were more important for us than ballet people. To say nothing of the fact that cinema was simply more interesting for us—as it was for any Russian. After all, for Russians any kind of didactic art is much more interesting than simply pure art. I never took ballet seriously. I once saw *Sleeping Beauty,* and I saw *The Nutcracker*—as a small boy, my mother took me—and of course, an infinite number of *Swans* on television.

Volkov. They also used to play Tchaikovsky on the radio . . .

Brodsky. Yes, he blared from all the loudspeakers right along with the Soviet Army's Red Banner Song and Dance Ensemble and those countless suites performed by orchestras of folk instruments.

Volkov. With that type of attitude toward ballet, how did you ever meet and become friendly with Baryshnikov?

Brodsky. I don't even remember, it happened so long ago. The point was that we had a few rather close friends in common in Leningrad. To say nothing of the fact that we were dating girls who lived in the same building, on the same stairwell. I didn't know this at the time. Misha told me later. It turns out his girlfriend pointed me out to him. Mine didn't know Barysh-

nikov—or me, I don't think. All this was happening in the Mariinsky Theater district. Ultimately, Leningrad is a small town, so virtually everyone
knew everyone else. I don't think Smakov stood out especially in this milieu;
he didn't arouse suspicion. The only cause there could have been for that
was the fact that he was seen with too many foreigners, which could easily
earn you a prison sentence. In every other respect Smakov felt perfectly at
home in Leningrad—to a much greater degree than where he came from,
Sverdlovsk, and much more than in New York. His teachers, friends, and
colleagues lived in Leningrad. He swam in that milieu like an eel in the
Baltic or a smelt in the Gulf of Finland, although he stood out because of his
tremendous knowledge and his attitude toward life. Smakov was a romantic, but at the same time he was a happy hedonist, someone whom nothing
in life could grieve except one simple thing, empty pockets, and the moment he got some money—six hundred rubles in Leningrad, two hundred
dollars in New York—and he could buy whatever it was he wanted, some
expensive trinket, at that moment he was completely happy. He forgot what
happened yesterday and didn't worry about what might happen tomorrow
or the day after. That is, by all standards the man behaved frivolously but by
my standards like a Hellene. At least, that's how I imagine Hellenes. Even
when he was dying and he and I started talking about the gravity of his illness, he said to me, "Joseph, I look on death the way a French aristocrat
looks on the guillotine. It's inevitable, so why discuss it?"

Volkov. You are somewhat idealizing the situation with respect to homosexuals in Leningrad. Of course, officially no such situation existed, exactly the way other complex problems officially did not exist, but the real
status of homosexuals in society—do you remember, Joseph? I'm not even
talking here about masses, but take me, I lived in a boarding school in
Leningrad "for musically gifted children," as it was called, and these sweet
musically gifted children went out regularly in gangs to beat up "homos."
They tracked them down and beat them up savagely. They boasted about
it afterward. And these were the refined natures of future musicians. Many
of them knew that their beloved Tchaikovsky was a "homo." That didn't
stop them. When *glasnost* and *perestroika* were already in full swing in the
Soviet Union, I caught a live broadcast from Moscow in English on my
short-wave radio, a radio bridge: people from the States were asking questions, and Soviet experts in Moscow sitting in the studio were answering
them on the air. The theme was life-styles, and suddenly some gay guy
from San Francisco asks, "What about the gay life-style in the Soviet

Union?" What came over the Soviet experts is beyond description. They all started giggling nervously and tossing the question back and forth like a hot potato. None of them had the nerve to tell the American that in the Soviet Union homosexuality was a criminal offense, even between mutually consenting adults. And that's how the matter stands to this day, if I'm not mistaken. There's the whole Russian gay life-style for you.

Brodsky. That's absolutely correct, but in this sense any life-style in the Soviet Union was a criminal offense. Objectively speaking, if you're interested in literature it's already a deviation from the norm. Everyone who is involved in literature in earnest more or less feels underground to one degree or another. For me this is an obvious fact, but in Russia the situation was even more exacerbated for one simple reason. Literature, and art in general, is ultimately private enterprise, and the Russian—at least at the time when Smakov and I were being brought up and were bringing ourselves up—had only a few forms of private enterprise available to him. For me, this was *belles lettres,* for Smakov, art, adultery, and also going to the movies. (For all the limitations of the movie menu, you could still choose where to go and what to see.)

We felt ourselves to be in a somewhat attenuated relationship with the system and the state—and not even the state and the system so much as the people around us. I'd like to say this, too, to clarify our thoughts about who feels like a stranger and where. The point is this. I remember back in Leningrad, I wrote a poem and went out afterward in the evening to Liteiny Prospect and I felt—and not even simply felt but knew for a fact—that I was among people with whom I had very little in common. Just fifteen minutes before my head had been filled with what for one reason or another had never occurred to them—and obviously wasn't about to any time soon. And meanwhile, these were my fellow countrymen. When you go outside with the same feeling in New York, then here at least you find justification for this, since in this instance the passersby speak a different native language, right? So that the feeling of strangeness here isn't as painful as the feeling of strangeness in your own homeland. Don't forget this when you hear all these endless, bitter-tasting arguments about the dreadful drama of writers in exile, because this is not in fact so. I even think that the audience here, in the West, for writers, musicians, and dancers from Russia or Eastern Europe is a more or less adequate audience, generally speaking, and frequently even exceeds what these people had back home. I often catch myself thinking this.

People could object to our arguments on this issue, saying, yes, you do have an audience in the West, but those people don't understand anything because they aren't speaking the same language as you. My answer to that is this: no one speaks anyone else's language! Even when your wife talks to you, she isn't speaking your language! When you talk to your wife you adapt. You adapt to your friend. In each situation you attempt to create a special jargon. Why do jargons exist? Why are there all kinds of professional terminologies? Because people know that they are all different animals, but they try to shield themselves from this rather terrifying fact by creating a certain common idiom that can be a code language for "your own kind." This is how you arrive at the illusion that you are among your own kind, that in this certain group they understand you. Naturally, when you're talking and you tell a joke and the audience starts smiling and chuckling—demonstrating they "understand" you, then this is obviously pleasant, but basically it's a pleasure one can do without.

Volkov. When Smakov moved from Peter to New York, he lost a lot, naturally, but he gained a lot, too. In particular, in New York, he didn't have to hide his homosexuality. Moreover, this particular gain was twofold. On the one hand, the constant threat of prison or labor camp that had been hanging over Smakov in Leningrad evaporated altogether. On the other, he still felt as if he belonged to a certain order, a brotherhood. It seems to me he took delight in this situation.

Brodsky. Smakov was by no means what you'd call your average flaming queen. Nothing of the sort. He was bisexual. That's for starters. Naturally, here in New York he no longer needed to make every effort to hide the side of his nature that was interested in and aroused by men, but even this statement of mine is to a certain extent an exaggeration. Because the point is not so much the restrictions imposed by the social structure as the self-restrictions imposed by someone from a specific culture. And he and I, our generation, we were all products of a generally puritanical culture, so Smakov was not the kind of person who would shout out his preferences and attachments on every corner. Don't forget, he adored Proust and translated a great deal of him. That is, he was a captive of culture first and last, not a captive of his erotic preferences, and this culture, this literature, reared him in a specific fashion. Ultimately, Proust, when he wrote his novel, well, it was no accident he turned Alfred into Albertine. So, too, when it came to sex, secrecy was more characteristic of Smakov, that is, he was more inclined to veil his amorous escapades with a certain secrecy than to get on his soapbox and proclaim his sexual freedom. He never did become one of those typical local gays for whom the essence of life is asserting their sexual identity.

Volkov. I remember meeting with Smakov before he left Russia for New York. That was in the spring of 1975. He was overjoyed. He told me that in New York he was going to be teaching in a university. Nothing ever came of that, though.

Brodsky. I assumed that as soon as Smakov arrived in the States everything would fall right into place. He would start teaching at some university—Columbia, I hoped—but circumstances here proved unfavorable in the extreme because the key positions in the Slavic departments in several of the leading American educational institutions turned out to be occupied by people who in the past had milked Smakov. When they came to the Soviet Union, Smakov gave them all kinds of materials, which they had gone on to use for their dissertations, never crediting Smakov or his consultations at all. For them, Smakov showing up in New York was worse than the Second Coming. The fact that they behaved like scoundrels goes without saying. For his part, when at the very beginning he was invited to certain Slavic conferences, Smakov aggravated the situation by calling the blathering he heard coming from the dais just that. He pulled that trick a number of times, which did nothing to help him make friends in the Slavic academic world. But none of this wounded Smakov especially, oddly enough. He was a very proud man, so he wouldn't have accepted crumbs in any case. He truly was indifferent to success. That is, naturally he liked it when people treated him well. We all do. But when people treat us badly, it just doesn't throw us off. In this sense, Smakov was a typical representative of our generation. There, in Peter, we all grew up committed individualists—we may even have been more American than many real Americans born in the States, at least on the philosophical and maybe psychological level. Smakov, too, having suffered failure in New York in the academic arena, made several attempts to realize his own individualist aspirations. I remember him getting all fired up over the idea of doing Russian cooking in New York—what they call catering here. He was an absolutely sensational chef.

Volkov. Yes, I'll never forget the Smakov soups and cutlets!

Brodsky. I never knew a cooking wizard like him. With one exception, perhaps: Chester Kallman, the friend of the late Auden. Kallman and Smakov were in many ways congenial beings. Unfortunately, nothing ever came of that idea of Smakov's; his culinary enterprise went bankrupt. Then he started writing articles about the Russian ballet for various magazines. Remember, you once quoted Slutsky: "They fed him. But they fed him badly"? Well, they didn't feed Smakov all that badly in point of fact. That is, he didn't feed himself all that badly. But they did pay him badly, especially in the beginning. I introduced him to Alex Liberman and his wife, Tatiana. Liberman ran American *Vogue,* and Smakov began supplying the magazine with material on a more or less regular basis.

Volkov. As far as I know, Smakov also began to write down Tatiana's memoirs. After all, she had lived a stormy life—in Europe and America. Mayakovsky's great love—what more could you want!

Brodsky. Nothing ever came of that either, unfortunately, for many complicated reasons, but the Libermans became Smakov's new family. In his final years he simply lived at their country house in Connecticut, rarely checking in at his New York apartment. When it came to Smakov, the Libermans were angels. They really are awfully fine people. You come to the West, you argue with people here over some issues, come to blows with someone over principles—but the charm of life is, that as it passes by, what becomes most important are purely human affairs and relationships, not the ideological or philosophical aspects of the matter. Lately I've begun thinking about this specifically in connection with me and the Libermans. I'm happy they took the edge off Smakov's final days. Moreover, they took a most active part in Smakov's book projects, of which he managed to bring three to fruition. The first to come out was Natalia Makarova's autobiography, which Smakov actually wrote, although he was only listed as editor. Then came his biography of Baryshnikov—in my opinion an extremely worthy book whose virtues proved to be part of the reason for its lack of commercial success. There was no gossip in it, no hanging out of the star's dirty laundry and so forth. And finally, this magnificently published volume entitled *The Great Russian Dancers.*

Volkov. The situation that came about with *The Great Russian Dancers* was tragic, as I see it. Not only did it not find a reader, but there were practically no reviews. This, in my opinion, reflected the hostility and disregard for Smakov that had built up at that moment in the ballet world of New York.

Brodsky. Certainly! Since Smakov was a man of absolute opinions, plus he never made any attempt to conceal them. I also feel it's pointless to open your mouth to say what you don't think. That's a total waste of the time and energy given you. People started to fend off Smakov with irony and jokes. His name, as you know, has a comic ring to the American ear. It appeared twice on a list of local critics with the most indigestible names. Which very much poisoned Smakov's life. He even changed the spelling [from *Shmakov*], but that didn't save him. Then he started signing his essays with a pseudonym, which we joked about endlessly. In addition, Smakov's next work about the ballet, a biography of Marius Petipa, the first of its kind as far as I know, was greeted by his publisher without particular enthusiasm. I don't know what the problem was there. At one time I saw several hundred pages of the manuscript, but after all, I don't read these things. I've already told you more than once that ballet doesn't grab me particularly. Smakov cooled somewhat toward writing about the ballet. I think what interested him most in the world in his final years—the years that turned out to be final—was opera, Maria Callas, whom he had started to write a book about.

Volkov. Smakov helped Baryshnikov a great deal.

Brodsky. Yes, he was extremely generous. As you know, Smakov had a phenomenal memory for ballets and stage sets. He knew and remembered many classical ballet productions by heart. He remembered every *mise en scène* in them, every movement. It was amazing. Listening to the conversations between Smakov and Baryshnikov about one classical ballet or another was incredibly interesting. I remember thinking, what strange qualities people can have! Imagine, before this I didn't know that there was such a concept as a musical memory, that musicians remember the order in which music unfolds, beat by beat, the way we remember how a verse unfolds—word by word. And a musical memory is even more detailed and precise. For me this was a great surprise. Wait a minute, Solomon, I'm going to light up.

Volkov. An understandable human weakness.

Brodsky. Yes, an understandable human weakness that leads to an even greater weakness.

Volkov. When Smakov died, I was astonished by one coincidence. This was just a detail, but telling. An obituary appeared in the *New York Times* that stated the cause of his death as a brain aneurysm, whereas Smakov died of AIDS.

Brodsky. I wrote that obituary, actually. Well, they rewrote it, obviously. They even wrote a sentence that didn't belong to me at all—that one, about the brain aneurysm. I could never say such a thing, since the fact that

Smakov died from AIDS was more or less known. We never made a secret of it. I was very much surprised at that kind of censorship on the part of the *New York Times.* Well, when you come right down to it, death is a private affair. It doesn't matter what you die of.

Volkov. At approximately the same time, the Moscow magazine *Ogonyok* ran a long interview with the main sexologist there, Igor Kon, on the topic of AIDS in Russia. This was a breakthrough. For the first time, people in Russia started talking about AIDS openly. For the first time in my memory the official press spoke without condemnation or panic about homosexuals in Russia. Kon said that according to his estimates, two to five percent of the male population there were homosexuals. Never before had such figures been cited. I don't even know how precise they are—more than likely they're quite conservative. Who in Russia would ever admit to being a homosexual! By the way, Smakov was by no means the first well-known Russian émigré to die of AIDS. In early 1988, the young pianist Yuri Egorov died in Amsterdam.

Brodsky. Yes, I knew him.

Volkov. A fantastically talented musician. He promised to become the new Horowitz. I received news of his death signed by Egorov's Dutch friend, and a few months later a letter arrived informing me of the death of that friend. As for Kohn's article in *Ogonyok,* many problems are laid out in it. They don't even have condoms for sale.

Brodsky. You don't mean the famous Bakovsky Rubber Goods Factory stopped producing? Remember? But as far as I remember, those items never enjoyed any special confidence among the Russian population.

Volkov. Yes, imported Chinese condoms were prized rather more highly. People felt they were of superior quality, since the Chinese had to control their birthrate.

Brodsky. This is a global problem. Recently I read somewhere some rather intriguing information about how in Chicago, at some research institute, they simply put condoms on a windowsill by way of an experiment, and they started to disintegrate from the effect of the air—the smog and so forth. That is, the rubber doesn't withstand the air we breathe.

Volkov. The rubber doesn't but we somehow do.

Brodsky. Not for long, though. Not for long. And this onerous thought that we shouldn't rely on condoms is bringing additional pressure, a topic Smakov and I told quite a few jokes about at one time.

Volkov. It would be good now to publish Smakov's Cavafy translations in Russia, and his other works, too. This is theoretically possible now, seeing as how they're sucking up the cultural wealth accumulated by the Russian emigration over the past seventy years. The turn will come, certainly, for Smakov's writings, too, which will be a restoration of a certain historical justice, since when Smakov emigrated they started crossing his name out everywhere in Russia and his works were tossed out of the libraries. What is most surprising is that at one time this kind of barbarous policy, which was applied to all émigrés without exception—it was as if they had all disappeared into a black hole—was viewed in Russia as something natural, that went without saying. All kinds of grotesque situations arose. For instance, in 1976, a collection of essays about Maya Plisetskaya came out in Moscow in which the leading ballet critics participated, including Smakov, but because he was living in New York by that time, his essay was signed with another name.

Brodsky. Yes, Smakov was ecstatic about Maya, and she was very favorably disposed toward him. When he was already quite ill, he and Baryshnikov went to Boston for Maya's gala performance, but he was laid low there by an attack, and he had to be whisked back to New York.

Volkov. Andrei Voznesensky, who had gone to Boston with Smakov, told me about that.

Brodsky. I must say that I still find Yevtushenko more to my liking than Voznesensky. The Russian language Yevtushenko has is better. And what's Yevtushenko? One big self-promotion factory, right? He works exclusively on his own behalf and makes no secret of the fact. He is absolutely frank. And unlike Voznesensky, he doesn't make himself out to be some *poète maudit,* a bohemian, an aesthete and connoisseur of the arts. I think Yevtushenko knows and understands more about art than Voznesensky.

Volkov. I'm sure that some future ideal anthology of twentieth-century Russian poetry will include—in anyone's, even the strictest selection—a good ten poems by Yevtushenko and Voznesensky both.

Brodsky. Well, that goes without saying! No question. I know poems by Yevtushenko and Voznesensky both by heart—two or three hundred lines from each.

Volkov. And in the history of Russian culture and sociopolitical life in the twentieth century both "Babi Yar" and "The Heirs of Stalin" by Yevtushenko will last forever.

Brodsky. I'm not so sure, because if that anthology you're talking about includes Klyuev's "Burned Ruins" and, say, poems by Gorbovsky, then there's no point in having "Babi Yar" in there.

Volkov. The difference is that Klyuev's and Gorbovsky's works have been distributed across the country all these decades at best in typescript, or else orally, whereas "Babi Yar" and "The Heirs of Stalin" appeared in newspapers with circulations in the millions. The entire Soviet Union read them. These poems by Yevtushenko played a historical role.

Brodsky. Well, that's true. Those boys were throwing stones in the officially sanctioned direction, knowing they'd land half a step ahead of the ordinary guy, who went nuts over it! That's their entire historical role. All this is very simple, banal even! Yevtushenko and Voznesensky had friends in the Central Committee of the Party all along the way—second, or third, or sixteenth secretaries—so they were always more or less in the know about which way the wind would blow tomorrow.

Volkov. The end of the twentieth century is very soon upon us. People's thinking is structured in such a way that they're always expecting some kind of supernatural event, like the end of the world, in connection with these round dates.

Brodsky. What's most interesting is that something of that kind has always happened.

Volkov. Still, the change in the situation as we approach the end of a century has been especially striking in the former Soviet Union and the countries of the Soviet empire. I'm not talking about economics, but the cultural scene. It's interesting that the changes did not by any means occur in the direction in which—

Brodsky. —the boys had intended? Yes, that's absolutely correct, but it's a normal miscalculation, a miscalculation by the entire state cultural apparatus, a miscalculation by the innumerable bureaucrats from all those socalled creative unions, and a miscalculation by those boys themselves, but that's natural, too. They couldn't help but miscalculate because the only way to predict the future with any kind of precision is to view it through fairly pessimistic eyes.

Volkov. It's especially funny now to look at the relatively recent editions in the Library of the Poet series—whom they put down as classics of twentieth-century Russian poetry. Before Gumilyov and Khodasevich were finally published in this series, there were chubby volumes of Lugovskoy, Lukonin, and Narovchatov, that is, poets with utterly overblown reputations.

Brodsky. Well, not all that overblown. There is some talent there. What happened to that talent later is another matter.

Volkov. Can you really compare Lugovskoy with even Selvinsky or Tikhonov? Those last two truly did something for Russian poetry. What did Lugovskoy contribute? Poems about secret policemen and fish-breeders—false romanticism, worse than Bagritsky.

Brodsky. It is worse than Bagritsky, of course. Bagritsky is much better than Lugovskoy, although nothing to write home about either. But I remember Lugovskov had a book called *Mid-Century*. This was blank verse that played a definite role in the formation—at least the purely poetic formation—of our generation. Of course, such a tremendous figure as Khodasevich tramples them all underfoot. Well, if we're going to talk about how toward the end of the century everything on the cultural scene seems to fall into place, then I would say this: no one need to get too worked up on this score. Time itself sets things to rights, regardless of the presence or absence of an iron curtain. There is the law of conservation of energy: energy sent out into the world does not vanish without a trace no matter what the political or cultural isolation, and if this energy has in addition some kind of specific quality, then there's absolutely no cause for concern. Therefore poets yield in vain to the *Weltschmerz* over not being published or recognized. The only thing they should be concerned about is the quality of what they're doing. Given quality, everything will fall into place sooner or later. Especially now, when thanks to the population explosion people have nothing to do and so many of them are going into criticism and literature studies. No one will pass unnoticed. All's well in that respect. There are no unknown geniuses. That's just a kind of mythology we inherited from the nineteenth century—a rather unconvincing mythology.

Volkov. It's curious to observe how people in Russia fussed over the collapse of the established cultural hierarchy. At first it was fashionable to try to show that you had always been a dissident or at least a nonconformist at heart, but that phase passed relatively quickly, and now you can once again recall your former lofty status and proximity to the powers that were. Not that long ago, some writer was describing enthusiastically how he played a hard game of tennis with Young Communist League leaders—I don't remember anymore, I think it was Gladilin.

Brodsky. As far as Gladilin goes, I just now remembered a characteristic episode that involved him. This was 1965, and I had just been released and had arrived in Moscow. So, Yevtushenko invited me to a banquet at *Yunost* magazine thrown by Gladilin because they were publishing his new novel. This was a kind of hustle I'd never dreamed of, and for me it was all an eye-opener, that a writer would arrange a banquet for the people who helped push and promote his work with a magazine or publishing house. (Here, in the West, this all works the other way around. Here the publisher holds a banquet if he's going to hold anything for you at all.) Sitting there were mainly associates of *Yunost,* rather terrible creatures. Gladilin stood up and addressing all these pigs and bastards began embroidering: "Only thanks to your wisdom, your keen sense and understanding of contemporary Russian literature," and so forth. I realize this is a set phrase. I realize all these people were just doing their job, but objectively—these are bastards, right? And Gladilin was raising this toast to them, this spiel that lasted about fifteen minutes. The whole business began to make me feel physically sick. I stuck it out, thinking, Well, any minute now we'll be chowing down. But not yet! Yevtushenko got up and gave a speech on the same level of lackey eloquence, which made me extremely uncomfortable. I started experiencing chest pains. Akhmatova was still alive at the time and I was often in her company so I always carried Validol around. I had to go out to the lounge, sit down on a bench, and start licking the Validol, because looking those bastards in the face across a feast-laden table was intolerable, greatly beyond the pale. This was the ionosphere of immorality, if I can put it that way. But that's not even the point. Words, of course, are meaningless, we know that—but only at the level of concept! When you're physically present at this foray beyond the pull of gravity, it gets bad; the overload begins to take its toll.

Volkov. Right now in Russia, people talk a lot about money, who earns how much and so on. Some people condemn these kinds of conversations, as if to say, where did our traditional Russian idealism go? Indeed, in the Soviet Union, talking about money, savings, and the like was not simply not encouraged, it was expressly forbidden. There still wasn't actual equality, since even then there were enormous gaps in income, but the illusion of this equality was maintained. It was a kind of social hypocrisy. In conversations nowadays about people's former lofty status, their membership in the Writers Union and so forth, I hear echoes of that hypocrisy, because in fact what the person wants to say is, "Hey, look at all the money I was making then!"

Brodsky. There's another nuance here that I really feel is the basis for this psychology. What these people have in mind is not so much what they once were and how much they used to earn but the fact that they were play-ers. They were real people. It's an attempt to prove the reality of their own existence, if only in the past. For instance, someone says, "I used to be chief engineer at a major plant." In Soviet mythology, a chief engineer was some-one who dealt with real problems, right? The same thing happens when someone says, "I was a prominent member in the Union of Soviet Writers." Of course, I find all this profoundly antipathetic, but when I hear all these speeches now, I try to detect a certain sentiment in them because—well, what kinds of judges of these people are we?

Volkov. "Judge not lest ye be judged."

Brodsky. That was not said about the communal apartment; that is on a somewhat higher level. Nonetheless.

Volkov. It's just that in dealing with people we perform a certain selec-tion. But judging them in the process is not at all mandatory.

Brodsky. I think that the selection you're talking about is performed on a purely physiological basis. Not out of any considerations of principle. As for considerations of principle, I don't really understand very well their ex-ceptional role in personal relationships, especially among one's fellow countrymen. No matter what, we were taught one thing in Russia all along the way and that is to forgive, to pardon, to vindicate. Not to judge. No, if I don't have anything to do with someone there, then it is only because that person simply makes me sick. There are people like that. But what can you do? It's incompatibility.

Volkov. Now you're being published, praised, and quoted a lot in Russia, but the attacks continue as well. It's just that before, these attacks were by the state—"parasite," "hooligan," "renegade," "anti-Soviet," and so forth—and now the blows are coming mainly from the right flank: the na-tionalists, communists, and neofascists. Their attacks on you boil down basically to this: you can't be called a Russian poet inasmuch as you're nei-ther a poet nor Russian. That is, the writings of many of your enemies are based on a conservative aesthetics with a very tangible admixture of anti-Semitism.

Brodsky. I'll read you a few lines from a letter I received today in the mail from Moscow. Here they are: "You kike! You should have been finished off properly! Damn you!" That's all.

Volkov. What, the letter came directly to your New York address?

Brodsky. Yes.

Volkov. At times like these you thank fate you're living on the other side of the ocean . . . Now maybe I understand better why you still haven't made the trip to Russia, and especially to your native city.

Brodsky. Well, we know, after all, that you cannot step twice into the same river, even if that river is the Neva. Moreover, you cannot step twice on the same asphalt, inasmuch as it changes after every new wave of traffic. Contemporary Russia is another country now, an absolutely different world, and to find myself there as a tourist—well, that would drive me completely mad. After all, as a rule, you go somewhere out of some internal or, rather, external necessity. To be perfectly frank, I don't sense either one in connection with Russia, because in fact you're not going somewhere but leaving somewhere. At least, that's what always happens with me. For me, life is a constant leave-taking, and in that situation it's better to more or less retain your past in memory and try not to come face to face with it again.

Volkov. Akhmatova used to say approximately this: "Absence is the best medicine for oblivion, and the best way to forget something forever is to see it every day."

Brodsky. After all, what drives you out of your wits the most in Europe? That the countries are different, their cultures are different, and their histories are different, but the leather jackets and haircuts on all the young European punks are the same everywhere you go, and if you didn't enjoy seeing that rabble here, then seeing it in your native city—that would really be the limit, wouldn't it? Well, I don't know . . .

Volkov. I've wanted to ask you something for a long time. In Russia now, your books are coming out in quick succession, but they're all compiled by other people, not by you. One often hears you complaining about how this or that book of yours was compiled. Nonetheless, you yourself never take up this work. If I'm not mistaken, in your entire publishing history, only once or twice have you taken on the responsibility for putting together your own book. Is this your position?

Brodsky. The simplest answer would be that yes, this truly is my position. That's just the way it is. I honestly don't care how my next book is going to look—since from the very beginning everything got off on the wrong foot. Maybe all this ought to have been published at the time in cycles, according to the chronology of their appearance, but since that didn't happen, what's the point of worrying about it? The game was spoiled once and for all, and correcting anything, putting it in order—I have no intention of doing that. I absolutely don't care, especially since I don't really look on myself or my affairs as any kind of linear process. I don't have any particular feelings or remarkable ideas—for example, that something in my books is out of place or something is printed incorrectly. It's out of place—well, that's great that it's out of place.

Volkov. That is, you categorically refuse to compile your own books of poetry?

Brodsky. Yes, I am utterly incapable of doing that. The only thing I am capable of doing is writing a cycle of poems, and then, of course, it would be nice if it were published immediately. That has virtually never happened, though, and it makes no sense to do this retrospectively, and really, if you're going to do this, you have to think better of yourself than I do. How can I put it? Writing just isn't a process that's terribly smooth, so if you do have an opportunity to do something, then you'd do better to write poetry than compile books. At the moment when you might compile a book . . . As a rule, at that moment you're having trouble writing poems, something isn't working, and when the poems aren't working, you think they never will. You think they're "gone," as Akhmatova would say. Therefore, taking the time to compile books during that period—well, you're living off your yesterday's reputation, your past merits. It's bad taste.

Volkov. I know that those periods of creative despair, when you think you'll never compose anything again, befell Shostakovich periodically. Does this happen to you often?

Brodsky. Fairly often. Every time I can't get a poem written, every time one doesn't work. Not more often but approximately as often as it does, and when a poem does work, you feel like doing another one right away. Therefore, psychologically, there's no internal time for compiling books. Better to let someone else do it.

Volkov. I can understand that you've had problems with the publication of your poems in the Soviet Union, but after all, when you moved to the United States, at least here you might have attempted to start all over, isn't that so?

Brodsky. Not entirely. In the States everything got started on the wrong foot from the very beginning too, somehow. Lev Loseff compiled my first books. First of all, for starters, this ought to have been one volume, not two, but out of the publisher's considerations they broke the book into two: *The End of a Beautiful Epoch* (poems from 1964 to 1971) and *A Part of Speech* (1972–1976). Well, I could agree with that, because 1972 was a kind of boundary, but it certainly was not a psychological boundary, even though that year I did make my way from one empire to another. I don't see any psychological boundary in my poems of that period, although I do think that, starting with "The Thames at Chelsea," written in 1974, there is a somewhat different poetics at work. Here, I think, we have more or less different poems, but once again, the fact that this is a different poetics is only noticeable when this poem neighbors on something previous that more or less prepared for this shift, or that was on the wane, or its last gasp, as they say. Only then can you see that it's something different. I don't really understand how you divide all this up into sections and volumes, or even why you have to divide it up at all. Let them follow one after another—like life.

Volkov. What about the books in English and other foreign editions of your poems?

Brodsky. Well, that's such an ordinary business. Basically, you include the poems that at the given moment have been translated in a more or less civilized way. I have no illusions or ambitions whatsoever on this score. The books just come out as books. In this sense I am no professional.

Volkov. You deviate in a way from the tradition of Russian poetry. Look at the maniacal fault-finding of the poets of the modern era—Blok, Annensky, Pasternak, Akhmatova—toward the composition of cycles and volumes. They were constantly switching their poems around.

Brodsky. With the exception perhaps of Mandelstam.

Volkov. Well, at a certain point circumstances became unpropitious for him—somewhat like yours. Otherwise I think he would have compiled all his books quite painstakingly. Remember the classics, remember Baratynsky's books! In fact, right now I can only think of one single example of a poet with an attitude toward his own books similar to yours—that's Tyutchev, for whom you have so little love. He too allowed other people to compile his collections, refusing to correct them and later complaining privately that it was done all wrong. He too insisted that he was not a professional man of letters. In this respect he was perhaps even more consistent than you.

Brodsky. Without a doubt, without a doubt. No question about it. This is actually a very intelligent and very fair observation. Indeed, I am not a man of letters. I don't have those sorts of ambitions, as I've already said. My sole ambition concerns the process. It consists exclusively of the course of the process, the process itself. The life of the product, so to speak, does not concern me at all. I absolutely don't care what happens to my poems after they're written. In this sense there are a few coincidences—or at least I hope there are—between my attitude toward my work and that of the ancients. Definitely not Tyutchev's.

Volkov. Do you mean the anonymous medieval authors or the ancient Greeks and Romans?

Brodsky. I'm talking about the ancient authors. All those editions of ancient poets, to a certain extent they're posthumous editions. It is impossible to approach them in any other way. After all, how does all this come about? Scholars find something, then all this gets sorted out in an order that the authors themselves didn't know much about, right? What there is gets stuck between two covers. Well, the same thing, I would like to hope, happens in my case. But all this concern of the poet over his biography is bad taste, as I've already said, especially for the twentieth century, since in this century, especially in Russian poetry, everything is in the process of development stylistically, and this development, it seems to me, continues to this day. I have absolutely no wish to dwell on any particular manner of expression, no matter what it is, and I think that this is characteristic of many other poets, too, not only me. That is why the chronology in poetry collections is not all that important, to be honest. You follow a poet's development either according to his stylistic movement or else according to the increasing depth of content, and in this sense neither the collection's compiler nor its reader can make mistakes.

Volkov. Or shouldn't, in any case.

Brodsky. Yes, shouldn't! Shouldn't. It's impossible, for instance, in a collection of Pasternak to put the poems from *Doctor Zhivago* before the poems from *Over the Barriers.* This simply wouldn't make sense. Or else it would make that higher ancient sense we were just talking about.

Volkov. I approach the question of chronology in poetry collections selfishly. I always like to know in precisely what year a poet wrote a given poem. Then I can calculate how old he was at that moment and what his circumstances were—historical and private. It annoys me when poets purposely obscure those circumstances. Many of them approach the chronology of their poems with complex emotions, and you are somehow particularly ambivalent in this regard.

Brodsky. I was just rereading some of my very old poems. Well, it's total raving! It's night, absolute night! I had no shame! If I had had the opportunity to publish everything in the homeland that I'd gotten it into my head to write, it would have been a total disaster. I should be grateful for all these censor turnstiles there were in the homeland. Of course, subsequently, when I became older and started composing more or less in earnest, there was a moment when it would have been good if I could have compiled and published my own books as the various cycles appeared. Even here, in the West, I've felt the urge a few times to sort through what I've done in retrospect and publish it in some specific order, but that's wrong, that's not the right way to go about it. The poems have already been published—in a certain disorder rather than an order, but crazy disorder is order, as Wallace Stevens said, and unlike the ordinary reader, I understand such things literally, so I take them very much to heart. In my life, in my behavior, I've always proceeded from this—whatever happens happens, and everything basically is going to fall into place, at least when it comes to the publishing of my books. I can't imagine anything more terrifying than posthumous commentaries. I think that even in Pushkin's case the chronology is very badly garbled. What's there to say about people like Lermontov, where we have absolutely no idea what's happening or where? Now they're sweating over Tsvetaeva. God willing, some kind of distinct chronology will emerge from it. As for me, I do not care.

Volkov. It seems to me you're denying responsibility for the final product. Perhaps it's the fear—even subconscious—of the reader's judgment.

Brodsky. I have no fears or complexes in this regard. Nor do I place myself above the reader—or below him for that matter. In this sense I may be a product of the Soviet system, but I've never looked on myself as an author. Word of honor! Although this statement, said out loud, might be perceived as rather coquettish, in fact, all my life I've looked on myself—and this is the main thing!—as a metaphysical unit. What has interested me primarily has been what happens to a person, to an individual, on the metaphysical plane. My poems are a by-product, although it's always viewed the other way around. That's nonsense though, and it's not that I consider this occupation—compiling my own books and so forth—frivolous. Nothing of the kind, quite the opposite! This is an extremely noble, sensible, and serious—choose whatever epithet you think best!—activity, but the whole story is that I have neither the time nor the inclination to do this. Akhmatova used to say, "When the poems don't come, living is very uncomfortable." When does a poet compile a book? When can you? When you aren't writing poems as such. But when you aren't writing poems, you're completely nuts. You turn into a brute—especially toward yourself. When you can't write, you think your life is over. I have a somewhat romantic attitude toward myself. Not so much toward myself personally even as toward existence as such, and my attitude toward myself is Calvinistic, if you like, and this is by no means pride.

Volkov. How do you make that psychological leap—I mean when you can't come up with poems?

Brodsky. When you can't come up with poems, you try to. Or you attempt to distract yourself, to get your mind off it. You do translations, prepare lectures, read books—I don't know what else. By the way, to read a book is more important for the individual, in the purely metaphysical sense or any other you like, than to compile one. There was a time when I thought that I wouldn't compile a single book in my life. I simply wouldn't live that long, inasmuch as the older you get the harder it is, but I actually have compiled one collection.

Volkov. New Stanzas to Augusta?

Brodsky. Yes. As you probably know, this is a collection of poems written over a span of twenty years with more or less a single addressee, and to a certain extent, this is the chief accomplishment of my life. When I was contemplating this, I decided that even the very best hands shouldn't touch this, that I should do it myself. Once again, if I hadn't, they would have made such a jumble of it! Moreover, one thought occurred to me—quite suddenly, during a conversation with Lev Loseff. I was looking through all these poems and suddenly saw that they formed a kind of plot in an astonishing way, and it seems to me that, as a result, *New Stanzas to Augusta* can be read as a separate literary work. Unfortunately, I didn't write *The Divine Comedy*, and evidently I never will, but here I had a book of poetry with its own plot—in principle more like prose than anything else. I have this secret hope that the readers will figure this out, that is, that they will in some infinite sense also find themselves on that level.

Volkov. By the way, one circumstance amazes me. Your poetry is highly epic and keeps epicizing more and more, which—

Brodsky. "Epicizing"—that's marvelous.

Volkov. At the same time, though, you have yet to break out with some monumental novel in verse.

Brodsky. I twice made such an attempt. Well, in the innocence of youth I composed that insanity, "The Procession." I was a little over twenty at the time. Later, when I was a little more serious, I wrote something that even now, when I look back on it—although doing so is almost impossible—seems to me an extremely serious work.

Volkov. "Gorbunov and Gorchakov"?

Brodsky. Yes. As for *The Divine Comedy*, well, I don't know, but evidently, no—I won't ever write it. If I'd lived in Russia, at home, maybe then I would have made a third such attempt. You know, these kinds of things can only be composed when you find yourself in some natural context, when you start thinking, All right, now I'm going to let them all have it—the old and the young alike, that is, my predecessors and my heirs, right? A sentiment like this can only overtake you when you are in your natural environment. When you fall out of it—or leave it behind—then existence acquires a somewhat more desperate nature and you're no longer up to such grandiose plans.

Volkov. On the other hand, what in Russian is somewhat highfalutingly called "exile" lends a fantastic advantage in the form of detachment.

Brodsky. Perfectly true, but I already had plenty of this detachment. I've pretty much overdone the detachment bit, you know. It's become an instinct. You don't have to renounce anything, of course, and I don't, but insofar as life goes on I'm not going to be composing any major works now, and the reader won't be reading them. To say nothing of the fact that they aren't reading what has already been written by our betters—*Gilgamesh,* say, or Homer, or Dante.

Volkov. People always prefer to read their contemporaries.

Brodsky. Maybe I'll try my hand at something like Auden's *For the Time Being,* God willing. That does not depend on me, you know. After all, you write more or less according to how your own prosody develops and certainly not because you have something to say. You know, there is an immediate dictate of language: the words begin to resonate—and then this, that, and the other follows. I don't know, maybe my prosody will keep changing until it attains something epic. On the other hand, Eugenio Montale never wrote anything epic. Eliot never wrote anything especially epic either, although he, of course, is no example. Yeats didn't write anything epic either.

Volkov. Or Mandelstam. Pasternak has his novel in verse, *Spektorsky*—not one of his better efforts.

Brodsky. Well, Pasternak wrote *Doctor Zhivago.*

Volkov. But that's prose.

Brodsky. No, this is precisely that instance, that very movement and that very reason we were talking about: the dictate of language.

Volkov. One contradiction continues to bother me. On the one hand, you insist that existence is more important than art; on the other, you assert that when you can't write you don't feel like living.

Brodsky. That is what existence is, and compiling books isn't existence or art. I can even say what specifically dictates arguments like yours: the principle of prose applied to *belles lettres.* We live in a society that has gone crazy over the idea of culture as a product. As a result, it demands books, books, and more books. This game has driven culture into an impasse. In point of fact, when you're writing, you have no idea who's reading and who's understanding what. Are they understanding nothing? Or everything? And that's as it should be! But if you live for the sake of putting out books, then you need to read the reviews of the book too, most likely, and then, based on the review, behave accordingly. Good Lord! For me personally—you know what suits me most of all? Suits me very well indeed! The fate of an ancient author, Archiloches or someone. All that's left of him is rat's tails. There's a fate I could envy.

Fall 1988–Winter 1992

BIOGRAPHICAL NOTES

Adamovich, Georgy (1894–1972). Russian émigré poet and essayist; member of Parisian literary circle known as the Parisian Note.

Akhmatova, Anna (1889–1966). One of the greatest poetic voices of the twentieth century; Brodsky's mentor.

Andropov, Yuri (1914–1984). Soviet party leader; chairman of the State Security Committee (KGB).

Annenkov, Yuri (1889–1974). Russian émigré artist; author of interesting memoirs.

Anrep, Boris (1883–1969). Russian émigré artist; Akhmatova's lover.

Ardov, Victor (1900–1976). Soviet humorist; Akhmatova's friend.

Bagritsky, Eduard (1895–1934). Soviet poet.

Bakhtin, Mikhail (1895–1975). Influential Russian literary theorist.

Baratynsky, Yevgeny (1800–1844). Great Russian poet of an intellectual bent with whom Brodsky strongly identified.

Baryshnikov, Mikhail ("Misha") (b. 1948). Russian émigré ballet star; Brodsky's friend.

Batyushkov, Konstantin (1878–1855). Russian poet who wrote beautifully consonant, harmonious verse.

Bely, Andrei (1880–1934). A leading Russian symbolist; prolific as a poet, novelist, essayist, and memoirist. His novel, *Petersburg,* belongs to the twentieth-century modernist canon.

Benkendorf, Alexander (1783–1844). Russian chief of the gendarmerie in Pushkin's time.

Berdyaev, Nikolai (1874–1948). Great Russian religious philosopher who died in exile in France.

Beria, Lavrenty (1899–1953). Notorious chief of the Soviet secret police.

Bitov, Andrei (b. 1937). Russian writer.

Blok, Alexander (1880–1921). One of the most popular and important Russian poets of all time.

Bobyshev, Dmitry (b. 1936). Russian émigré poet; member of the "magic choir" of young poets around Akhmatova, which also included Brodsky.

Bolshintsova, Lyubov (1908–1983). Akhmatova's friend.

Brik, Lili (1891–1978). Moscow socialite; lover of the poet Vladimir Mayakovsky.

Bulgarin, Faddei (1789–1859). Russian writer, editor, and police informer.

Bunin, Ivan (1870–1953). Russian émigré writer; Nobel Prize winner (1933).

Cavafy, Constantine (1863–1933). Great Greek poet, one of Brodsky's favorites.

Chaliapin, Fyodor (1873–1938). Mighty Russian bass; died in exile in France.

Chorny, Sasha (1880–1932). Russian satirist; died in exile in France.

Chukovskaya, Lydia (1907–1995). Russian writer; daughter of Kornei Chukovsky; author of monumental *Akhmatova Journals.*

Chukovsky, Kornei (1882–1969). Russian critic; author of popular verse for children; active in the defense of Brodsky against harassment by Soviet authorities.

Czapski, Jozef (1896–1992). Polish émigré painter and writer; Akhmatova's lover.

Daniel, Yuli (1925–1988). Soviet dissident writer.

Delvig, Anton (1798–1831). Russian poet, a member of the Pushkin "Pleiad."

Derzhavin, Gavriil (1743–1816). Great Russian poet, one of Brodsky's favorites.

Dmitriev, Ivan (1760–1837). Russian satirical poet.

Dobuzhinsky, Mstislav (1875–1957). Russian artist whose images of St. Petersburg became emblematic; died in exile.

Dovlatov, Sergei (1941–1990). Russian émigré writer; Brodsky's friend.

Dubelt, Leonty (1792–1862). Russian chief of the gendarmerie.

Dzerzhinsky, Felix (1877–1926). First head of the Soviet secret police; also known as Iron Felix.

Efron, Sergei (1893–1941). Husband of the poet Marina Tsvetaeva; worked for the Soviet secret police abroad and was executed by them upon returning to Moscow.

Egorov, Yuri (1954–1988). Russian émigré pianist of great promise; died of AIDS.

Esenin, Sergei (1895–1925). One of the most beloved Russian poets.

Favorsky, Vladimir (1886–1964). Russian engraver who illustrated the Bible and Pushkin.

Fet, Afanasy (1820–1892). Great Russian lyric poet.

Frank, Semyon (1877–1950). Russian religious philosopher; died in exile in England.

Garshin, Vladimir (1887–1956). Leningrad physician; Akhmatova's lover in the late 1930s.

Gitovich, Alexander (1909–1966). Leningrad poet and translator; Akhmatova's friend.

Gladilin, Anatoly (b. 1935). Moscow writer; emigrated to France in 1976.

Godunov, Alexander (1949–1995). Russian ballet star who defected to the West in 1979.

Golenishchev-Kutuzov, Arseny (1848–1913). Russian poet whose verse was set to music by the great Russian composer Modest Mussorgsky.

Gorbovsky, Gleb (b. 1931). Russian poet.

Gordin, Yakov (b. 1935). Russian writer; Brodsky's friend.

Gorenko, Andrei (1848–1915). Akhmatova's father.

Gorenko, Khanna (1896–1978). Victor Gorenko's wife.

Gorenko, Victor (1896–1976). Akhmatova's younger brother.

Grebenshchikov, Boris (b. 1952). Russian rock singer and composer.

Griboedov, Alexander (1795–1829). Author of the famous Russian comedy *Woe from Wit.*

Grin, Alexander (1880–1932). Russian writer of popular adventure stories.

Gudzenko, Semyon (1922–1953). Soviet poet; member of the "war generation."

Gumilyov, Lev (1912–1992). Russian historian; Akhmatova's son.

Gumilyov, Nikolai (1886–1921). Russian poet, founding member of the acmeist group; Akhmatova's first husband; executed by the Bolsheviks.

Herzen, Alexander (1812–1870). Great Russian writer, editor, and journalist.

Ivanov, Georgy (1894–1958). Russian émigré poet; member of the Parisian Note; author of colorful memoirs.

Ivanov, Vyacheslav ("Koma") (b. 1928). Influential Russian linguist; Brodsky's friend.

Ivinskaya, Olga (1913–1994). Lover of Russian poet Boris Pasternak; immortalized by Pasternak in *Doctor Zhivago.*

Katenin, Pavel (1792–1853). Russian poet; one of Brodsky's favorites.

Kharms, Daniil (1905–1942). Leningrad dadaist writer, member of the Oberiu group; died in prison.

Khlebnikov, Velimir (1885–1922). Great Russian experimental poet.

Khodasevich, Vladislav (1886–1939). Important Russian émigré poet.

Khomyakov, Alexei (1804–1860). Russian Slavophile poet.

Klyuev, Nikolai (1884–1937). Russian religious poet; died in a labor camp.

Koussevitzsky, Sergei (1874–1951). Russian émigré conductor.

Kramskoy, Ivan (1837–1887). Russian realist painter.

Krylov, Ivan (1769–1844). Most popular Russian fabulist.

Kuzmin, Mikhail (1875–1936). Influential Russian poet and translator.

Leontiev, Konstantin (1831–1891). Influential Russian philosopher.

Liberman, Alex (b. 1912). Art director of *Vogue;* Brodsky's friend.

Liberman, Tatiana (1906–1991). Addressee of some of Mayakovsky's love poems; Alex Liberman's wife; Brodsky's friend.

Lipkin, Semyon (b. 1911). Russian poet; Akhmatova's friend.

Lokhvitskaya, Mirra (1869–1905). Russian poet whose verse had strong erotic overtones; precursor of Akhmatova.

Lomonosov, Mikhail (1711–1765). Russian poet; in 1755 founded Moscow University, which now bears his name.

Loseff, Lev (b. 1937). Russian émigré poet; Brodsky's friend.

Lossky, Nikolai (1870–1965). Russian religious philosopher; died in exile in France.

Lourié, Arthur (1892–1966). Russian émigré composer; Akhmatova's lover.

Lugovskoy, Vladimir (1901–1957). Soviet poet.

Lukonin, Mikhail (1918–1976). Soviet poet.

Makarova, Natalia (b. 1940). Russian émigré ballet star.

Mandelstam, Nadezhda (1899–1980). Osip Mandelstam's wife; author of important memoirs.

Mandelstam, Osip (1891–1938). Russian poet and essayist whose work belongs among the greatest achievements of twentieth-century culture; died in a labor camp.

Markish, Simon (b. 1931). Russian émigré writer and translator; lives in Switzerland.

Marshak, Samuil (1887–1964). Soviet translator of Shakespeare and Robert Burns; author of popular verse for children; signed letter in defense of Brodsky when the young poet was being persecuted by the Soviet authorities.

Maximov, Vladimir (1930–1995). Russian émigré writer; Brodsky's friend.

Mayakovsky, Vladimir (1893–1930). Great Soviet poet; committed suicide.

Merezhkovsky, Dmitri (1865–1941). Russian symbolist writer; died in exile in France.

Mezhirov, Alexander (b. 1923). Russian poet; member of the "war generation."

Milosz, Czeslaw (b. 1911). Polish émigré poet, Nobel Prize winner (1980); Brodsky's friend.

Narovchatov, Sergei (1919–1981). Soviet poet.

Nayman, Anatoly (b. 1936). Russian poet; member of the "magic choir"; Akhmatova's literary secretary; wrote memoirs about Akhmatova; Brodsky's friend.

Nedobrovo, Nikolai (1882–1919). Russian critic and poet; Akhmatova's friend.

Neizvestny, Ernst (b. 1926). Russian émigré sculptor.

Oleinikov, Nikolai (1898–1942). Leningrad dadaist poet, member of the Oberiu group; executed during Stalin's purges.

Olesha, Yuri (1899–1960). Soviet experimental writer.

Orlov, Sergei (1921–1977). Soviet poet.

Pasternak, Boris (1890–1960). Great Russian poet and novelist; author of *Doctor Zhivago;* awarded Nobel Prize for Literature in 1958.

Pavlova, Karolina (1807–1893). Russian poet.

Pikul, Vladimir (b. 1928). Leningrad writer of popular fiction.

Pilnyak, Boris (1894–1937). Soviet experimental writer; executed during Stalin's purges.

Platonov, Andrei (1899–1951). Russian writer, considered by Brodsky to be one of the most important literary voices of the twentieth century.

Plevitskaya, Nadezhda (1884–1940). Russian singer in folk style.

Plisetskaya, Maya (b. 1925). Russian ballet star.

Popkov, Pyotr (1903–1950). Leningrad party leader, executed on Stalin's orders.

Proffer, Carl (1938–1984). American publisher; Brodsky's friend.

Punin, Nikolai (1888–1953). Russian art historian; Akhmatova's third husband; died in a labor camp.

Rein, Yevgeny (b. 1935). Russian poet; member of the "magic choir"; introduced Brodsky to Akhmatova; Brodsky's first literary mentor.

Repin, Ilya (1844–1930). Russia's greatest realist painter.

Rodchenko, Alexander (1891–1956). Russian avant-garde artist and photographer.

Samoilov, David (1920–1990). Soviet poet whose work was championed by Akhmatova.

Selvinsky, Ilya (1899–1968). Soviet experimental poet.

Shestov, Lev (1866–1938). Russian religious philosopher whose ideas greatly influenced Brodsky; died in exile.

Shileiko, Vladimir (1891–1930). Russian Assyriologist; Akhmatova's second husband.

Shklovsky, Viktor (1893–1984). A leading Soviet literary theoretician.

Shostakovich, Dmitri (1906–1975). Great Soviet composer; signed letter in defense of Brodsky.

Simonov, Konstantin (1915–1979). Soviet writer; member of the "war generation."

Sinyavsky, Andrei (1925–1997). Russian émigré writer.

Slutsky, Boris (1919–1986). Soviet experimental poet whose work influenced the early Brodsky.

Smakov, Gennady (1940–1988). Russian émigré ballet critic and historian; Brodsky's friend; died of AIDS in New York.

Sologub, Fyodor (1863–1927). Important Russian symbolist poet and novelist.

Sontag, Susan (b. 1933). American cultural commentator and novelist; Brodsky's friend.

Stenich, Valentin (1898–1939). Soviet translator; executed during Stalin's purges.

Sudeikin, Sergei (1882–1946). Russian painter; emigrated to the West in 1921.

Sudeikina, Olga (1885–1945). St. Petersburg socialite; Sergei Sudeikin's wife; Akhmatova's friend; emigrated to France in 1924.

Surkov, Alexei (1899–1983). Soviet poet and cultural bureaucrat.

Suvorov, Alexander (1729–1800). Russian military leader.

Sviridov, Georgy (b. 1915). Russian composer.

Tarkovsky, Arseny (1907–1989). Soviet poet whose work was championed by Akhmatova.

Tikhonov, Nikolai (1896–1979). Leningrad poet.

Tolstoy, Alexei Konstantinovich (1817–1875). Russian poet, playwright, and novelist. Very popular and influential in his homeland, but practically unknown in the West.

Tolstoy, Alexei Nikolaevich (1883–1945). Soviet writer; master of historical prose.

Tomashevskaya, Zoya (b. 1922). Russian friend of Akhmatova and Brodsky.

Tsvetaeva, Marina (1892–1941). Russian poet who Brodsky often claimed was the greatest of the twentieth century; emigrated, then returned to Russia, where she hanged herself.

Tvardovsky, Alexander (1910–1971). Important Soviet poet and editor.

Tyutchev, Fyodor (1803–1873). Great Russian poet; master of philosophical, meditative verse.

Ufliand, Vladimir (b. 1937). Russian experimental poet; Brodsky's friend.

Vaginov, Konstantin (1899–1934). Leningrad dadaist writer whose novels constitute an important part of the St. Petersburg mythos.

Vinokurov, Yevgeny (1925–1993). Soviet poet.

Voznesensky, Andrei (b. 1933). Russian poet.

Vvedensky, Alexander (1904–1941). Leningrad dadaist poet, member of the Oberiu group; died during Stalin's purges.

Vyazemsky, Pyotr (1792–1878). Russian poet; member of the Pushkin "Pleiad"; one of Brodsky's favorites.

Walcott, Derek (b. 1930). West Indian poet, Nobel Prize winner (1992); Brodsky's friend.

Yevtushenko, Yevgeny (b. 1933). Russian poet; when Yevtushenko was elected to the American Academy of Art and Sciences in 1987, Brodsky resigned in protest.

Zabolotsky, Nikolai (1903–1958). Leningrad experimental poet, member of the Oberiu group; one of Brodsky's favorites.

Zamyatin, Yevgeny (1884–1937). Russian émigré writer whose most popular work is his anti-utopian novel *We*.

Zhdanov, Andrei (1896–1948). Soviet party leader and ideologue; harshly attacked Akhmatova and Zoshchenko in 1946 and Shostakovich in 1948.

Zhirmunsky, Viktor (1891–1971). A leading Russian literary theoretician; Akhmatova's friend.

Zoshchenko, Mikhail (1895–1958). One of the most beloved Russian satirical writers.

ACKNOWLEDGMENTS

I am convinced that great books by others are what most sustains our own writing efforts. While these exemplary books may sometimes reinforce our sense of woeful inadequacy, more often they remain a constant source of moral encouragement and intellectual sustenance. For me, such an indispensable role during the long years required for bringing conversations with Joseph Brodsky into print was played by my old and battered edition of Johann Peter Eckermann's *Gespräche mit Goethe in den letzten Jahren seines Lebens,* first acquired some forty years ago in the spectral city of Riga by the Baltic Sea. This book survived miraculously through all the tribulations of my émigré life.

Also always with me was another great example of the conversation genre—Robert Craft's dialogues with Igor Stravinsky, condensed in a one-volume Russian edition in 1971. Read much earlier in their original English language version by Anna Akhmatova and discussed with considerable animation in her circle, these dialogues, I am sure, were instrumental in persuading Brodsky to adapt the format of questions and answers as a vehicle for expressing some of the complexities and visionary qualities of his creative outlook.

My first glimpse into these complexities came from Akhmatova herself, during our conversations about Brodsky and other matters in 1965. To her and to others who gave me a keener understanding of Brodsky's personality and work—Anatoly Nayman, Yevgeny Rein, Dmitry Bobyshev, Sergei Dovlatov, Andrei Bitov, among many others—goes my deepest gratitude.

My wife Marianna, some of whose photographs of Brodsky are reproduced in this volume, was a true partner throughout this endeavor, tape-recording and transcribing the interviews. Adam Bellow of The Free Press was a steadfast supporter of the project, and Stephen Morrow made numerous acute suggestions. My heartfelt thanks go also to Harry Torczyner, my attorney and longtime friend. His commitment and wise counsel were, as always, of enormous help

INDEX

301